UNDERSTANDING THE MEDIA

UNDERSTANDING THE MEDIA

Second Edition

Eoin Devereux

SAGE Publications
Los Angeles • London • New Delhi • Singapore

First published 2003. Reprinted 2003, 2005
This edition, 2007. Reprinted 2008

SAGE Publications Ltd
1 Oliver's Yard
55 City Road
London EC1Y 1SP

SAGE Publications Inc.
2455 Teller Road
Thousand Oaks, California 91320

SAGE Publications India Pvt Ltd
B 1/I 1 Mohan Cooperative Industrial Area
Mathura Road, New Delhi 110 044
India

SAGE Publications Asia-Pacific Pte Ltd
33 Pekin Street #02-01
Far East Square
Singapore 048763

British Library Cataloguing in Publication data

A catalogue record for this book is available from
the British Library

ISBN 978-1-4129-2990-5
ISBN 978-1-4129-2991-2 (pbk)

Library of Congress Control Number: 2006937331

Typeset by C&M Digitals (P) Ltd, Chennai, India
Printed in Great Britain by TJ International, Padstow, Cornwall
Printed on paper from sustainable resources

For Liz, who always understands

CONTENTS

ACKNOWLEDGEMENTS

Special thanks to Julia Hall, my former commissioning editor at Sage (London) for her faith from the very start.

Ian Antcliff and Gurdeep Mattu at Sage (London) for their attention to detail.

Brian Keary, Carmen Kuhling, Padraig Lenihan, John O'Brennan, Patrick O'Connor, Ruan O'Donnell, John Logan and Anne McCarthy at University of Limerick, Ireland for their help and encouragement.

Michael Breen, Ger Fitzgerald, Leo Halpin, Amanda Haynes, Matt Kelly, Sandra Loftus, Sarah Moore, Niall McGowan, Noreen O'Loughlin, Michael O'Flynn and Mike Ryan for their unwavering friendship and support.

Liz, Gavin and Joe Devereux for their love and all the laughs.

PLATES

FIGURES AND TABLES

Figures

Tables

BOXES

PREFACE TO THE SECOND EDITION

In this era of rapid globalization, this volume brings together a wealth of material to bear on questions concerning the role and influence of the media in cultures and contemporary societies. Eoin Devereux deftly argues that while the concept of globalization is problematic, complex and contested, it can be characterized in its complexity in terms of the key role that transnational media organizations are playing in the process, as media ownership has become increasingly concentrated despite overwhelming deregulation.

The author brings examples from societies around the world to illustrate developments in each chapter. From music to soaps, sports to serious news and current affairs programming, and reality shows to teen drama, this introductory text gives students an opportunity to think critically about the daily representations of the world in film, on television and radio, in print and online. Media representations of class, ethnicity, gender and sexuality are discussed along with media representations of poverty in the 'Third World' and the 'developed world'.

Devereux provides an abundance of detailed examples in case studies from around the world. The assignments force students to reflect upon their media consumption and how it may influence their ways of thinking and their behaviour. The volume offers students a way to develop a reflexive and critical approach to create and empower agency in light of the 'dominance of the global media'. New media technologies – such as blogging and podcasting – appear to be pushing this process to enhance the power of individual audience members, but the author warns that 'it would be naïve to ignore the power of the global media giants'.

The volume provides a thorough and accessible discussion of 'ideological' approaches to understanding and theorizing about the role of the media in society. Devereux offers a re-conceptualization of the media introducing such concepts as 'audience resistance'. He makes it possible for students to easily digest material that is usually found in much more complex elaborations of Althusserian concepts as 'ideological state apparatus', 'relative autonomy', and 'hegemony'.

Incidentally, as a brief morbid aside to these serious Althusserian concepts, readers may be interested to know that Louis Althusser (1918–1990), an influential Marxist philosopher and advocate of the French Communist Party, claimed mental instability after killing his wife, Hélène Legotien nee Rytmann, by strangulation in 1980. After a few years in a French psychiatric ward, he returned to normal daily life before his own death of natural causes in 1990. When the French deconstruct the name Althusser they say 'tu-serres' which means to grip or hold fast. His name is therefore not only a synonym for his personal actions but also for his theory, one that leaves little room for individuals to breathe while in grip of the apparatus of the all-powerful ideological state.

Serious questions about how to analyse media content and media reception are raised in this volume. A variety of qualitative approaches to analysing audiences and their reception of media content are discussed, with the author's preference clearly stated for understanding media influence through more emphasis on rich forms of reception analysis and ethnographic research. Methodological approaches to audience research are dichotomized into 'quantitative' and 'qualitative' paradigms. It is important to note that the increasingly popular and widespread use of the 'qualitative' methodologies of unstructured interviews, participant observation, focus groups and diary keeping are by no means limited to a particular ideological or critical corner of the field. Indeed, these methodologies constitute the very means by which market researchers identify opportunities to influence buying behaviour through persuasive advertising. These methodologies are also central to how those working in the field of development and poverty eradication in low-income countries assess progress, and identify successful approaches to bringing about real change.

The wide array qualitative methods discussed in this valuable introductory text engage interest and encourage students to become involved with them and at the same time critically reflect upon the research process.

Holli A. Semetko
Emory University
March 2007

INTRODUCTION TO THE SECOND EDITION

A note to the teacher

Understanding the Media is an introductory text for first-time undergraduate media and communications students. Using a variety of pedagogic devices, it invites novice students to engage with a range of questions about the mass media in the early twenty-first century. This book aims to be student-friendly and is consciously written in an accessible and straightforward manner. Drawing upon a wide variety of examples, it encourages students to think critically about recent changes and developments in the traditional and newer forms of mass media. This second edition has been significantly expanded and updated.

The 'imagined readers' of this textbook are largely those living, studying and using the media in the developed or Western world. With this in mind, we have carefully selected a range of illustrative materials that will pertain to a maximum number of student readers. The practical exercises that form a core part of this book have already been used with some success in the classroom by the author. They are intended primarily to encourage greater reflexivity or critical reflection among media students and their teachers. It is hoped that they will be used as the basis of either collective or individual assignments either at home or in the classroom and help stimulate some lively and informative discussions and debates on the contemporary mass media. In my own experience as a teacher, I have found that these practical exercises have worked to bring theoretical concepts – such as discourse, hegemony, ideology, structure or agency, for example – to life for undergraduate students and for that key reason a particular emphasis is placed upon them in this textbook.

The need for critical eclecticism

Reflecting my training as a sociologist and my experiences in teaching about the mass media at the University of Limerick and elsewhere, there is an obvious emphasis in this book on the importance of examining the mass media in a social context. Although not exclusively written from a sociological perspective, the importance of examining the media in a social context is clearly reflected in many of the themes chosen for discussion. This textbook recognizes the contribution that a sociological approach can give us in our analysis of the media in the form of tried and well-tested methodological and theoretical principles (see, for example, Croteau and Hoynes, 2003; Gamson, 2004; Hanson, 2005; McCullagh, 2002). That said, sociology is not alone in having an interest in the significance of the mass media. Rather, *Understanding the Media* – as well as being indebted to the sociological tradition – draws upon a range of illustrative materials that owe much to the diverse range of academic disciplines and approaches – such as communications studies, cultural studies, feminist studies and media studies to name but four – that seek to make sense of the media. It is only through using what Halloran (1998: 19) terms a 'critical eclecticism' of this kind that we will further our own and our students' appreciation of the complexities involved in studying the contemporary mass media. This complexity demands that we be far-reaching and open-minded in our overall approach in attempting to critically understand the mass media and its central role in everyday life.

Media saturation and the complexities contained therein form a recurring theme of this book. An approach to understanding the complexities of the mass media requires us to be both critical and systematic and we would argue that the socio-logical tradition, bolstered by a range of approaches developed within other acad-emic disciplines and fields of study, arms us with the toolkit necessary to attempt this important and challenging task. We are, in this textbook, attempting to put the noted US sociologist C. Wright Mills's (1976) call to 'defamiliarize the familiar' into practice, in our examination of the media-saturated world in which we live. This requires all of us to stand back and examine our everyday, familiar and often mundane media experiences and ask critical and hopefully sometimes awkard questions. Continuing in this vein, Gitlin proposes that we:

> . . . stop – and imagine the whole phenomenon freshly, taking the media seriously, not as a cornucopia of wondrous gadgets or a collection of social problems, but as a central condition of an entire way of life. Perhaps if we step away from the ripples of the moment, the week or the season, and contemplate the torrent in its entirety, we will know what we want to do about it besides change channels. (2002: 210)

In attempting to look critically at our media-saturated world, Gitlin's key phrase is that the mass media represent 'a central condition of an entire way of life'. His challenge to all of us as scholars, as students and as citizens is to engage critically with the everyday media world in which we live. Given the conditions – such as ongoing media globalization, the restructuring of media ownership and rapid tech-nological change – that have given rise to the historically unprecedented levels of media saturation and social change, this is not a simple task.

Aims and objectives

Understanding the Media's main aim is to familiarize neophyte students with a variety of salient questions about the media. As well as introducing them to the theoretical debates that are taking place about specific issues, the structure of the book actively encourages its readers to go further in their quest for understanding and knowledge. Each chapter contains detailed case studies, class and individual exercises, boxes with further discussion of key concepts and theories, details on the key thinkers who have informed specific debates, critical questions for consideration, three carefully chosen extracted readings from experts in the field, discussion points and questions for further consideration as well as signposts for further reading and research. The practical exercises have an important role to play not only in getting students to think more critically about their own (and others') experience of the mass media, but also in introducing them to some of the methodological approaches that may be used in media analysis. This practical dimension to *Understanding the Media* will make it appealing to students and teachers alike and should ideally form the basis of tutorial or practical work, typically associated with course lectures delivered through both traditional and non-traditional means. As we document below, a website for teachers and students which accompanies this textbook, focuses on regularly updated illustrative materials as well as a 'Quick Questions' section for student readers.

Understanding the Media aims to equip its student readers with the appropriate theoretical and methodological tools in their initial efforts to deepen their understanding of the media. Although individual chapters are written as self-contained units, and may be read as such, the book – as is demonstrated in more detail in Chapter 1 – follows a deliberate organizational sequence. The succession of chapters in this book is based upon giving equal weighting to the 'trinity' of production, content and reception. *Understanding the Media* is therefore an unapologetically traditional textbook in this regard. As we document in Chapter 1, we encourage our readers to think critically about media texts in terms of how they are created, their structure and content and their reception by audiences. All three aspects are crucial in taking what some might term a more holistic approach to media analysis in an age of media globalization. While the postmodern approach to media analysis may, on the face of it, seem tantalizing, this textbook takes the view that we need to continue to examine the production, content and reception of mass media texts in a systematic way. The mass media are changing with great rapidity but the old questions remain:

- questions about the ownership and control of the global media industries;
- questions about the power of media content to disseminate dominant and other forms of ideology which shape audience attitudes and beliefs about the social world;
- questions about how the mass media represent and perpetuate social inequalities in terms of class, ethnicity and gender, and
- questions about the power of audiences to negotiate and renegotiate media texts.

Having introduced the student to the rudiments of media analysis, through a number of case studies and an examination of their own personal media use and exposure by means of keeping a media diary, *Understanding the Media* goes on to examine the themes of media globalization; media ownership; media professionals and the production of media texts; ideological and discursive analysis; media

3

representation of class, gender and ethnicity, and media audiences. The final chapter has been extended to provide a more detailed account of audiences and fandom.

The practice of media studies

The term 'explosion' is sometimes used to describe both the expansion of the mass media themselves and the consequent rise of media studies. In reflecting the excitement typically associated with media analysis, *Understanding the Media* draws upon illustrative materials from a wide range of media and from diverse geographical territories, thus ensuring its broad appeal as an undergraduate textbook. Its aim is to whet the appetite of the first-time media student and to nurture, in the longer term, a more critical interest in the analysis and study of the mass media.

A note to the student

This textbook is designed with first-time media students in mind. The book's main aim is to develop your understanding of the media through a mixture of theoretical discussion, empirical research findings and practical research exercises. To facilitate this, each of the chapters contains the following:

1 A synopsis of the theoretical debate about specific chapter themes.
2 Critical questions throughout the text – signified by this icon **?**
3 Boxes containing further theoretical discussion, research findings or details about the key thinkers who have attempted to understand the issues at hand.
4 Useful links between chapters identified by this icon ⚬⚬⚬
5 Three extracted readings.
6 Research exercises.
7 Discussion points/questions for further consideration.
8 Under the heading 'Going Further' you are provided with a short list of annotated references if you wish to delve further into a specific chapter theme.

In addition to these features, there is a glossary at the end of the book which aims to define and demystify the key concepts used throughout the text. To obtain the greatest benefit from this textbook, it is best to read the individual chapters in the sequence in which they are presented here. *Understanding the Media* introduces you to some of the main approaches that you can follow in asking critical questions about the media. As a student reader, you will gain most by engaging with the theoretical discussion, examples of research findings and the suggested practical research exercises at the end of each chapter. Individual chapters are punctuated with guidelines as to when you should undertake the suggested exercises and study the extracted readings. For the purposes of introducing the variety of analytical approaches to the media, we present each approach separately. However, we encourage you to read the textbook in its entirety and consider the ways in which the approaches discussed here may be used either separately or in combination in order to further your understanding of the media.

Asking questions about the mass media: an example

Let us consider briefly an example of the sorts of questions you might ask of a widely circulated media text. As a media student, you might wish to undertake some research into a popular television series such as *Buffy the Vampire Slayer* (see Box 0.1). In addition to examining the production values employed in making the series (the quality of the camera work, scripts and storylines etc.), your research might focus on the ownership, production and distribution of such a series. In this regard you might want to pay particular attention to the commodification of popular culture and examine how products such as *Buffy* are a major source of profit for their owners. Profits are generated not only from selling the series' syndication rights throughout the world but also through a wide range of merchandising associated with the series. You might want to examine the diversity of personnel who are involved in the making of *Buffy* – the owners, the creator, the scriptwriters and the team who cast the series. You might focus

Plate 0.1 *Buffy the Vampire Slayer* reproduced with permission © 1997 Twentieth Century Fox Television. All rights reserved.

on *Buffy the Vampire Slayer* as a multimedia phenomenon by examining how it has crossed over into a range of media genres such as DVD, computer games, official and fan-created websites as well as books, comics, soundtracks and magazines. Alternatively, you might examine cross-cultural audience response to the programme or how it represents gender relations, alternative sexualities or spiritual beliefs in the postmodern era. Does the reading or interpretation of *Buffy* vary according to the location of audience members in terms of region, age, gender and cultural contexts (such as religious beliefs or ethnicity)? Given the programme's emphasis on the many trials and tribulations associated with being an adolescent, you might focus specifically on the meaning that female teenage fans take from *Buffy*. You might choose all or any of these four approaches in analysing the series in question. In reading *Understanding the Media*, you will learn about the implications of choosing one or other or all these approaches in analysing a media text.

BOX 0.1 BUFFY THE VAMPIRE SLAYER

Joss Whedon's *Buffy the Vampire Slayer* began life as a movie in 1992. This was followed by a seven-year run as a television series – initially on Warner Brothers and then on the United Paramount Network (UPN) in the USA. The seven seasons of *Buffy* had immense appeal to teenage female audiences across the globe chronicling the story of its heroine Buffy Summers, between the ages of 16 and 22. The recurring theme of adolescent angst was of major importance in helping to create the connection that teenage fans felt with the series.

Whedon's creation inverts the usual ingredients of the horror genre which typically portrays female characters as being helpless. As a media text that uses the key elements of a number of genres such as horror and comedy as well as some aspects of intertextuality, *Buffy* is seen by many critics as being representative of so-called 'girl-power', where young women are portrayed in heroic roles. Of significant commercial importance to both Warner Brothers and UPN, the programme gave rise to a range of spin-offs such as the television series *Angel*, *Buffy* comic books and novels, as well as official and unofficial websites and discussion forums.

Many of *Buffy*'s fans continue to communicate with each other on the web. Following the series discontinuation in 2003, some fans went so far as to write their own eighth series of the programme. The programme has also attracted a considerable amount of interest from academics within the field of media and cultural studies. Labre and Duke (2004), for example, examine the construction of *Buffy* in a video-game based on the television series. Bloustien (2002) explores the relationship between female adolescent fans of *Buffy* in an Australian context. She uses an ethnographic (see chapter 7 in your textbook) approach in attempting to understand more about the significance of globalized texts such as *Buffy* in the everyday lives of younger female fans. The academic interest in *Buffy* has even given rise to a peer-reviewed journal called *Slayage*. (For more details see: http://slayageonline.com)

Organization of the textbook

In the light of the overall approach adopted in this textbook, the chapters are organized as follows. Chapter 1 examines the ways in which we can better understand the contemporary mass media. Chapters 2 and 3 examine the changing contexts in which the media operate. They discuss the significance of media globalization, the rapid changes occurring in the structure of ownership and control of the media, and the social impact of changing forms of media technology. Chapter 4 is concerned with the initial 'making' of media texts and concentrates upon an examination of the constraints on media professionals both within and without media organizations. Chapter 5 revisits the somewhat problematic issue of the ideological power of the media. Chapter 6 explores how the media represent inequality in terms of class, ethnicity and gender. Chapter 7 examines the role of the audience in general and of reception in particular. The revised chapter has a focus on audiences and fandom.

Understanding the Media Website

A companion website for your textbook may be found at www.sagepub.co.uk/devereux

The website contains resources for both students and lecturers, including access to online journal articles, useful links, quick questions, and diagrams and tables.

References

Bloustien, G. (2002) 'Fans with a lot at stake: serious play and mimetic excess in *Buffy the Vampire Slayer*', *European Journal of Cultural Studies* 5 (4): 427–49.

Croteau, D. and W. Hoynes (2003) *Media Society: Industries, Images and Audiences*, 3rd edn. Thousand Oaks, CA: Pine Forge Press.

Gamson, W. (2004) 'On a sociology of the media', *Political Communication* 21(3) July/September.

Gitlin, T. (2002) *Media Unlimited*. New York: Metropolitan Books.

Halloran, J. (1998) 'Mass communication research: asking the right questions' in A. Hansen, S. Cottle, R. Negrine and C. Newbold (eds) *Mass Communication Research Methods*. London: Macmillan.

Hanson, R. (2005) *Mass Communication: Living in a Media World*. Boston: McGraw-Hill.

McCullagh, C. (2002) *Media Power: A Sociological Introduction*. London: Palgrave.

Labre, M.P. and L. Duke (2004) '"nothing like a brisk walk and a spot of demon slaughter to make a girl's night": the construction of the female hero in the *Buffy* video game', *Journal of Communication Inquiry* 28(2): 138–56.

Mills, C. Wright (1976) *The Sociological Imagination*. New York: Oxford University Press.

1

UNDERSTANDING THE MEDIA

Summary

This introductory chapter should help you appreciate the following:

- The key kinds of questions that we must address in developing more fully our understanding of the mass media.
- The eclectic nature of media studies.
- The importance of investigating the mass media in a social context.
- The overall approach taken in this book.
- The benefits of beginning to examine your own mass media use and consumption in a more critical light.

Key concepts

- Media saturation
- Mass media
- Social context
- Media globalization

- Media texts
- Production–content–reception model
- Theoretical and methodological tools
- Media use and media exposure

How are we to begin to make sense of the media-saturated world in which most of us live? What sorts of questions should we be addressing as students of the twenty-first-century media? What kinds of theoretical and methodological tools should we be using in order to develop our understanding of both the traditional and the newer forms of media? In attempting to begin to answer these three key questions, this chapter introduces you to some of the ways in which we can unpack the media's ever increasing complexity.

The chapter starts by looking at the main issues that we need to address in order to begin to understand more fully the ever-burgeoning media. Although the diverse nature of media studies is acknowledged, a particular emphasis is placed on the need to examine the media in a social context. A sociological approach to media analysis continues to offer us a set of approaches that are both critical and fruitful. The 'production, content, reception' model, which underpins the overall approach taken in this textbook, is outlined. We use the Irish rock band U2 and *The Simpsons* television series in order to demonstrate the kinds of questions we can and should be raising about the contemporary media. As a key starting point, you are encouraged to begin your own intellectual journey through a structured and critical examination of how you personally experience and use the media by keeping a media diary.

In spite of or indeed because of the ubiquity of the mass media in our lives, we need to take mass media analysis seriously. Every day we are presented with a plethora of images and messages about the social world. The array of images and messages we encounter – increasingly created and distributed by a handful of multimedia conglomerates – is unprecedented within human history. We are constantly reminded of the need to consume certain products and look a certain way. The covers of magazines aimed at a female readership, for example, mix the themes of celebrity gossip and the possibility of weight loss each week ('Lose 3 stone before Christmas'; 'How I lost 100lbs . . . '). A globally circulated television programme such as *The Swan* plucks a group of 'ordinary women' from what is represented as a dysfunctional context (such as a failed relationship or addiction to food or alcohol) and reconstructs the 'ugly ducklings' psychologically (through counselling) and physically through an exercise programme as well as by means of radical plastic surgery. The BBC's *Honey We're Killing the Kids* (also remade in a US version for the cable channel TLC) focuses on poor parenting (often amongst working-class or blue-collar families) as the basis of obesity amongst British children. It employs computer-based technology to virtually 'fast-forward' to the future. Parents are shown images of what their children may look like as adults if they don't mend their ways in terms of eating and exercise.

These are just two example of the media contexts in which we find ourselves. More importantly, there are fundamental questions to be addressed about the democratic nature of the mass media. The media saturation that shapes our lives is increasingly colonized by commercial interests that are driven not by altruism but by profit.

The mass media

In this book we are concerned primarily with the mass media – 'old' media such as film, magazines, newspapers, radio and television and 'new' media such as the Internet, digital television and radio, MP3 players, video on demand and WAP-based technology – which have the capacity to enable communication with potentially large numbers of people in a diverse range of social settings. Traditionally, the mass media have been defined as those media that allow the communication of messages or texts between 'senders' and 'receivers'. While this conceptualization of the mass media helps you to think about the idea of the media as being quite literally the 'medium' of communication between, for example, media organizations such as a film company, a newspaper, a television network or a radio station and their respective audiences, it runs the risk of oversimplifying what has become in reality a very complex set of affairs. It reveals little of the impact of new media technologies, their convergence with more traditional forms of media, and the potential power that they hold for some audience members. It sheds little or no light on the internal dynamics of media organizations; it does not allow for much consideration of the sheer multitude of often contradictory media texts to which audiences are exposed; and it is silent on the capacity of audiences to engage actively with these texts.

The increasing availability of relatively cheap media technologies that have the potential for greater audience activity and agency raises further problems for the way in which the mass media have traditionally been conceptualized. With information and communication technology (ICT)-based media such as the Internet, a small though significant number of audience members have the capacity – or, to use the traditional Marxist term, the means of production – to produce their own media texts such as websites, blogs, e-zines, independent movies or music programmes through the use of podcasts, for example, on home or other pages hosted on the World Wide Web.

You will know from even a cursory examination of your own everyday experience that media organizations, media genres, media texts and media audiences are quite diverse in their make-up. The objectives of media organizations also vary. Some exist explicitly to generate a profit. Others exist to inform their publics.

Consider the range of media genres that you encounter in just one day. Television genres, such as documentaries, 'reality' shows, news or soap operas, for example, obviously differ in terms of their make-up and in terms of the discourses or forms of knowledge that they reproduce about the social world. Some media texts uphold the status quo in society. Others directly challenge what they perceive as being unequal systems of power. Audiences may have differing expectations about different media genres. They may in turn be active or passive (or both), depending upon certain sets of circumstances. The growing volume of media content of varying quality that audiences encounter is in a constant state of flux. In addition to this, the twin processes of media globalization and technological change – most specifically in the shape of the convergence of new and older technologies such as the personal computer and television set and the digitalization of the latter – raise fresh questions for those who wish to understand the changing relationship between what were traditionally conceptualized as the 'senders' and 'receivers' of media messages or texts.

Defining the mass media

McQuail (2000), in acknowledging the rapidly changing environment in which the mass media operate, offers us a useful set of criteria through which we can define the contemporary mass media. He sees the mass media's significance as arising from 'its near universality of reach, great popularity and public character' (2000: 4). McQuail argues that these features have profound consequences for the cultural life and political organization of contemporary societies:

> In respect of Politics, the mass media have gradually become:
>
> * an essential element in the process of democratic politics by providing an arena and channel for wide debate, for making candidates for office widely known and for distributing diverse information and opinion;
> * a means of exercising power by virtue of the relatively privileged access that politicians and agents of government can generally claim from the media as a legitimate right.
>
> In respect of *culture*, the mass media:
>
> * constitute a primary source of definitions of and images of social reality and the most ubiquitous expression of shared identity;
> * are the largest focus of leisure time interest, providing the shared 'cultural environment' for most people and more so than any other single institution.
>
> In addition, the media are steadily increasing in economic significance, as media industries grow, diversify and consolidate their power in the market. (2000: 4)

Therefore, as well as allowing the communication of messages or texts between senders and receivers, the mass media need to be seen in terms of their public character and in respect of their political, social and economic importance. Extracted Reading 1.3 by McChesney at the end of this chapter stresses the important role that the mass media can (and should) play in ensuring the existence of a democratic society. Media professionals working in the media industries produce media products, which are increasingly seen as commodities to be bought and sold in a globalized marketplace. Many of these products or texts have significance in the day-to-day lives of many audience members in different parts of the globe. The

11

texts may be a primary source of information and knowledge about the social world and most significantly about relationships of power. Media texts have a further potency in the way in which cultural and political differences are constructed and defined. The experience of living in modern and postmodern societies is defined primarily by the very existence of the mass media. Our understanding of the mass media then has to go further than a narrow technical definition of the media as the medium of communication between senders and receivers.

Figure 1.1 summarizes the five key ways in which we can conceptualize the mass media. Moving from the narrow technical definition of the mass media as the medium through which messages or texts may be sent between senders and receivers, we favour a much broader understanding of the mass media where they are understood as industries or organizations, where media texts are commodities as well as cultural products, and where the media act as powerful agents of social change and transformation. In short, we are concerned with understanding the mass media in a *social context*. Such a concern will invariably be taken up with questions of power and unequal power relationships.

CRITICAL QUESTIONS 1.1   THE MASS MEDIA AND EVERYDAY LIFE

The media diary exercise at the end of this chapter may surprise you as to the degree to which you are exposed to the mass media in your everyday life. Because of their ubiquity, it is difficult for us to separate ourselves from our everyday, largely mass-mediated, experiences (see Gitlin, 2002). The challenge for media students is to stand back from this media saturation for a while and ask critical questions of what we otherwise take for granted in our day-to-day lives. In doing so we have the potential to gain new and hopefully critical insights into an otherwise all too familiar world.

By asking questions such as those just outlined, we stand to gain much from our study of the media. Try to imagine your everyday life without the mass media.

1   What sorts of differences would there be in a medialess society?
2   How would you find out about national and world events?
3   Where would you get your ideas and opinions about those who are 'different' from you?
4   How would you know about the views and opinions of the powerful?
5   Would your conversations with family and friends be any different?
6   How would you entertain yourself?
7   How would your use of time be different in your daily life?

• Mass media as means of communication between 'senders' and 'receivers'	• Mass media as industries or organizations	• Mass media texts as commodities produced by media industries
• Mass media texts as cultural products with social, cultural and political significance	• Mass media as agents of social change and globalization	• Mass media as agents of socialization and powerful sources of social meaning

FIGURE 1.1 Conceptualizing the mass media

The mass media in a social context

The questions posed above about the role of the media in everyday life remind you about the extent to which the mass media are an intrinsic part of the web of your day-to-day experience. Living as we do in a media-saturated society, we run the very real risk of taking the social significance of the mass media for granted (see Hanson, 2005). In this chapter we have already referred to the importance of understanding the mass media in a social context. By viewing the mass media in this way, we need to be more fully aware of their social significance at both macro and micro levels. Although we use admittedly broad brushstrokes, our intention is to highlight the key ways in which we can understand the mass media more fully by specific reference to their sociological significance.

At the macro level, the mass media are an important agent of transformation and social change. They are inextricably bound up with the capitalist project and they play a centre-stage role in the reproduction and continuation of various kinds of social inequalities at local, national and global levels.

The mass media have played – and continue to play – an important part in the transformation of societies from being traditional to modern and from being modern to postmodern. The experience of living in modernity and postmodernity is shaped significantly by mass mediation.

For most people the 'texture' of modernity and postmodernity is a result of the very existence of the mass media in their everyday lives. Silverstone states that the media are:

> a constant presence in our everyday lives, as we switch in and out, on and off, from one media space, one media connection, to another. From radio, to newspaper, to telephone. From television, to hi-fi, to Internet. In public and in private, alone and with others. (1999: 6)

We could add many more recent examples to Silverstone's list. An updated list could include in-car DVD players with screens placed in the headrests of SUVs;

13

the capacity of many mobile or cellphone to act as an MP3 player, digital camera or radio; the capacity for players of the Nintendo DS to compete against one another wirelessly at different points on the globe; the presence of in-store television screens in supermarkets as we shop for groceries; and the merging of mass media and the built environment, best exemplified in the gigantic screens on the front of buildings in the main square in Shibuya, Tokyo, in Times Square, New York or in Piccadilly Circus, London.

The mainstream media industries – many of which in their own right are examples par excellence of global capitalist organizations – play a pivotal role in the continued spread of a consumer culture that drives and perpetuates global capitalism. We can find very obvious examples of consumerism within advertising across the mass media, but at a more general level the mass media promote certain kinds of lifestyles and taste cultures within a broad range of media genres as being more legitimate and desirable than others. The increasingly complex ownership structure of the media industries and their interconnections with other kinds of capitalist industries have in recent times reinforced these patterns even further.

The media play a central role in defining societies as traditional, modern or postmodern. Modern and postmodern societies continue to be marked by inequalities in terms of class, ethnicity and gender. The mass media's role in reproducing these inequalities may be seen on two main fronts. We can view the question of the mass media and inequality in terms of access to the mass media and we can and should ask questions about the extent to which the mass media either challenge or reproduce social inequality in their representation of the social world.

As you will see in more detail in Chapters 5 and 6, the mass media continue to play an important ideological role in contemporary societies in terms of how they contribute to or challenge unequal relations of power in the public and private spheres.

The much favoured illusion of the global community or 'global village', used repeatedly by the media industry itself, needs to be balanced with a more realistic perspective that recognizes that not all social groups or societies have equal access to media technology or the increasing amount of media content being made available for purchase and consumption.

At a micro level the mass media act as agents of socialization, constitute a powerful source of social meaning, and occupy a significant amount of people's leisure time. Writing about mediated childhoods and leisure in a comparative European context, Livingstone (2002) reminds us of the increasingly complex nature of the media environment in which many children now live. She begins with the following example to make the point that we need to recognize the importance of contextualizing the uses of 'new' and 'old' media in everyday life:

Two eight-year-old boys play their favourite multimedia adventure game on the family PC. When they discover an Internet site where the same game could be played interactively with unknown others, this occasions great excitement in the household. The boys choose their fantasy personae and try diverse strategies to play the game, both co-operative and competitive, simultaneously 'talking' on-line (i.e. writing) to the other participants. But when restricted in their access to the Internet, for reasons of cost, the game spins off into 'real life'. Now the boys, together with their younger sisters, choose a character, don their battledress and play 'the game' all over the house, going downstairs to Hell, The Volcanoes and The Labyrinth, and upstairs to The Town, 'improving' the game in the process. The new game is called, confusingly for adult observers, 'playing the Internet'. (1998: 436)

We should also pay attention to the agency or creativity of both media professionals and media audiences when we consider the mass media at this micro level.

The mass media are important agents of socialization in that they reproduce dominant (and other) social norms, beliefs, discourses, ideologies and values. Although media content may sometimes be constructed with the expressed aim of educating or duping audience members – as evidenced in anti-smoking advertising campaigns or in propaganda films, for example – most of the time the transmission of norms, beliefs, ideologies, discourses and values happens in an unconscious fashion. The mainstream media draw upon a wide range of taken-for-granted assumptions about the social world: assumptions that, more often than not, go unquestioned by media professionals and audiences alike.

One of the key aims of this book is to introduce you to the tools of analysis that you might use to interrogate the otherwise all too familiar media content of your daily life. Consider, for example, the array of messages within media content that you will encounter today about gender roles. Do these messages challenge or perpetuate what are currently viewed as the 'appropriate' gender roles in your specific social setting or cultural context? What do these messages tell you about masculinity and femininity? What sorts of assumptions are inherent in these media messages about being a 'man' or a 'woman' in the early twenty-first century? What aspects of being male or female are downplayed or ignored altogether in these media messages? What sorts of normative assumptions are made about sexuality? Is universal heterosexuality assumed? What sorts of discourses predominate about ideal body shapes and weight? Within the mainstream print and broadcast media, how are these messages articulated at a symbolic level? Do you think that they alter in any way the understanding you have about the social world in terms of gender divisions and gender-based inequality? If you were to compare how these messages concerning gender politics vary with those reproduced in the mass media, say, twenty years ago, how would they differ? Why?

Media content acts as a powerful source of social meaning. The mass media are centrally involved in the social construction of reality for audience members, giving them an understanding – however limited – of both their immediate and their more distant social contexts. Media audiences are informed and entertained by the mass media industries. A significant amount of people's leisure time is taken up with mass media consumption, and mass media content itself plays an important role in the day-to-day conversations and interactions in which members of society engage. Mass media content draws upon and contributes to the discourses or forms of knowledge that we have about the wider social world.

Finally, it is important to remember that the media industries and media audiences are comprised of living, breathing people who shape and are shaped by media content as well as a wide range of other social forces. Given the centrality of the mass media in people's everyday lives, it is important to stress the capacity that audience members have to engage actively with media content. As you will see later on, an appreciation of the specific social contexts in which media consumption takes place is a crucial starting point in attempting to understand the power of the mass media over their audience and the circumstances in which audience members can exercise agency in their interactions with media texts. Similarly, it is this tension between structure and agency that frames our concerns in beginning to understand the world of the media professional.

Later on in this chapter the overall approach being taken in this book is explained in greater detail. Let us begin, however, by exploring an example of changes and developments in the mass media from the world of popular music.

CASE STUDY

Making sense of the media: the Irish band U2

In a remote South African village a group of teenage boys listen to the U2 song 'One' on a shared wind-up radio. Afterwards they talk about U2 and the fact that they find them appealing because of their meaningful lyrics. They usually listen to U2 on the radio or on cheap pirated cassette copies of the band's recordings. At the same time in Tokyo a female fan participates in an Internet chatroom discussion about the band's film *Rattle and Hum*. Using a pseudonym, she converses with other U2 fans in America, Australia, Germany and Sweden. A heated debate ensues about the overall quality of the film. The participants debate whether the film represents a high or low point in the band's journey through the roots of American rock-and-roll culture. Some of the fans argue that U2's reinvention of themselves as being postmodern and ironic in their 1990s recordings *Achtung Baby* and *Zooropa* was in fact the zenith of their creativity.

Meanwhile in London a young man listens to the band's music on his recently purchased limited edition U2 branded iPod as he travels to work on the underground. His passage to work is itself a media-rich environment. There are hundreds of adverts in the various Underground stations in addition to the posters within his individual carriage. His fellow travellers read newspapers, books, magazines. Like him, many of them are listening to music on their MP3 players. The young man is thinking about the

Plate 1.1   U2. The Irish band U2 are a prime example of a globalized popular culture. Photograph by Anton Corbijn, courtesy of Principle Management (Dublin) Ltd. © U2 Ltd 2005.

fact that later that evening he will watch U2's Vertigo tour in a 'pay per view' concert, live from Bucharest, via his recently purchased digital satellite television system. The latest technology will allow him to choose from a range of camera angles while watching the concert in his sitting room. The irony that one of the main themes of U2's 1992 Zoo TV tour was about the subversive power of the audience is not lost on him. He watches the concert wearing a U2 t-shirt that he has bought from the official U2 website. Afterwards he converses online with other U2 fans about the concert.

(Continued)

UNDERSTANDING THE MEDIA

These fans all share a common interest in the globalized popular culture and multimedia phenomenon that is U2. However, they interact with and about U2 using different media and in clearly different social contexts. In spite of their shared interest in U2, they do not have equal access to the range of media settings in which U2 may now be found. The fans differ in terms of which of them can afford to pay for legitimate recordings, official band merchandise or live concert broadcasts by the band. Although U2 has an importance for all these fans, we cannot presume anything about the meanings that these fans take from either U2's lyrics or the images contained within their promotional videos or films.

In approaching U2 in this way, we recognize the importance of the apparent globalization of popular culture and the significance of technological change in its spread and distribution. We also recognize the complexities involved.

Asking questions about U2

What sorts of questions might we usefully ask about this specific example of media use? Depending on our chosen theoretical perspective or methodological approach, we might have concerns, for example, about U2 being representative of a globalized (or Americanized) form of popular culture that now predominates over all other popular cultures. If we follow a feminist line of argument, we might be interested in whom – in gender terms – U2 appeal to. Is their audience what is presumed to be a traditional male-dominated, rock-and-roll audience or have they also significance for female fans? What differences, if any, emerge between male and female U2 fans? What other kinds of demographic factors such as age, class or ethnicity shape their fan base? Do U2 fans constitute a specific subculture as would many of the fans of Marilyn Manson, Morrissey or The Cure? (See Hodkinson, 2002 and Chapter 7 of your textbook for further discussion on fandom.)

> ∞
>
> *See Box 1.1 on Baudrillard*

A student taking a postmodern position might be interested in exploring to what extent U2's media products contribute towards creating what Baudrillard termed a 'hyperreality' for their fans. She might ask to what extent their promotional videos, DVDs or films make use of intertextuality. To what extent do U2's audiences appropriate or localize the main themes of their songs in terms of either their own personal experience or their own cultural context?

Alternatively, we might focus on the band's use of new media technology and examine how it shapes the media texts that they produce for their fans.

We could decide to focus on the selling of music (and its related products) as a phenomenon in itself. We could also usefully ask questions about the ownership and control of the production and distribution of media products such as U2's recordings and associated merchandise. In U2's case they are signed to Mercury Records, which is owned and controlled by the multinational global corporation Vivendi Universal – a global conglomerate with diverse interests ranging from music, games, pay-tv, digital television and telephony.

We could possibly do an analysis of their records and videos to examine their content in terms of dominant themes and representations. U2 have already been a focus of attention for some musicologists and sociologists. The songs 'Sunday, Bloody Sunday' and 'Zoo Station' have, for instance, been examined as examples of discourses (Fast, 2000). On the other hand, we might also want to ask some questions about the meaning that U2 have for their audiences in the totality of markets in which their products are bought, sold and exchanged. In doing so we would need to acknowledge the fact that their audiences vary in terms of age, class, gender and ethnicity and location, for example. The contexts in which these fans are exposed to the variety of media products associated with the band – whether they are alone or in a group, for example – might also be of possible significance in our deliberations.

CRITICAL QUESTION 1.2   THE RECORD INDUSTRY

Apply the questions posed about U2 to your favourite recording artist. What sorts of issues emerge?

Asking questions about the media

The way in which we might approach the media behaviour of these hypothetical U2 fans offers us some clues as to how we should try to understand the media more generally. The example suggests that in undertaking media analysis, we should pay sufficient attention to the questions that arise about *context* as much as *text*. That is to say that, while textual analysis is important in its own right, we also need to ask other, equally fundamental questions about the media. These questions might be about the ownership, control and distribution of media products. The questions might be about the dynamics involved in the creation of media products or they might be concerned with audience response(s) or activities. In approaching the media in this way, we have the potential to gain deeper insights into what are increasingly multifaceted phenomena. This more broadly defined approach to understanding the media means that we must learn to choose between a wide range of theoretical and methodological models of media analysis.

The importance of theory and method

By learning to apply a range of theoretical perspectives to the media, you will deepen your understanding of what you might otherwise take for granted. The use of theory will help you think more critically about the media. At the practical level of doing media-based research, it typically involves using a research design that draws upon the strengths of a number of research approaches. Ultimately, through combining theory and method, you will be able to ask critical questions, gather reliable empirical data, and compare and contrast how the media work and are experienced by audiences in diverse social settings. That the media play a central role in the social construction of reality is a key tenet of this book. This stance has important implications in terms of how we approach the analysis of the mass media and of society in general. How do we arrive at a position of knowledge and understanding?

We use a variety of theories and methods in an attempt to add to our overall understanding or knowledge base. Our choice of theory and method not only provides the means of identifying 'truths' but also provides the context within which those 'truths' are reliable and valid.

Theories allow us to move from the specific to the general. They permit us to think about 'facts' at a higher level. They help us to make connections between sometimes otherwise seemingly unrelated phenomena. One useful way to think about the use of theory in this context is to imagine that your overall subject area, discipline or approach is a camera. As a student of the media, you have a range of lenses that you may place on the camera. These will allow you look at something in a variety of ways and perhaps result in your coming to a multiplicity of conclusions, depending upon your chosen lens or lenses. Theories work like a camera lens in this regard: they help to illuminate different aspects of the same phenomena.

To extend the camera metaphor for a moment, research methods may be likened to the other techniques involved in camera work in that they allow you to zoom in or out of specific phenomena. Your choice of method will determine whether you go for the very detailed or the very general aspect of your research question. Research methods allow us to undertake research that is credible. Research should be carried out in a transparent and reputable way. A research design may be replicated in other contexts (in other cultures, societies or communities, for example) and this allows researchers to compare their findings and to test the theoretical implications of their results. Whether you are a student who prefers a qualitative to a quantitative approach, or whether you prefer to combine research approaches to suit your particular research question, the overall aim is to engage in work that is trustworthy and rigorous.

Your choice of theoretical perspective(s) and methodological approach(es) will have an important bearing on how you arrive at a position of understanding and knowledge. Imagine that you are asked to undertake a short piece of observation-based research on the followers of punk music. If your interest is in the sociology of subcultures or countercultures, you might concentrate on how punks invert the meanings of symbols that already have currency in wider society such as safety pins, the swastika or bin-liner bags, for example. Alternatively, you might be interested in how individual punks conform to the norms and values of the subculture or counterculture to which they belong. If your interest is in gender politics, your focus might be on whether punk culture replicates or challenges patriarchal relationships of power. The choices that you make about theory and method therefore have important implications for furthering your knowledge and understanding.

Paradigms and perspectives

The mass media have been analysed by a wide range of academic disciplines using a variety of theoretical and research approaches. Mass media analysis is best described as eclectic. While individual authors and members of particular 'schools' may be dedicated to a specific theoretical or methodological model, the practice of doing media analysis is not the preserve of any single discipline or approach. Where actual research is concerned, authors vary not only in terms of their theoretical position, research question(s) and research design, but also in the extent to which their work may be described as being quantitative or qualitative in its orientation.

Mass media analysis began in the first half of the twentieth century within established subject areas such as philosophy, political science, psychology and sociology. Early examples of empirical research on the mass media – such as those using the experimental design model most associated with social psychology – are usually described as following an 'effects' model of media research in that they sought to examine the effects that the mass media content were reputed to have on the audience.

The last thirty years or so of the twentieth century witnessed more highly specialized media analysis with the emergence of a range of approaches – as opposed to particular academic disciplines – that are more specifically focused on particular aspects of the mass media. These approaches include, for example, communication studies, cultural studies, film studies, journalism, linguistics, media studies and social informatics. They have borrowed theories and methods of research from the more traditional subject areas in the social sciences and humanities as well as generating novel ways of approaching the media. Ethnography, for example, which has its roots within traditional anthropology and was originally applied to the study of 'primitive' societies, has been used to analyse the internal workings of media organizations and to understand more about the mass media audience. The textual orientation of a great deal of cultural studies research on the mass media has its roots within literary criticism and semiotics (the study of signs and symbols) in particular. These developments have given rise to a growing body of research literature, much of it concerned with popular forms of culture and especially those to be found on television.

Older disciplines such as sociology and psychology continue to have an interest in the mass media and it is also a well-established concern for the 'younger' and related subject areas and approaches such as discourse analysis, gender studies and postmodernism (see Box 1.1 Key thinker: Jean Baudrillard). The broad field of mass media analysis is not without its tensions, however. As the Extracted Reading 1.1 by Tester (1994) illustrates later in this chapter, there have been hostile exchanges between the more established disciplines such as sociology and newer approaches like cultural studies as to the form and direction of media analysis. Debates have taken place, for example, between those who favour textual analysis and those who emphasize the importance of examining the structure of ownership and control of the mass media. Others have concentrated their research energies on the sense that audiences make of media texts. All in all, the continuing growth and expansion of the mass media have been mirrored by the development of more sophisticated means of media analysis within both the older disciplines and the newer, more recent approaches. The robust nature of the debate amongst those interested in media analysis is testament to the vitality and health of the subject area.

BOX 1.1   KEY THINKER: JEAN BAUDRILLARD (1929-)

The contentious French thinker Jean Baudrillard looms large over recent controversy about the role of the mass media in everyday life. Influenced initially by Marxism and semiotics – and by Roland Barthes and Marshall McLuhan in particular – Baudrillard's writings have come to serve as *the* manifesto for adherents of postmodern theory. According to Baudrillard, the postmodern experience is defined by and through the 'ecstasy of communication'. In living media-saturated lives, the media texts that surround us simulate a 'hyper-reality' for audiences in which 'media reality' is more 'real' than 'reality' itself.

Baudrillard's most controversial book is, arguably, *The Gulf War Did Not Take Place* (1995). Here, he examines the extent to which the (first) Gulf War took place in a virtual space, i.e. on our television screens. This war was different from previous wars in that it was represented within some media coverage as a virtual reality game. The symbols and language used (e.g. a target-rich environment) were unprecedented in terms of war coverage.

It is not surprising that Baudrillard's ideas have caused considerable controversy. He has been criticized for over-generalizing, for being politically disengaged, and for not testing his ideas against any empirical research findings on how audience members actually experience media saturation and whether or not they engage critically with media content.

> You should now read EXTRACTED READING 1.1, *A Sociological Approach to Media Analysis* (Tester, 1994) and consider the following issues:
>
> 1   How does Tester characterize a sociological approach to media analysis? How does it differ from a cultural studies approach?
>
> 2   Tester stresses the need to use the 'sociological imagination' – a term first coined by the sociologist C. Wright Mills and discussed in the introduction to this book – in our approach to the mass media. What sorts of benefits does its use bring?

What sorts of questions?

We have just seen that academic study of the media embraces a wide range of disciplines and research paradigms. In the midst of an ever-expanding body of media research, and in the light of the explicit emphasis upon social context in this textbook, eight interrelated concerns stand out, in our opinion, as being the most salient in attempting to explain recent changes and developments in the media. These are:

1   What is the extent and significance of media globalization?
2   Who owns and controls the media?
3   What sorts of forces within and without media organizations shape the creation of media products?
4   How is media content best analysed?
5   How do media texts represent the social world? What do they tell us about social relationships concerning power?
6   How democratic are the media in terms of audience access and participation?
7   To what extent and in what circumstances are audiences active agents in the construction of meaning?
8   What is the impact of new forms of media technology upon society and more specifically how are they responsible for social change?

These eight themes underscore the focus of the chapters that follow. These themes – all concerned with the concept of 'power' in one shape or another – point to the complexities involved in doing critical media analysis. They also indicate why the study of the media with all its inherent complexities and contradictions is ultimately a fascinating and rewarding enterprise (see Devereux, 2006 for an elaboration).

Model of media analysis: production, content and reception

These eight key questions about the media clearly overlap and intersect with one another. Taken singly, and in combination, all these issues have the potential to

Contexts	Focuses
• Media globalization	• Production, content and reception of media texts
• The restructuring of media ownership	• Media representations of the social world
• Technological change	• Audiences are capable of agency
• Unequal social structure in modern/postmodern societies	• Audiences' interpretations of media texts

FIGURE 1.2   Model of media analysis employed

throw further light on how we understand the media. In this book, however, we are concerned, in the main, with the analysis of mass-mediated texts that are circulated among large numbers of people. When we come to analyse such media texts, we do so increasingly in the twin contexts of media globalization and technological change. Both are responsible for the shaping and reshaping of the media environment in which we operate as audience members and as students of the media.

In terms of an overall model of media analysis, this book encourages you to think sequentially about media texts in the contexts of their production, content and reception. While there will be the inevitable variations between media and divergences in emphasis among individual media researchers, arguably these are the three zones of critical importance in doing media analysis.

The proposed model suggests that you begin by thinking about the production context of media texts. Here you might consider the various contexts – cultural, economic, legal, organizational, political, social and technological – in which a specific media text is created. This approach will help inform your understanding of the dynamics involved in the making of a particular media text and it may also be used as a backdrop towards furthering your understanding of its actual content and reception.

The second suggested stage in undertaking media analysis is to examine the content of the media text. In focusing on media content, we are usually concerned with the potency (or not) of a media text in shaping people's understanding of social reality in some way. It might be used, for example, as the basis for investigating the ideological content of a media text concerning patriarchy or gender inequality. As before, this research strategy may be used in isolation or in combination with analyses of production or audience reception.

The power of both media organizations and media texts to shape perceptions of social reality hinges ultimately on their capacity to influence audiences. The media occupy a privileged position in the socialization of both young and old in society. While media texts have the potential to alter one's perception of the world, they are not operating in a vacuum. Media texts are in competition with other media texts; audiences can accept, appropriate or reject media texts depending upon a wide range of sometimes complex circumstances.

Media construction of social reality

1. Read the following extract concerning asylum seekers in the UK then rewrite the 'story' as if you were a newspaper reporter. How does your version compare with (a) the orginal version and (b) the versions produced by your fellow students?

2. What is the significance of including or omitting specific descriptors of asylum seekers?

3. If you are not based in the UK, compare the ways in which asylum seekers are portrayed in the print media where you live. What are the main similarities and differences?

4. Consider the significance of the use of language in the construction of meaning for audience members in the piece.

5. Media researchers such as Haynes, Devereux and Breen (2006) suggest that media coverage of immigrants makes use of 'othering' discourses – i.e. reports will routinely set up an opposition between 'them' and 'us'. Is this in evidence in this article?

£16,000
That's what the average asylum seeker's family gets a year in handouts (and it's all tax-free!)

Families of asylum seekers are getting more than £16,000 in tax-free handouts every year, it was revealed yesterday.

Startling Government figures showed immigrants are better off than newly qualified teachers or experienced NHS nurses as they wait for their applications to be processed.

Immigration Minister Beverly Hughes admitted the support given to an average asylum-seeking family amounts to £1,340 a month – the after-tax equivalent of a £20,500 salary.

A teacher would take three years to achieve that level of earnings and nurses would need five years of hard work and rapid promotion.

The figure includes cash benefits and housing given to an average asylum-seeking couple with 2.13 children – but not the burden on the NHS, schools or the costs to the Home Office and courts of processing asylum claims.

For some families, the figure is far higher than the average. The family of extremist Muslim cleric Abu Hamza, a father of eight, receives £1,000 a week in benefits, although the hook-handed preacher's own support has been blocked while the Government fights to deport him.

The total cost of the asylum system to the tax-payer is estimated at almost £2 billion a year, or £5 million a day, covering cash benefits, housing and legal bills. This includes the £174 million in legal aid last year and the huge bureaucracy needed to process claims and appeals. . . .

At the start of this year [2003], 91,860 asylum seekers were receiving state support – 42,130 members of families and 49,730 single adults.

There are also tens of thousands of families who have been granted asylum but are claiming benefit. Once asylum has been granted, they would move over to the normal benefits system. The Government has struggled to deport large numbers of failed asylum seekers because of problems in tracking them down and the expense of locking them up in secure units and laying on special flights.

Mr. Blunkett recently admitted that he 'hadn't a clue' how many failed asylum seekers were still in Britain, although officials believe the figure runs to hundreds of thousands. . . .

The chances of winning an asylum appeal have soared from 6 per cent when Labour came to power to 22 per cent last year. Numbers of successful appeals have rocketed from 1,180 to more than 13,000 – a 12-fold increase. . . .

Tory MP Andrew Rosindell said 'A lot of lower-paid workers doing important jobs will be pretty cross to hear of families getting this kind of support just for turning up and claiming asylum.'

Report by Matthew Hickley, Home Affairs Correspondent, *Daily Mail* (UK), published 16 December 2003. Extract reproduced with permission © *The Daily Mail*, 2003.

You should now read EXTRACTED READING 1.2, *Asking the Right Questions* (Halloran, 1998) and consider the following issues:

1   Do you understand what Halloran means by the term 'media-centredness'? What are the problems with taking a media-centred approach in media analysis?

2   Think of an example of how you would apply Halloran's model in attempting to understand more about the communications process. In doing so, outline the various stages involved in undertaking such a piece of research.

CASE STUDY

The Simpsons: Not just a dysfunctional blue-collar family . . .

The cartoon series *The Simpsons* is a classic example of the globalization of popular culture. Its importance, however, extends beyond its obvious popularity with younger and older audience members in different societies and cultures. *The Simpsons* also makes an interesting case study in the increasingly transnational nature of cultural production, given that the main animation of the series is undertaken in South Korea, while its distribution is owned and controlled by Twentieth Television (formerly known as Twentieth Century Fox) in North America (see Elber, 2001). Produced by Gracie Films for Twentieth Television – a media giant that is in turn owned by Rupert Murdoch's News Corporation – the programme is a valuable commodity for its owners and creators. *The Simpsons* began life as a short insert on the *Tracey Ullman Show* in 1989 and is contracted to run until 2008. The show's central protagonist was initially Bart but this soon gave way to a greater focus on Homer, who represents a latterday bungling but immensely popular 'Everyman'. In 1998 *The Simpsons* generated syndication sales of US$3 million per episode (Schlosser, 1998). In 2003 it was estimated that sales from *Simpsons* T-Shirts in the US alone were worth US$20 million with global syndication revenues estimated to be US$1 billion. (Bonne, 2003). The series has helped maximize audiences, advertising and sponsorship for a variety of television networks and it has generated additional profits for its owners and creators in the shape of the merchandising of toys, t-shirts, pyjamas, chocolate, breakfast cereals and PlayStation games, for example. In a range of territories such as Australia and Western Europe, *The Simpsons* series has played a pivotal role in the ratings war between publicly and privately owned television channels.

The Simpsons is not just a television phenomenon, however. It has crossed over into other media settings such as film, video, DVD and the Internet. There are many websites where dedicated fans dissect individual episodes of the series and discuss the meaning of specific storylines. As a complex media text about the lives and experiences of America's most famous dysfunctional blue-collar family, the television programme attempts to engage with its audience on a wide variety of issues. Individual episodes of the programme are replete with intertextual references and parodies. The cartoon within the cartoon – the Itchy and Scratchy Show – is a clear send-up of the effects debate within media and communications studies about children and television violence. The decoding of *The Simpsons* requires of its readers a vast array of reference points from Western popular culture. The history of the Beatles, for example, has been used as the basis of the storyline of Homer's barbershop quartet group 'The B-Sharps'. The storyline included a reference to barfly Barney Gumble's decision to marry a Japanese performance artist based presumably on the John Lennon and Yoko Ono story. The Beatle's pilgrimage to India in search of knowledge and wisdom was parodied in an episode which saw Homer and Apu travel to India in order to speak to the founder of Kwik E Mart.

There is also – to a certain extent – evidence of reflexivity in that *The Simpsons* manages to critique many of the dominant ideologies at play in North America about class, ethnicity, gender and religiosity. Bad capitalism is personified in the programme through the character of Mr Burns – owner of among other things, the local nuclear power plant. The hypocrisy of the media dropping in on the homeless on Thanksgiving while rendering them invisible for the rest of the year was satirized in an episode entitled 'Bart vs. Thanksgiving' (see Box 1.2). Issues concerning ethnic differences and gender inequality in the United States are recurring themes.

BOX 1.2   BART VS. THANKSGIVING

In 'Bart vs. Thanksgiving' (episode 7507: 1990), Bart Simpson has run away from home. Having sold a pint of his blood for US$12 at a plasma centre, he ends up at a local Rescue Mission soup kitchen. His family only realizes where he is when they see him on the perennial Thanksgiving news report being broadcast live from the soup kitchen. The Springfield news station – Channel 6 (kwz) – has, once again, sent their news anchorman Kent Brockman to cover the annual 'event' of the Thanksgiving Homeless story. What follows is an interesting parody on the media's treatment of homelessness. In his report, Brockman says: 'Oh, we have lots of names for these people. Bums, deadbeats and losers, scums of the earth. We'd like to sweep these people into the gutter, or if they are already in the gutter, to some other out-of-the-way place. Oh, we have our reasons. They're depressing, they wear ragged clothes they're [he makes a quotation sign with his fingers] "crazy", they smell bad.' He is interrupted by a homeless man who says 'Hey, listen, man . . .'. Brockman continues however by whispering 'Wait, I'm going somewhere with this . . . Kent Brockman's Emmy-winning news report from a soup kitchen.' He then interviews Bart Simpson who claims to have been homeless for nearly five years. Brockman packs away his things and says, 'This reporter smells another local Emmy.'

There is also a sense in watching *The Simpsons* that it is consciously written as a multi-layered text. One of the best examples of the latter might be the ongoing reference to the ambiguous nature of Mr Smithers' sexuality. Within a single episode the text can reproduce some of the slapstick humour traditionally associated with cartoons in combination with a discourse about being a closeted gay man. Many of the episodes contain a consciously 'camp' discourse (see Henry, 2004). Thus the programme manages to mix the usual ingredients of the cartoon genre – which presumably appeal to its younger fans – with other narratives that have more of an adult interest (Mullen, 2004). *The Simpsons* has (rightly) been celebrated by many commentators for the way in which it has challenged racism and ethnic stereotypes – the one exception being its repeated representation of the Irish as being simian or ape-like and particularly prone to violence and drunkenness.

There is more to the series than its clever scripts, however. In a rare moment in one episode of *The Simpsons*, viewers saw its news anchorman Kent Brockman reporting on location from a South Korean animation house where the animators were drawing and colouring at bayonet point (episode 9503: 1992). Although the programme has in the past parodied media mogul Rupert Murdoch and his dominance of the world's media, the 'moment' of Brockman's report was a defining one. While it did not contain any direct reference to its own production context, the parody struck an important chord. While some might see this as being just one more example of post-modern irony, it is also a very telling comment on the American animation industry that increasingly makes use of what it euphemistically refers to as 'overseas anima-tion'. In an important essay, Cherniavsky gives us an account of how and where *The Simpsons* is produced:

> Film Roman subcontracts the labor-intensive aspects of production of the series, including the drawing and coloring of cells, to one of six 'animation houses' in South Korea. According to studio owner Phil Roman, underpriced Asian labor has become indispensable to the animation industry in the United States: 'If we had to do animation here,' Roman notes, 'It would cost a million dollars instead of $100,000 to $150,000 to produce a half-hour, and nobody could afford to do it except for Disney.' (1999: 141)

Cherniavsky argues that *The Simpsons*, in spite of its occasional reflexivity about cap-italism, is:

> profoundly implicated in a system of global capital that requires and perpetu-ates the existence of a casual and chronically impoverished labor force – for example, at Akom, the largest of the South Korean animation houses, where *The Simpsons* is produced, 1,100 of the 1,200 employees are temporary work-ers, paid around $1.50 per cell for the tedious job of inking and painting – *The Simpsons* cannot reflect on its own transpacific origins. (1999: 153–4)

Film Roman became known as DPS Film Roman in 2004. The current production arrangements for *The Simpsons* involve upwards of 120 animators working for AKOM in Seoul, South Korea. Here, animators are paid less than one-third of what their North American counterparts would receive for the same work. They work according to instructions sent from the US on the desired camera and colouring requirements. The wider political context of the relationship between the US and South Korea should also be noted. In addition to availing itself of cheap labour, the US seems intent on bolstering the economic development of South Korea whilst it is in ideological conflict with communist North Korea.

By looking at *The Simpsons* in this way, we have highlighted a number of impor-tant issues. *The Simpsons* can be seen as a well-constructed media text containing a

(Continued)

29

Plate 1.2 *The Simpsons* relies heavily on the cheap labour provided by the South Korean animation industry. Photo by You Sung-Ho (2005). Reproduced by kind permission. © Reuters.

range of meanings for its global audience, which is in itself segmented into various groups depending on age, social status, geographical location, gender and ethnicity, for example. *The Simpsons* can also be viewed as a valuable commodity produced by one of the key players in the global media industry. Like many other commodities, its overall production takes place in more than one country. The programme is a source of profit for its owners and creators as well as the television networks that buy the right to broadcast the series. Animated television and film are more amenable to translation and therefore travel well in the globalized media marketplace. While at this juncture we can only speculate on the intentions of the programme's writers and producers, there is nonetheless some evidence to suggest that, as a text, *The Simpsons* reproduces an ideological viewpoint that may be considered to be liberal rather than critical in orientation.

Our approach to *The Simpsons* has stressed the importance of knowing equally about production, content and reception. It draws upon a framework that gives equal weighting to political economy, content analysis and reception analysis in order to understand this globalized multimedia phenomenon more fully. This three-part approach is the paradigm upon which this textbook is based.

BOX 1.3 DON'T HAVE A (SACRED) COW MAN: *THE SIMPSONS* AND HEGEMONY

Brook's (2004) examination of the ideological positioning of *The Simpsons* argues that the programme has, in fact, been quite successful in challenging the hegemonic order present in the USA. Using both auterist and ethnographic approaches, he examines how a combination of subversive encodings by the programme's creative producers and a set of resistant and oppositional readings by an audience group made up of non-fans, function to challenge dominant ideologies. *The Simpsons*, he suggests, is 'consistently satirical' and is 'occasionally subversive' (2004: 172) and it manages to challenge many of the sacred cows apparent in the USA. It has managed to do this from within the system.

Furthermore, it is worth noting that Brook makes reference to how Bart Simpson has been appropriated by some black audience members. He tells us that 'In summer 1990, unlicensed T-shirts with black images of Bart Simpson popped up in Five Points, Colorado, where they became a hot seller at an African American Juneteenth celebration. Among the most popular T-shirt decorations were 'Air Bart' – a black Bart in a Michael Jordan-Nike takeoff; Bart as a 'Young Gifted and Black Dude'; and a dreadlock-sporting 'Rasta Bart'. (2004: 178)

You should now read EXTRACTED READING 1.3, *Playing the Piano Wearing Mittens* (McChesney, 2000) and answer the following questions:

1 What is the nature of the relationship between the mass media and democracy?

2 Why do students and scholars of the mass media have a special role to play in the analysis of the contemporary mass media?

Understanding the media in a social context: blogging

Let us conclude this chapter by briefly considering a recent addition to many people's daily media lives. Since 1997 'weblogs', or 'blogs' as they are more commonly known, have emerged as a significant feature of daily Internet activity. 'Blogs' and the practice of 'blogging' are of interest because they allow ordinary people to become media producers in their own right. At the most basic level we can see the production of content for consumption by others who may be known or unknown to the producer.

The technology is free (or cheap) and is easy to use. Blogs allow for the creation of new content, for commentary or reactions to previous entries and for links to other blogs or websites. Blogs are concerned with an ever-widening range of topics and are governed by a blog etiquette. Matheson (2005: 171–4)) shows how the freelance journalist Christopher Allbritton's blog *Back to Iraq* offered his readers a detailed understanding of the conflict during 2003. His success in developing a relationship with his on-line readers resulted in 320 of them sending him money in order for him to return to Iraq. Matheson (2005) argues that over time the content of the blog is shaped by the reactions of its readers.

In addition to reflecting the views and concerns of ordinary citizens, they are increasingly being used by powerful interest groups in society such as politicians and political parties as well as an adjunct to existing mainstream media such as newspapers and television news programmes. Alongside podcasts, blogs are an interesting example of where audience members can exercise their agency and express their points of view to the wider public.

Blogs are often mistakenly characterized as being the on-line equivalent of a personal diary replete with confessions of a personal nature for all to see. However, Nardi et al. (2004) in an ethnographic study of North American bloggers point to the numerous variations involved in this kind of media activity (see Chapter 7 of your textbook for an elaboration on the ethnographic approach).

Blog content as well as levels of access to blogs vary. Nardi et al. focus on blogging as a social activity, noting how blog content can change as a result of reader/audience reactions. An on-line etiquette is observed by most bloggers. Nardi et al. (2004) also found that the exchanges between bloggers carry over into other forms of media such as email and text-messaging. Bloggers communicate with people they know and to a wider public they will never encounter in their daily lives referred to as the 'blogosphere'. Nardi et al. (2004) differentiate between bloggers who create content for people they know, such as family and friends, and those who generate content in order to influence public opinion about a political or human rights issue, for example. Far from being a confessional diary-like space, blogging is, they argue, a social activity and needs to be understood as such.

Conclusion

The twenty-first-century media present the media student with an increasingly complex set of questions. Globalization, technological change and the restructuring of media ownership underscore many of the questions that have been asked about the mass media as well as raising new kinds of issues for all of us in our roles as students and citizens. There are clear tensions in the field of media analysis as to how we should approach a critical understanding of the mass media. While a sociological approach to media analysis would recognize the so-called 'pleasure(s) of the text' experienced by audience members, there is more to media analysis than a sole focus on the 'ecstasy of communication' which many postmodernists would hold as sacrosanct. A sociology of media informed by political economy stresses the need to examine these new mass media realities by reference to the increasingly concentrated nature of media ownership. It asks us to consider whose interests exactly are served by mass media conglomeration.

In this chapter it has been suggested that we need to undertake media analysis in a critical and systematic way. By using a framework that gives equal recognition to the production, content and reception of media texts, we can begin to make sense of the increasingly complex media environment in which we live our lives. It is within these parameters that we can now proceed to consider questions – both old and new – about the twenty-first-century mass media. The overarching theme of this first chapter is that there is much to be gained by considering these questions in a sociological light.

Extracted readings

1.1   A sociological approach to media analysis

Keith Tester, *Media, Culture and Morality*. London: Routledge, 1994, pp. 4–5

. . . There is much more to be said about the media than cultural studies can allow. Most of these additional things can be said if a sociological light is brought to bear on the media. This is because sociology holds out the possibility of a lively study of culture which is informed by a seriousness of moral and cultural purpose of a kind that is inconceivable from the point of view of cultural studies.

. . . Sociology might do this because, unlike cultural studies, if it is worth doing, sociology is not happy just to describe and explore what exists. Sociology ought to be driven by a sense of moral commitment and by a moral outrage at what presently passes for a good life; an outrage that cultural studies, with its increasing emphasis on things like clothes and shopping, can say absolutely nothing about.

Sociology ought to seek to know why things happen. In so doing it offers the chance that it will be possible to develop an argument for why things ought to have happened differently in the past or could be made to happen differently in the future. Consequently, a sociological approach can mean that we will refuse to take anything at all for granted. Certainly, we will be unable to take it for granted that something is 'good' or 'boring' simply because it is. Sociology can in principle rescue the media – and therefore the cultural and moral values – from the trivialization to which they are otherwise all too susceptible.

. . . If a sociological imagination is brought to bear on the question of the media and their impact on cultural and moral values, then it is potentially possible to encourage people to think about the media for themselves. People in principle will be able to develop their own attitudes towards the media rather than simply accept what they are told.

1.2   Asking the right questions

James Halloran, 'Mass communication research: asking the right questions' in Anders Hansen, Simon Cottle, Ralph Negrine and Chris Newbold (eds), *Mass Communication Research Methods*. London: Macmillan, 1998, p. 19

. . . Over the years there has been a growing appreciation that the whole communication process needs to be studied, and that includes those who provide (including their institutions) as well as the nature of what is provided, and those who receive what is provided. For example, the production of programmes in broadcasting fulfils functions for the institution, the broadcaster, the audience and society at large. This needs to be recognized and dealt with in research. Intentions, aims, purposes, policies, organizational frameworks, modes of operation, professional values, funding, general circumscriptions, external pressures and ideological considerations all need to be taken into account.

Ideally, the media should not be seen in isolation, but as one set of social institutions, interacting with other institutions within the wider social system. The failure to recognize the relevance of context and interaction between institutions has resulted in a neglect of the part played in the communication process by non-media institutions, and an underestimation of the importance of mediation, support factors, follow-up activities and the like. The other side of this coin is the problem of media-centredness. The media do not work in isolation, but in and through a nexus of mediating factors. What any medium can do on its own is probably quite limited.

Let it be repeated that, simply stated, this means that we should not be asking what the media do to people, or what they could do to people, but what will people, variously located in society, with different experiences, opportunities, skills, competencies and needs, make of what the media and other sources provide, and which are available to them? This is really at the heart of the problem, and if we fail to get this question right, our research will be worthless.

1.3   Playing the piano wearing mittens

Robert W. McChesney, 'The political economy of communication and the future of the field', *Media, Culture and Society* 22 (1) (2000): 115

Communication scholars must play a central role in analysing, debating and popularizing issues concerning the relationship of media and democracy. This is an area that conventional politicians and the corporate media have shown little inclination to pursue. Only communication scholars have the resources and institutional basis to move forward with honest independent scholarship and instruction, with a commitment first and foremost to democratic values. The field of communication needs to apply the full weight of its intellectual traditions and methodologies to the daunting questions before us. They desperately require scholarly attention . . . if the field of communication does not do it, nobody else will.

. . . Political economy and communication have a special relationship. Each of them is located uneasily but necessarily between capitalism and democracy; each deals with commercial and material issues and each is ultimately concerned with issues of social justice and political self-government. While one can be a political economist and have only a passing interest in communication issues, the need to at least have a passing interest has grown considerably in this, the so-called Information Age. And if one is a scholar of communication, it strikes me as highly questionable not to have a working knowledge of political economy, in order to understand how capitalism works. To approach communication without political economy is similar to playing the piano wearing mittens. If scholars are to move beyond description to explanation, political economy must be at the center of the enterprise. It is not only the necessary aspect of the field of communication, but it is one of the cornerstones.

Exercise 1.2

The media diary

A basic starting point in beginning to understand the media more critically is to examine the role of the media in your own life. The object of this exercise is to establish the extent and range of your interactions with the media. With this in mind, you should keep a diary of your media use and consumption for a period of one week. Your diary should consider all forms of media use and consumption in the selected seven days. Remember to document as many situations as possible where you are exposed to mass media texts. It is important to consider your use of traditional as well as newer forms of media.

The diary itself should attempt to be as comprehensive an account as possible of your everyday media interactions. For each day note the kinds of media that you use; estimate the amount of time spent in specific kinds of media use and, especially where the print and broadcast media are concerned, highlight the kinds of media genres that you typically engage with. Where you consume specific media texts such as radio or film – whether in a private or a public context – may also be of significance. It is also worthwhile noting whether you discuss the content of specific media texts with your family, friends or colleagues. Your media consumption extends way beyond the media that you might actively use, so you should also document the other kinds of situations in which you consume media texts. (It might be an advertising hoarding on your way to college or work, for example.)

In beginning to explain your own media use and consumption patterns, you should start by examining your findings in the context of where you 'fit' in social terms. You should consider the significance (or not) of your age, class, ethnicity, gender and regional location in trying to understand your personal media use and consumption. An example of a diary is contained in Figure 1.3.

UNDERSTANDING THE MEDIA

Student Name: Joseph Gavin (Media Studies student)
Day: Monday
Date: 14 April 2007

Time	Media	Ownership	Genre	Estimate length of time (minutes)	Were you alone or in the company of others?	Public or private?	What else were you doing at the time?	Discussed with others?	Exposure to other media?
7.00 a.m.	Radio	Public service	News bulletin	30	Alone	Private	Showering and breakfast	No	None
8.00 a.m.	PC	N/A	E-mail	14	Alone	Private	Nothing	No	On-screen banner advertising when I logged on
9.00 a.m.	Radio	Pirate radio	Country and western music	45	With 43 others on the bus	Public	Commuting to college	Yes. I complained to the person sitting beside me about the bus driver's choice of music!	Advertising on the bus itself. Outdoor advertising hoardings for beer, cars and condoms. Several people on the bus were reading newspapers
10.00 a.m.	News-papers	News Corporation.	Broadsheet and tabloid	37	With two classmates	Public	Having a coffee	Discussed the story of the day	College radio station being played in the background in canteen

(Continued)

Time	Media	Ownership	Genre	Estimate length of time (minutes)	Were you alone or in the company of others?	Public or private?	What else were you doing at the time?	Discussed with others?	Exposure to other media?
11.00 a.m.	DVD	Universal Pictures	Horror film	60	With fellow students	Public	In tutorial discussion on neogothic film	Yes. Marks are awarded for participation	None
12.00 p.m.	MP3	N/A	Punk Rock	30	Alone	Public	Studying	No	None
1.00 p.m.	PC	N/A	Surfing the web; downloading music files	55	In college library	Public	Nothing	Talked to my friend about a new online fantasy game.	Onscreen banner advertising when I logged on
2.00 p.m.	Book	Sage Publications	Media studies textbook	41	In college library	Public	Nothing	No	No
3.00 p.m	Lectures	N/A	Lectures	Lectures	Lectures	Lectures	Lectures	Lectures	Lectures
4.00 p.m.	Lectures	N/A	Lectures	Lectures	Lectures	Lectures	Lectures	Lectures	One of my fellow student's mobile phone rang
5.00 p.m.	CD	Universal	Rap music	16	With classmate	Private	Getting lift home in car	Discussed the lyrics heard on CD	No
6.00 p.m.	Television	Public service	News	37	My parents, who were visiting me	Private	Eating the main evening meal	Discussed the main news stories with my parents	No

(Continued)

Time	Media	Ownership	Genre	Estimate length of time (minutes)	Were you alone or in the company of others?	Public or private?	What else were you doing at the time?	Discussed with others?	Exposure to other media?
7.00 p.m.	Television	Independent commercial channel	Soap opera	30	My parents	Private	No	Talked about the soap's latest storyline	Commercial breaks and programme sponsorship
8.00 p.m.	Radio	Independent licensed station	Rock music	20	Alone	Private	Cleaning up	No	No
9.00 p.m.	Television	News Corporation	Pay-per-view film	60	With girlfriend	Private	Relaxing	Compared it with the director's previous film	No
10.00 p.m.	Television	News Corporation	Pay-per-view film	30	With girlfriend	Private	Relaxing	Compared it with the director's previous film	No
11.00 p.m.	Internet	Site hosted by fans of *Star Trek*	Weblog	60	Alone	Private	No	Talked about the next *Star Trek* Convention	Yes. Banner advertising re. *Star Trek* memorabilia

FIGURE 1.3 Example of a media diary

In writing up the general summary of your diary, you should pay attention to the following issues:

1 Can you estimate the amount of time in which you interact with the various media on a daily basis?
2 How do your use patterns compare in terms of using traditional and newer forms of media?
3 To what extent are your media use and consumption undertaken alone or in a social setting (i.e. with family, with a partner, friends or with fellow students)?
4 Is your use of television primarily about being informed or entertained or both?
5 If you are an atypical student (such as a mature student, part-time student or adult-learner) how does your media diary compare with full-time undergraduate students?

Key issues to be addressed

Identify clearly the media organizations with which you mainly interact. Can you identify who owns them?

1 What proportion of your media consumption involves globalized media products?
2 Select one 'story' during your week of diary-keeping and compare how it was treated by at least four media organizations. How and why does coverage differ between them?
3 How does your media consumption compare with that of your fellow students? What sorts of differences emerged and why?

Questions for consideration and discussion

1 Has reading this chapter altered in any way the manner in which you look at your own media consumption?
2 Having read the Tester (1994) and Halloran (1998) extracts, what are the key differences between a cultural studies and a sociological approach to media analysis?
3 Choosing any one example from your own media consumption, apply the production, content and reception analysis model outlined earlier in this chapter.

References

Baudrillard, J. (1995), trans. P. Patton, *The Gulf War Did Not Take Place*. Bloomington and Indianapolis: Indiana University Press.

Bonne, J. (2003) 'Simpsons evolves as an industry,' www.msnbc.msn.com, Nov. 7.

Brook, V. (2004) 'Myth or consequences: ideological fault lines in *The Simpsons*' in J. Alberti (ed.) *Leaving Springfield: The Simpsons and the Possibility of Oppositional Culture*. Detroit: Wayne State University Press, pp. 172–96.

Cherniavsky, E. (1999) '"Karmic realignment": transnationalism and trauma in *The Simpsons*. *Cultural Critique*, 41 (4): 139–57.

Devereux, E. (2006) 'Media and mass media' in A. Harrington, B. Marshall and H.P. Muller (eds) *The Routledge Encyclopaedia of Social Theory*. London: Routledge.

Elber, L. (2001) 'Television's *The Simpsons* goes global', The Simpsons Archive, www.snpp.com/other/articles/goesglobal.html.

Fast, S. (2000) 'Music, contexts and meaning in U2' in W. Everett (ed.) *Expression in Pop-Rock Music: A Collection of Critical and Analytical Essays*. New York: Garland Publishing Inc., pp. 33–57.

Gitlin, T. (2002) *Media Unlimited*. New York: Metropolitan Books.

Halloran, J. (1998) 'Mass communication research: asking the right questions' in A. Hansen, S. Cottle, R. Negrine and C. Newbold (eds) *Mass Communication Research Methods*. London: Macmillan.

Hanson, R. (2005) *Mass Communication: Living in a Media World*. Boston: McGraw-Hill.

Haynes, A., E. Devereux and M. Breen (2006) 'Fear, framing and foreignness', *International Journal of Critical Psychology*. Spring.

Henry, M. (2004) 'Looking for Amanda Hugginkiss: gay life on *The Simpsons*' in J. Alberti (ed.) *Leaving Springfield: The Simpsons and the Possibility of Oppositional Culture*. Detroit: Wayne State University Press, pp. 225–43.

Hodkinson, P. (2002) *Goth: Identity, Style and Sub-Culture*. Berg: Oxford and New York.

Livingstone, S. (1998) 'Mediated childhoods: a comparative approach to young people's changing media environment in Europe', *European Journal of Communication* 13 (4): 435–56.

Livingstone, S. (2002) *Young People and New Media*. London: Sage.

McQuail, D. (2000) *McQuail's Mass Communication Theory*. London: Sage.

Matheson, D. (2005) *Media Discourses*. Maidenhead: Open University Press.

Mullen, M. (2004) 'The Simpsons and Hanna-Barbera's Animation Legacy in *The Simpsons*' in J. Alberti (ed.) *Leaving Springfield: The Simpsons and the Possibility of Oppositional Culture*. Detroit: Wayne State University Press, pp. 63–84.

Nardi, B.A., D. J. Schiano and M. Gumbrecht (2004) 'Blogging as social activity, or would you let 900 million people read your diary?' *Proceedings of the 2004 ACM Conference, Computer Supported Co-Operative Network*. New York: ACM Press, pp. 222–31.

Schlosser, J. (1998) '"King" poised to beat Bart', *Broadcasting and Cable* 128(26): 48.

Silverstone, R. (1999) *Why Study the Media?* London: Sage.

Tester, K. (1994) *Media, Culture and Morality*. London: Routledge.

Going further

Alberti, J. (ed.) (2004) *Leaving Springfield: The Simpsons and the Possibility of Oppositional Culture*. Detroit: Wayne State University Press. An edited collection of essays on a wide range of aspects of *The Simpsons,* including its ideological orientation and its representation of gay issues.

Cherniavsky, E. (2006) *Incorporations: Race, Nation and the Body Politics of Capital.* Minnesota: University of Minnesota Press. This book contains an updated essay on the Asian production context of *The Simpsons.*

Croteau, D. and W. Hoynes (2003) *Media/Society: Industries, Images and Audiences*, 3rd edn. Thousand Oaks, CA: Pine Forge Press. This is a very thorough and student-friendly introduction to mass media analysis from a sociological perspective.

Deacon, D., M. Pickering, P. Golding and G. Murdock (1999) *Researching Communications*. London: Arnold. A very useful introduction to the research methods needed for mass media analysis.

Fenton, N. (1999) 'Mass media' in S. Taylor (ed.) *Sociology: Issues and Debates*. London: Macmillan. An excellent introduction to the study of the mass media, especially in terms of the tensions between political economy and cultural studies approaches.

Ferguson, R. (2004) *The Media in Question*. Oxford: Oxford University Press. An important defence of media studies in the twenty-first century.

Wood, A. and A.M. Todd (2005) 'Are we there yet?: searching for Springfield and *The Simpsons*' Rhetoric of Omnitopia', *Critical Studies in Media Communication* 22 (3): 207–22. Wood and Todd's essay is a fascinating examination of the role played by the Simpsons' hometown of Springfield as a commentary on the (post) modern condition in the overall text.

2

MEDIA GLOBALIZATION

Summary

In this chapter you will discover:

- The main features of media globalization.
- The pivotal role played by transnational media organizations in the more general globalization process.
- That globalization is a problematic, complex and contested concept that defies simple definition.
- The importance of examining the experiences of audiences in terms of their access to, consumption of and the meanings they derive from globalized media products.
- That while the dominance or hegemony of the globalized media industry is of obvious significance in the twenty-first century, we should never underestimate the ability of local media audiences to resist, appropriate or reconstruct globally distributed media messages.
- There are also hopeful signs that at least *some* citizens have begun to resist the hegemony or dominance of the global media through the creation of their own media texts and through the use of new media technologies. Such developments however – while obviously very welcome – should not be overstated and it would be naïve to ignore the sheer power of the global media giants.

- Globalization is not a one-way street. One of the possible net results of globalization is *glocalization* – whereby localizing and globalizing forces merge to create new hybrid identities. There has been a particular focus in this regard on how diasporic media audiences engage with globalized and other media texts.

Key concepts

- Globalization
- Media globalization
- Transnational media industries
- Media imperialism
- Homogenization
- Information rich and poor
- Audience resistance
- Hybridization
- Localization
- Glocalization
- Diaspora/diasporic media audiences

In writing your media diary in Chapter 1, you were asked to reflect on what portion of your regular media consumption is produced and distributed by media organizations that operate at a global level. In watching television news, going to the cinema, reading a book, surfing the Net, downloading music, playing the latest computer game or listening to a new recording by your favourite band, DJ or singer, the chances are that you were using or consuming a media product created, controlled and distributed by the global media industry. The production, distribution and consumption of an increasing number of media products now take place in a transnational context. An understanding of what media globalization is all about is a crucial starting point in our attempts to come to terms with media in the twenty-first century. Media globalization has resulted in a radically changed media landscape for media audiences. It is in the context of this rapidly changing milieu that we will address questions surrounding media ownership, technologies, production, content and reception.

So what is the real significance of media globalization? Is it responsible for unprecedented social change, the shrinkage of time and space, the perpetuation of global capitalism, the creation of a hierarchy of media 'haves' and 'have nots', the further hastening of cultural homogenization or sameness, or the intensification of local, ethnic and national identities? Whatever its shortcomings as a process, media globalization represents one of the most complex, fascinating and dynamic questions facing us in the twenty-first century. It is at once both immensely powerful and laden with many contradictions and ambiguities. Media globalization is characterized by convergence. It has come about because of the convergence of old and new media technologies as well as the convergence of old and new media organizations to form immensely powerful transnational media conglomerates. It raises new possibilities and new (and not so new) questions for media audiences and media organizations. It poses new and important challenges for students of the mass media.

In seeking to further explain what media globalization is, this chapter takes the view that we need to fuse elements of both the macro theoretical accounts of media globalization with the emerging accounts of the workings of media globalization at the micro or local level. The latter draws upon a largely ethnographic research model that seeks to understand how audiences actively engage with and have the capacity to resist aspects of the globalized media. We need to appreciate the arguments being made at both ends of the media globalization spectrum – between political economists and those following a cultural imperialism perspective and pluralists – in order to more fully understand what is happening to and with the media.

Having introduced the phenomenon of globalization, this chapter outlines the key features of media globalization in particular. It is crucial that we engage critically with the hyperbole evident in a significant amount of the commentary on what the globalization project is all about. We will place special emphasis on the degree to which a great deal of the reported globalization of people's local lives is as a result of mass mediation. Given the emphasis within some quarters of globalization theory on the supposed shrinkage between the distant and the local (Giddens, 1999), we examine in the form of a detailed case study, the reporting in one Western European setting of a Third World news story concerning an impending famine crisis in Sudan. Finally, the chapter considers the relationship between audiences and the globalized media. Our focus here will be on access to, the consumption of and the meanings that audiences make of globalized media products. As an antidote to the emphases traditionally placed by those following a cultural imperialist or effects model of media research on the process of media globalization, the localized appropriation of and potential for resistance to media texts produced by the global media industry by diasporic and other audiences are crucial aspects of this equation.

Following Tomlinson (1997), Lull (1995) and Silverstone (1999), we recognize the importance of examining the interplay between the macro and micro processes of media globalization.

What is globalization?

Explaining the social changes associated with industrial capitalism has been a central preoccupation within sociology since its beginnings in the nineteenth century. Traditionally, sociologists explained concepts such as class, community, family and the emerging mass media in terms of how they operated within individual societies and nation states. This emphasis has now firmly shifted and, in recent decades, globalization has become arguably *the* core concept that sociologists and others use in order to explain the experience of living in modernity or postmodernity (see Scholte, 2000). There is no one agreed definition of globalization, and as we will show later on in this chapter, the concept is a problematic one – especially when it comes to understanding the mass media.

You should now read EXTRACTED READING 2.1, *A Window on the World*? (Tomlinson, 1994) and consider the following issues:

1 To what extent are people's local lives more 'open' to global phenomena as a result of mass mediatization?

2 Why is the globalized mass media not a window on the world?

Globalization is 'the compression of the world and the intensification of consciousness of the world as a whole' (Robertson, 1992: 8)	Globalization is 'the product of a changing economic and political order, one in which technology and capital have combined in a new multi-faceted imperialism' (Silverstone, 1999: 107)
Globalization is 'best considered a complex set of interacting and often countervailing human, material and symbolic flows that lead to diverse, heterogeneous cultural positionings and practices which persistently and variously modify established vectors of social, political and cultural power' (Lull, 1995: 150)	Globalization 'refers to the rapidly developing process of complex interconnections between societies, cultures, institutions and individuals worldwide. It is a social process which involves a compression of time and space, shrinking distances through a dramatic reduction in the time taken – either physically or representationally – to cross them, so making the world seem smaller and in a certain sense bringing them "closer" to one another' (Tomlinson, 1999: 165)
'Globalisation is a jargon term which journalists and politicians have made fashionable and which is often used in a positive sense to denote a "global village" of "free trade", hi-tech marvels and all kinds of possibilities that transcend class, historical experience and ideology' (Pilger, 1999: 61)	'Globalization means different things to different people. Some say it is the movement of people, language, ideas, and products around the world. Others see it as the dominance of multinational corporations and the destruction of cultural identities' (Peters and Peters (2005)

FIGURE 2.1   Definitions of globalization

CRITICAL QUESTION 2.1

Starting with some examples from shopping or your daily consumption of food and drink, draw up a list of examples of where global phenomena are present in your own day-to-day life. How many of these are a result of your exposure to and interaction with the mass media?

The latest brand of colonialism?

The globalization of everyday life for a significant number of the world's citizens is as a result of the restructuring of economic and cultural activities along global lines. Following Weber, we recognize that globalization is founded upon increasing levels of rationality and the hyper-rationality of transnational corporations in particular. While the media and communications industries are part and parcel of this more general restructuring of economic activity at a global level, it is they who are primarily responsible for the promotion of the notion of globalism (see Figure 2.2) as well as contributing to the qualitative shift in how modernity or postmodernity is experienced by an increasing number of social actors.

It is worthwhile thinking about this for a moment. The dominant players in the global media industry continue to represent globalization as an unproblematic given. They repeatedly (and cynically) reproduce the idea – first mooted by the late Canadian scholar Marshall McLuhan (see Box 2.1) – of the 'global village' where it is assumed that all the planet's citizens can, if they want to, participate in a global society through their media use. This of course naïvely (or otherwise) presumes equal access to media technologies and products in all societies and cultures across the globe. It ignores the information deficit that exists between the information-rich and information-poor within the developed world and between the developed and Third World. It downplays the profit motives of the agents of globalization. Globalization is responsible for the exploitation of people and resources on an unprecedented scale. It should be seen as the continuation of the colonization project which involved the process of exploitation (including people as well as raw materials) in the eighteenth and nineteenth centuries in particular. While the process of globalization is a reality, we need to be cautious of the ways in which it is heralded and celebrated by those interests who benefit most from it.

BOX 2.1   KEY THINKER: MARSHALL MCLUHAN (1911–80)

Born in Canada in 1911, Marshall McLuhan published his best-selling book *Understanding Media: The Extensions of Man* in 1964. McLuhan is celebrated by many media scholars for the far-seeing nature of his work on the contemporary mass media. He argued, somewhat controversially, that what mattered most was not media content but the effect the medium itself has on human beings. The act of watching television, reading a newspaper or novel or listening to the radio was of greater significance than the content involved per se and in McLuhan's much quoted words 'The medium is the message.' McLuhan's foresight on the potential of electronically based media to reshape human experience is of major significance. He argued that the initial rise of print media had resulted in the privatization of media activity, whereas electronic media had the potential to restore collective media experiences and lead to the creation of a global village. This utopian view has resulted in McLuhan being celebrated by many recent theorists who are interested in the capabilities of ICT in terms of how it can reshape society.

Main features of globalization

As Figure 2.1 indicates, there are a variety of definitions and interpretations of what constitutes globalization. It is, however, usually discussed in terms of the following key features:

1 The growing level of connectedness between individuals, societies and nation states at a global level.

2 The reduction in the distance between individuals, societies and nation states in terms of both time and space facilitated by technological developments such as the Internet and other media. These are usually referred to as Information Communication Technologies (ICTs).

3 The development of ICTs has not only resulted in major changes in the workings of the mass media but also allows the rapid transfer of information, knowledge and capital.

4 Globalization involves not only the movement of capital and knowledge facilitated by technological developments within ICT, but also, crucially, the displacement and movement of people. Migration is a key feature of globalization.

5 Globalization is characterized by a series of flows: the flow of capital, knowledge, mass-mediated symbols and people (see Appadurai, 1996).

6 An increased awareness of global phenomena in people's (local) lives.

7 The globalization of culture and economic activity as a direct result of the activities of powerful transnational capitalist organizations. It has also meant the disaggregation of economic activities through a process of deterritorialization. US PC manufacturers, for example, build computers in Western Europe using parts and labour in at least four different economies, thus availing themselves of a combination of cheap labour, low or no tax and non-unionized workers. A PC sold in Scandinavia or Australia may have its support network based in a call centre in India. Call centre workers in New Delhi, for example, are trained to speak 'American', follow set scripts and mask their actual location in dealing with first world consumers (see Mirchandani, 2004).

8 Globalization tends to assume a decrease in the significance of other kinds of identities such as the ethnic, the local, the regional or the national in people's everyday lives. Globalization has increased the possibility of greater reflexivity among social actors. It offers the potential to human beings to become more critical of their immediate environment by allowing them to compare their experiences with those living in other societies or under different political arrangements. Media activities such as watching satellite television news or surfing the Internet offer the potential for this kind of reflexivity in an unprecedented way (see Kit-Wai Ma, 2000). The restrictions imposed by the Chinese authorities in 2001 and 2002 on Internet use provide a concrete example of how powerful interests in that country are fearful of reflexivity among its citizens. In 2006, global capitalism and state communism reached an accord when Google agreed with the Chinese government to limit the extent of access afforded to Chinese citizens who use its search engines. It was reported that Google.cn would not allow its users to access information about the Tiananmen Square student massacre, Tibet or the outlawed Falun Gong organization (Sabbagh, 2006). China is not alone in this regard. It is currently illegal to own a satellite dish in Iran and there are many other historical precedents of governments attempting to censor media content such as newspapers, films, radio or books.

9 Critics of globalization argue that it has resulted in even more exploitation of the Third World. Those whom journalist John Pilger (2002) terms 'the new rulers of the world' exploit both the raw materials and the labour power of the world's poorest people in order to feed the insatiable consumer demand in the West. The use of child labour in the manufacture of well-known global brands has been a particular focus of anti-globalization activists.

10 The stark realities behind much of the hype associated with globalization have been noted by many feminists. Far from being a utopian process which has smoothed out the power differentials between women and men, globalization has accentuated many inequalities.

Globalization has witnessed an increase in the trafficking of women and children for the global sex industry as well as their exploitation in the workplace.

11 Resistance to economic and cultural globalization has taken many forms (see Webb, 2005). What has been termed the 'Anti-Globalization' movement is in fact made up of various groups and alliances comprising anarchists, anti-consumerists, communists, green activists, socialists and women's groups. Their protests have been in evidence at various G8 Summits as well as engaging in specific protests about McDonald's restaurants or Nike products, for example. Critics of 'McWorld' have argued that McDonaldization is responsible for increased levels of cultural homogenization and obesity; the destroying of the rain forest to make way for the ranching of cattle in order to supply the increased demand for cheaper beef, and also the exploitation of children in China who are a source of cheap labour in the manufacture of toys given away with 'Happy Meals'.

Proponents of globalization theory – especially those who follow either a Global Society or Global Culture approach – argue, perhaps predictably, that the experience of day-to-day living in the early twenty-first century is markedly different from that which has gone before. People's local lives are increasingly lived in the shadow of global phenomena. We can see the 'spectre of globalization' in our everyday experience and it is particularly evident in terms of our working lives, our consumption – especially in our shopping and eating – and our mass media activities. The spaces and places of everyday life are awash with the images and messages of globalization. Everyday life has been Disneyfied, McDonaldized and Coca-Colonized (see Ritzer, 2000). The iconography associated with global brands such as Microsoft, McDonald's, Nike or Pizza Hut transcends both space and language. In Tokyo, the phrase 'I'm Lovin' It' appears side by side with Japanese in adverts for McDonald's. On the main street in Warsaw, a giant Nike shoe sits on top of a small kiosk selling local and national newspapers in Polish. In Latin America the Microsoft logo appears side by side on a PC screen whose on-screen language is Spanish.

A positive view of globalization would hold that the globalization process brings with it the possibility of creating a truly global society. A more critical perspective – best embodied in the shape of the International Political Economy viewpoint – would argue that globalization is just Western capitalist imperialism under another guise. Both perspectives would be in broad agreement about the crucial role played in the globalization process by the mass media and by television and the Internet in particular.

Theories of globalization

There are a wide range of diverse theoretical positions that seek to explain the concept of globalization. Following Sklair (1999), we can summarize these under four main headings: the Global Society approach; the Global Culture approach; the

'Think globally, act locally' (bumper sticker encouraging greater environmental awareness at local level).	'Reaching forty million people, in eighty different countries, twenty-four hours a day, this is Sky News!' (Sky News jingle).
The global telecommunications companies use an AAA paradigm: 'Anything, Any time, Anywhere' (see Negroponte, 1995: 174).	'The world's largest mobile community' (Vodafone corporate website, 2006).
Time Warner's website speaks of engaging with: 'Active Citizens in a Global Community' (Time Warner Corporate website, 2006).	'Producing and distributing the most compelling news, information and entertainment to the furthest reaches of the globe' (News Corporation website, 2002).
'We will help the people of the world to have fuller lives – both through the services we provide and through the impact we have on the world around us.' 'Passion for the World Around Us', Vodafone's Business Principles (Vodafone Corporate website, 2006).	'At the core of our business is a corporate philosophy that guides our conduct wherever we do business, which we call the *Soul of Dell*. Central to that philosophy is our commitment to global citizenship – understanding and respecting the laws, values and cultures wherever we do business; profitably growing in all markets; promoting a healthy business climate globally; and contributing positively in every community we call home, both personally and organizationally' (Dell corporate website, 2006).
'More than 70 per cent of our income comes from outside the US, but the real reason we are a truly global company is that our products meet the varied tastes and preferences of customers everywhere' (Coca-Cola corporate website, 2006).	'Our world is not for sale' (Anti-globalization slogan).
Little Britain Anywhere in the World, £149.99 (PSP Playstation Advert 2006).	'The world in your backyard' (Australian Broadcasting Corporation corporate website, 2006).

FIGURE 2.2   The language of globalism

World System approach; and the Global Capitalism approach, discussed below. These can be further subdivided in terms of the relative amount of stress they place on the cultural or economic aspects of globalization. One thing is certain – there is very little consensus as to what constitutes globalization.

Global Society approach

Proponents of the Global Society approach emphasize the extent to which we all as citizens of the planet inhabit *one* society that has common concerns and possibilities. The Global Society position points to the increasing consciousness of the global that is said to exist in everyday life. People's local lives are becoming more and more affected by global phenomena. According to this perspective, the global media industries play a key role in raising global awareness and in the extent to which global phenomena are said to impinge on everyday consciousness via media products. Environmental issues such as global warming might be an example of where the mass media have raised public awareness of the local implications of a global problem. The approach has been accused of seriously underplaying the continuing extent of global inequalities and of overstating the argument that we live in a 'global village'. The failure of the media in the Western world to report on Third World poverty and famine in a sustained and critical way is an example of one of the contradictions of the Global Society approach.

At a technological level it is now possible to beam stories back and forth across the globe in a matter of seconds. The 2004 Asian Tsumani received blanket media coverage (for upwards of four weeks) in the West – arguably because the catastrophe involved Western citizens and many of the areas affected were tourist destinations. The scale of the coverage stood in stark contrast to the general invisibility of Third World stories in the Western media.

Global Culture approach

Those who take a Global Culture standpoint see an increasing level of cultural homogenization taking place at a global level. Members of culturally and politically diverse societies participate in a global cultural experience never before witnessed in human history. Following the logic of this perspective, children in Belfast, Berlin and Budapest all play with the latest Digimon characters. They are likely to want to eat the same kinds of fast food in McDonald's, Burger King or Pizza Hut. Depending on their age and gender, they are also likely to be fans of specific kinds of popular music such as 'boy bands' that are marketed on a global scale. There is, according to this perspective, an increasing amount of homogenization or 'sameness' in the cultural practices evident in the early twenty-first century. The Global Culture approach allows little room for either local resistance to or local appropriation and reinvention of globalized cultural products.

The World System approach

Both the World System and Global Capitalism (see below) approaches are primarily concerned with explaining the continuing dominance of capitalism. While the World System position is not expressly concerned with explaining globalization per se, it has provided us with a model that divides the world into core, semi-peripheral and peripheral societies and economies that are exploited by the capitalist system. The parts needed to assemble media hardware such as personal computers or digital television sets may be produced in peripheral or semi-peripheral societies to

Plate 2.1 Mcnikecolasoft. Globalization is characterized by both the dominance and convergence of global capitalist organizations. Reproduced with permission © Polyp/Paul Fitzgerald (2002) from *Big Bad World: Cartoon Molotovs in the Face of Corporate Rule*. Oxford: New Internationalist Publications.

feed the consumer demand for such products in the core societies in the West. The production of certain media texts – the animation industry referred to in Chapter 1 is a powerful example of this phenomenon – takes place in peripheral and semi-peripheral societies in order to maximize profits for transnational multimedia conglomerates and to feed consumer demand in core and non-core countries.

The Global Capitalism approach

∞∞

See Chapters 3 and 6 for an elaboration of this theme.

The Global Capitalism approach argues that the globalization of capitalism lies at the heart of the globalization process. Its key actors are transnational corporations which in many instances are more powerful in economic and political terms than many of the countries they exploit, in terms of labour, raw materials or markets. At the heart of the Global Capitalism perspective is the viewpoint that globalization of this kind depends upon the promotion of the ideology of consumerism. The media industries relentlessly promote consumerism by emphasizing what is considered to be a desirable lifestyle. This is undertaken not only in the form of advertising, sponsorship and product endorsement, but also in the promotion of certain lifestyles as being more desirable than others within a wide range of media settings. Evidence of this desirable lifestyle is embodied, for example, in advertising, where specific kinds of body image for men and women are relentlessly promoted. There are implicit messages that if you buy this product (a car, aftershave, beer, perfume, to name but four examples), you will somehow be transformed and become more desirable to men or women. In spite of the overtones of globalism, Western and more particularly North American lifestyles are the ones given greatest prominence. As you will see in the next chapter, the increasingly complex ownership patterns of multimedia conglomerates or oligarchies means transnational media companies may not only be involved in the media industry per se but also own or control other kinds of companies producing goods and services for sale in the global market.

You should now read the EXTRACTED READING 2.2, *Culture Jamming and Semiotic Resistance* (Worth and Kuhling, 2004) and consider the following questions:

1 Naomi Klein's 'Culture Jammers' are examples of *some* audience members exercising agency. Can you think of other examples of where audience members exercise agency in the face of globalized media texts?

2 To what extent do new media technologies allow for greater audience agency?

3 Who do you think has the greater amount of power – audience members or the owners and producers of globalized media texts – and why?

Media globalization

We turn now to examine the pivotal role that the media play in the more general globalization process. The main features of recent media globalization raise important questions that we need to address as students of the media. The anxieties about media imperialism and cultural homogenization raised initially by the late Herbert Schiller and others concerning the dominant position assumed by the North American mass media industry in the postwar period has now given way to growing worries about the domination of the global media industry by a small number of powerful, transnational, vertically integrated media conglomerates. There are further well-founded anxieties about the extent to which access to the media is truly global and democratic. Having outlined the key features of media globalization, we tease out more fully the concerns raised around technological change, ownership and access to the global media. The concerns that have been raised about the global media conglomerates mirror more general fears about the rise of global capitalism itself.

Main features

Following Thompson (1995), we can say that media globalization is characterized by a number of distinct features. These are:

1 The emergence of and continued dominance of the global media industry by a small number of transnational media conglomerates.
2 The use by these media conglomerates of new information and communications technologies (ICTs).
3 The increasingly deregulated environment in which these media organizations operate.
4 A greater amount of homogenization and standardization in certain media products produced and distributed by the global media industries.
5 The uneven flow of information and communication products within the global system and the different levels of access that global citizens have to global networks of communication.
6 The promotion of the ideology of consumerism, which is therefore bound up with the capitalist project.

Technological change

Media globalization has been made possible by the ongoing changes and developments in information and communications technology. Broadband, cable, ISDN, digitalization, direct broadcast satellites as well as the Internet have created a situation where vast amounts of information can be transferred around the globe in a matter of seconds. The merging of the personal computer and the television set in tandem with the rolling out of digitalized television and radio opens up even wider possibilities for those who can afford new media technologies. Wireless technology such as the WAP mobile phone allows Internet access. The Multimedia Messaging System (MMS), for example, allows the delivery of text, audio clips and digital pictures via mobile or cell phone handsets. Mobile or cell phones work as radios, digital cameras and MP3 players.

The latest promise from the mobile phone companies is the widespread delivery of videostreaming to individual subscribers whereby audiovisual content such as films, music videos or television programmes may be viewed in transit in the car, on the bus or on the train for example. This development has radical implications for media audiences in terms of how and where media content is consumed. It also has the specific potential for media companies to target particular demographic cohorts, such as those who have greater spending power.

See Chapter 3 on media ownership

Media globalization is also defined in terms of the restructuring of media ownership. The global media industry is dominated by a small number of powerful transnational media conglomerates that own and control a diverse range of traditional and newer forms of media (Bagdikian, 2004). Conglomerates such as Time Warner, Bertelsmann, Disney, Sony, Viacom and News Corporation operate at a global level in terms of the production, distribution and selling of their media products. While these companies are transnational in character, they emanate from 'core societies' such as the United States, Australia, Japan or Western Europe. Unlike traditional publicly or privately owned media organizations, these conglomerates operate in an increasingly deregulated environment.

The structure of ownership of media organizations has become increasingly concentrated, and as convergence has taken place, groups such as Bertelsmann (Europe) or Time Warner (North America) might be more accurately described as multimedia conglomerates. As we discuss in Chapter 3, a growing number of global media companies are engaged in cross-ownership. They are constituent parts of more general conglomerates with vested interests in companies that produce among other things armaments, cars and cigarettes. General Electric, for example, is involved in, amongst other things, the production of satellite systems, jet engines, electricity from nuclear power, the provision of financial services as well as television news. It owns 80 per cent of multimedia conglomerate NBC-Universal, with Vivendi Universal owning the remaining 20 per cent. Such monopolization raises serious questions about the extent to which media companies that are part of larger conglomerates can critically report on the activities of their sister companies.

As Boxes 2.4 (a) and (b) demonstrate, the largest multimedia conglomerate Time Warner is characterized by its gigantism, its economic (and political) power, and its ability to dominate all aspects of the production, distribution and dissemination of both old and new media content throughout the world. Media representations circulated by the mainstream mass media are created by a handful of conglomerates – a development that raises important questions for all of us as audience members and as citizens.

Access to the global media

One obvious counterpoint to those who herald media globalization as being unproblematic is to examine the question of access. Those who are critical of media globalization now speak of the 'information-rich' and the 'information-poor' as well as the 'digital divide' that is evident both within societies in the developed world and between the northern and southern hemispheres (van Dijk, 2005; Campbell, 2003; Campbell and Breen, 2001).

BOX 2.2   *BIG BROTHER* GOES GLOBAL?

The *Big Brother* television series has been one of the most talked-about media phenomena of recent years. Created by John de Mol, it has attracted a considerable amount of attention from media researchers (see, for example, Scannell, 2002; Couldry, 2002; Chandler and Griffiths, 2004; Pecora, 2002; Griffen Foley, 2004; Mathijs, 2002). Strong on active audience participation both in terms of voting by telephone and email, the programme is a potent illustration of media globalization. *Big Brother* has, to date, been produced in the following locations:

Location	Programme Title
Africa	Big Brother
Australia	Big Brother
Belgium	Big Brother
Brazil	Big Brother
Bulgaria	Big Brother
Croatia	Big Brother
Denmark	Big Brother
Finland	Big Brother
Germany	Big Brother
India	Big Brother
Mexico	Big Brother
Netherlands	Big Brother
Nigeria	Big Brother
Norway	Big Brother
Philippines	Big Brother
Portugal	Big Brother
Scandinavia	Big Brother
Slovakia	Big Brother
South Africa	Big Brother
Sweden	Big Brother

Switzerland	Big Brother
Thailand	Big Brother
UK	Big Brother
USA	Big Brother
Argentina	Gran Hermano
Central America	Gran Hermano
Colombia	Gran Hermano
Ecuador	Gran Hermano
Pacific	Gran Hermano
Spain	Gran Hermano
Venezuela	Gran Hermano
Canada	Loft Story
Czech Republic	Big Brother/Velky Bratr
France	Loft Story
Greece	Big Brother/Big Mother
Hungary	Big Brother/Nagy Testver
Italy	Grande Fratello
Middle East	Big Brother/Al Raiss
Poland	Big Brother/Wielki Brat
Romania	Big Brother/Fratele Cel Mare
Russia	Bol'shoy Brat
Serbia	Veliki Brat

The programme has given rise to several offshoots such as *Celebrity Big Brother* as well as an array of copycat programming, all of which share the essential *Big Brother* ingredients of engaging in the surveillance of ordinary people who are challenged to survive either each other's company or specific tasks. Although it is usually referred to as 'reality television', the programme has a clearly identifiable script.

Big Brother is a multimedia phenomenon, being television, telephone and Internet-based. The first UK series of *Big Brother* on Channel 4 attracted television audiences of up to 10 million viewers. Its associated website recorded over 200 million page impressions, while over 20 million phone votes were made. In addition, the second

(Continued)

UK series on Channel 4 and E4 used a combination of interactive digital television, radio and mobile phone.

Endemol Entertainment, which owns the *Big Brother* brand, is a European-based multinational television production company. Endemol Entertainment is 100 per cent owned by the Spanish telecommunications and multimedia giant Telefonica, which in turn has a controlling stake in the Terra-Lycos group.

The *Big Brother* series is transnational in the sense that the format has been successfully sold to television networks at different points around the globe. Its track record in terms of attracting large volumes of audience share appeals to programme makers. Hill (2002) observes that programmes like *Big Brother* '... indicate the economic success of selling a global format that is locally produced. ... Buying an established format such as BB reduces the costs of production and attenuates the risks associated with new programming.' (2002: 324–25)

Some localizing has taken place in terms of the making of specific series. The homogeneity of the *Big Brother* format has been altered by local context (see Frau-Miggs, 2006). Series differ, for example, in terms of their overall duration and in terms of what is deemed as permissible to viewers. Thus, in some locations, viewers have seen real or simulated sex scenes which would not be allowable in other contexts. Although *Big Brother* has been criticized by many for being exploitative (and in some instances for being boring!), its appeal seems to rest in the way that it allows us to engage in surveillance of an (artificially created) private sphere. Van Zoonen (2001: 672) summarizes the appeal of *Big Brother* in the words of one 17-year-old Dutch fan who stated:

> If I could see what my sister is like with her girlfriends, how the maths teacher talks to his wife, how my parents behave among adults, I would not feel the need for a substitute for life. But I don't see all that. How do you learn how to read people if you only know three kinds: kids your age, teachers and parents? . . . *Big Brother* is the only programme we watch and discuss everyday with the whole family. At last, we have common friends, with whom we can talk, think and gossip. (Woltz, 1999)

As a global television phenomenon, *Big Brother* encapsulates many of the issues that have engaged audience members as well as intrigued academic researchers. (See van Zoonen and Aslama (2006) for a comprehensive overview of research undertaken on *Big Brother*.)

BIG BROTHER

Plate 2.2   *Big Brother* logo reproduced by kind permission of Channel 4 (UK) © 2005.

BOX 2.3   THE GLOBAL JUKEBOX

The recording industry is an important example of how multimedia conglomerates control the production, distribution and commodification of popular culture across the globe. While technological developments – such as peer to peer file-sharing using Internet-based MP3 files – allow for bands and fans to freely share music and video, the creation and dissemination of popular culture continues to be dominated by the conglomerates. The closure of Napster in 2001, its protracted legal battles and its eventual purchase by Roxio (part of the Sonic Solutions Group) in 2005 are further reminders of the power of the conglomerates. While free file-sharing continues on sites such as Kazaa, Limewire and Bearshare, the Goliaths remain in a position of dominance. Their dominant position is in evidence, for example, in the dependency of many smaller independent record labels in terms of marketing and distribution (see Hesmondhalgh, 1999).

Using a political economy perspective, Burnett (1996) examined the dominance of the global record industry by the then 'Big Six' oligopoly of Time Warner, Sony, Philips, Bertelsmann, Thorn EMI and Matushita. In the 1990s these six conglomerates controlled the production and distribution of recordings and their related products. As evidence of their dominant position Burnett notes that:

(Continued)

MEDIA GLOBALIZATION

the transnationals were found to dominate the market in the United States, the United Kingdom, Canada, Germany, Italy, Australia, Sweden, Japan, France and the Netherlands. When the total market share of transnationals was taken into account (own labels, licensing distribution), there were five countries (UK, Italy, Japan, Sweden, France) where the transnationals had between 60 and 80 per cent of the total market shares. In the rest of the sample, the transnationals controlled over 80 per cent of the market shares. (1996: 60)

In 1994 in excess of 90 per cent of the gross sales of music products worldwide were produced and distributed by these six organizations. While US$33 billion worth of sales were achieved in the United States in 1994, Burnett stresses the increasing significance of overseas or foreign markets for these transnational media giants, accounting as they do for half their total revenues. While it is a high-risk investment business, the 'Big Six' maintained their dominant position through relying upon an 'open system of development and production' (1996: 115).

Burnett argues that:

The contemporary strategy of the transnationals relies on their exclusive control over large-scale manufacturing, distribution and access to the principal avenues of exposure. With this exclusive control, the transnationals have adopted a multidivisional corporate form linked with a large number of independent producers. This open system of development and production remains under oligopolistic conditions because the transnationals find it advantageous to incorporate new artists, producers and styles of music in order to constantly reinvigorate the popular music market and ensure that no large unsated demand among consumers materializes. The innovation and diversity sustained in this open system [are] essential in order to maintain a profitable and secure market. (1996: 115)

Since the publication of Burnett's book, further convergence and monopolization has taken place. Time Warner have sold the Warner Music Group to a private group of investors. They are concentrating on developing their music download business; Philips have merged with Decca and the new consortium is now owned by Vivendi Universal; Bertelsmann merged its music group with Sony to form Sony/BMG; Thorn EMI is now part of the EMI music group and Matushita has sold its share of Universal Music Group back to Vivendi Universal.

Technological change in the form of the widespread adoption of MP3 players (such as the iPod or Zen) has meant that the means by which recorded music is purchased and used by audiences has changed radically. The market is dominated by Apple's iTunes. Seventy per cent of all MP3 downloads are to iPods. Concerns have been raised by both fans and the other multimedia conglomerates about the control exerted by iTunes in that the technology employed by Apple is incompatible with other MP3 players. Some conglomerates are now focusing on other means of selling and distributing music through MP3-enabled mobile or cell phones.

BOX 2.4(A) TIME WARNER OVERVIEW

- Time Warner is the world's largest multimedia conglomerate. It was estimated in 2005 to be worth US$86.8 billion, with assets of US$123,339 billion. Its revenues for 2005 were US$43.7 billion.
- Filmed entertainment represents its largest source of income at US$11,924 million; networks earned US$9,611 million; cable US$9,498 million; AOL US$8,692 million; and publishing US$5,846 million.
- Key companies within its corporate structure include: America On Line; Home Box Office; New Line Cinema; Time Inc.; Time Warner Cable; Time Warner Trade Publishing; Turner Broadcasting System; Warner Bros.
- Core businesses: interactive media; television networks; publishing; filmed entertainment and cable systems.
- Location: US-based with a considerable number of joint venture activities in Asia, Europe and Latin America. Language is not a barrier to global domination. Filmed entertainment output is either dubbed (in the case of television series such as *Six Feet Under*) or available in a number of languages (in the case of both home video and cinema-based movies) and several of its radio and television channels use local languages such as Spanish, Polish or Japanese.
- One billion instant messages are sent daily using AOL's AIM and ICQ systems. AOL has 110 million domestic users who use its services on a monthly basis – an increasing number (40 per cent plus) through broadband connections. AOL has 26 million members in the US and Europe. It also provides services in Canada, the UK, France and Germany – the latter under the AOL Europe brand.
- Although its parent company Time Warner has sold its recording and music publishing businesses, it is now concentrating on developing its AOL Music Now brand, which allows its users to download music to their PCs in an MP3 format.
- A significant proportion of the revenues generated by its television and filmed entertainment business in the United States and elsewhere is on either a

(Continued)

---

subscription or a pay-per-view basis. The Time Warner conglomerate has the lion's share (21.7 per cent) of DVD sales intended for domestic consumption in North America.

- In describing its activities, the organization is quite consciously a promoter of globalism. Its corporate website speaks of seeing 'a more converged and inter-active world emerging' and that the organization's task is to provide 'access to a breathtaking array of choices and new ways to connect to the ever-expanding online universe'.
- Time Inc. publishes over 166 magazines with an estimated total readership of 173 million. Two-thirds of US adults read a magazine produced by Time Inc. each month.
- The Turner Broadcasting System's Cartoon Network is available to more than 138 million households in 145 countries. In addition to content aimed at younger viewers, its Adult Swim programming is aimed at those in the 18–34 years age cohort.
- CNN reaches a potential audience of 1 billion people worldwide.
- Its filmed entertainment division is responsible for such movies as *Charlie and the Chocolate Factory* (2005), *Harry Potter and the Goblet of Fire* (2005) and *The Lord of the Rings: The Return of the King* (2005). It produces a wide range of globally circulated television series such as *Six Feet Under*, *Friends*, *The Drew Carey Show* and *Seinfeld*.

Sources: Time Warner Corporate website, 2006, and Annual Report (2005)

BOX 2.4(B)   TIME WARNER'S MEDIA AND OTHER INTERESTS

AOL America Online	ICQ
AIM	inStore
AOL	KOL
AOL.com	MapQuest
AOLbyPhone	Moviefone
AOL Call Alert	Netscape
AOL CityGuide	RED
AOL Europe	SingingFish
AOL Latino	Tegic Communications
AOL Music Now	Truveo
AOL Wireless	Weblogs
AOL Voicemail	Wildseed
CompuServe	Xdrive

HBO: Home Box Office
HBO
HBO Domestic and
   International Program
   Distribution
HBO HD
HBO Independent Productions
HBO Multiplexes
HBO on Demand
HBO Video
Cinemax
Cinemax HD
Cinemax Multiplexes
Cinemax on Demand
Picturehouse
WBTV Latin America

Joint ventures:
HBO Asia
HBO Brasil
HBO Czech
HBO Hungary
HBO India
HBO Ole
HBO Poland
HBO Romania
HBO Serbia
E! Latin America
Channel

New Line Cinema
New Line Cinema Picturehouse
New Line Distribution
New Line Home Entertainment
New Line International
   Releasing
New Line
Merchandising/Licensing

New Line Music
New Line New Media
New Line Television
New Line Theatricals

Time Inc.
25 Beautiful Gardens
25 Beautiful Homes
25 Beautiful Kitchens
4x4
Aeroplane
All You
Amateur Gardening
Amateur Photographer
Ambientes
Angler's Mail
Audi Magazine
BabyTalk
Balance
Bird Keeper
BMX Business News
Bride To Be
Bulfinch Press
Business 2.0
Cage & Aviary Birds
Caravan
Center Street
Chat
Chat - It's Fate
Chilango
Classic Boat
Coastal Living
Cooking Light
Cottage Living
Country Homes & Interiors
Country Life
Cycle Sport
Cycling Weekly

(Continued)

Decanter
English Woman's Weekly
Entertainment Weekly
Essence
Essentials
European Boat Builder
Eventing
EXP
Expansión
Family Circle (UK)
Field & Stream
Fortune
Fortune Asia
Fortune Europe
FSB: Fortune Small Business
Golf.com
Golf Magazine
Golf Monthly
Guitar
Hair
Health
Hi-Fi News
Homes & Gardens
Horse
Horse & Hound
IPC
Ideal Home
In Style
In Style (Australia)
In Style (UK)
International Boat Industry
Land Rover World
Life
Life and Style
Little, Brown & Company:
   Adult Trade Books
Little, Brown & Company:
   Books for Young Readers
Livingetc

Loaded
Manufactura
MBR – Mountain Bike Rider
MiniWorld
Mizz
MNI
Model Collector
Money
Motor Boat & Yachting
Motor Boats Monthly
Motor Caravan
Motor Boating
NME
Now
Nuts
Obras
Outdoor Life
Parenting
Park Home & Holiday
Caravan
People
People en Español
Pick Me Up
Popular Science
Practical Boat Owner
Practical Parenting
Prediction
Progressive Farmer
Quad Off-Road
   Magazine
Quién
Quo
Racecar Engineering
Real Simple
Ride BMX
Rugby World
Salt Water Sportsman
Ships Monthly
Shoot Monthly

Shooting Times
Ski
Skiing
Soaplife
Southern Accents
Southern Living
Sporting Gun
Sports Illustrated
Sports Illustrated For Kids
Stamp Magazine
Sunset
Sunset Books
SuperBike
Synapse
Targeted Media, Inc.
Teen People
The Field
The Golf
The Golf+
The Railway Magazine
The Shooting Gazette
This Old House
This Old House
Ventures
Time
Time Asia
Time Atlantic
Time Australia
Time Canada
Time For Kids
Time Pacific
Time Inc. Strategic
   Communications
Time Warner AudioBooks
Time Warner Book Group UK
Time Warner Book Group
   Distribution Services
TransWorld Business

TransWorld Motocross
TransWorld Skateboarding
TransWorld Snowboarding
TransWorld Surf
TV & Satellite Week
TV Easy
TV Times
Uncut
VolksWorld
Vuelo
Wallpaper*
Warner Books
Warner Faith
Web User
Wedding
What Camera
What Digital Camera
What's on TV
Who
Woman
Woman & Home
Woman's Own
Woman's Weekly
Women & Golf
World Soccer
Yachting
Yachting Monthly
Yachting World
Yachts

Joint Ventures:
Avantages S.A.
BOOKSPAN
Elle
European Magazines
   Limited
Marie Claire (UK)
Quo

(Continued)

Time Warner Cable
Road Runner
Road Runner – Business
   Class
Digital Phone

Local News Channels:
Capital News 9-Albany,
   Albany, NY
MetroSports, Kansas City, MO
News 8 Austin, Austin, TX
News 10 Now-Syracuse,
   Syracuse, NY
News 14, Carolina-Charlotte,
   Charlotte, NC
News 14, Carolina-Raleigh,
   Raleigh, NC
NY1 News, New York, NY
R News, Rochester, NY

Joint Ventures:
Urban Cableworks of
   Philadelphia
Texas and Kansas City Cable
   Partners, L.P.

**TBS Turner Broadcasting
System**
Adult Swim
Atlanta Braves
Boomerang
Cartoon Network
Cartoon Network
   Asia Pacific
Cartoon Network Europe
Cartoon Network Latin
   America
Cartoon Network Studios
CNN/US
CNN Airport Network
CNN.com

CNN en España
CNN en Español Radio
CNN Headline News
CNN Headline News in Asia
   Pacific
CNN Headline News in Latin
   America
CNN International
CNN Mobile
CNNMoney.com
CNN Newsource
CNN Pipeline
CNNRadio
CNNStudentNews.com
CNN to Go
NASCAR.com
GameTap
PGA.com
TBS
TCM Asia Pacific
TCM Classic Hollywood in
   Latin America
TCM Europe
TNT HD
TNT Latin America
Turner Classic Movies
Turner Network
   Television
Turner South
TCM & Cartoon Network/Asia
   Pacific
Williams St. Studio

Joint Ventures
BOING
Cartoon Network Japan
CETV
CNN+
CNN.co.jp (Japanese)
CNN.de (German)

CNN-IBN	Telepictures Productions
CNNj	The WB Television
CNN Turk	Network
Court TV	Warner Bros. Animation
NASCAR Races	Warner Bros. Consumer
NBC/Turner	Products
n-tv	Warner Bros. Games
Zee/Turner	Warner Bros. Interactive
	Entertainment
Warner Brothers	Warner Bros. International
Entertainment	Cinemas
DC Comics	Warner Bros. Online
Hanna-Barbera	Warner Bros. Pictures
Kids' WB!	Warner Bros. Television
Looney Tunes	Warner Home Video
MAD Magazine	Warner Independent Pictures

Source: Time Warner Corporate website (2006)

∞∞
*See Chapter 3 on the
political economy of the
Internet.*

The UN Development Programme, for example, estimated in the year 2000 that 0.1 per cent of Internet connections are in Sub-Saharan Africa, where 9 per cent of
the world's population is living. South Asia has 1 per cent
of Internet connections with 19 per cent of the world's
population (Cullen, 2000). The categories 'information rich' and 'information poor'
refer to the degree of access that citizens have to both old and new media. Cullen
(2001) notes that the digital divide may result from factors of social class, geography,
educational attainment, from attitudinal and generational factors and from physical
disability (see also DiMaggio et al., 2001; Dutta-Bergman, 2005). One's ability to participate in a wired world is not a given. It is socially and economically determined. As
we discuss in detail in Chapter 3, utopian perspectives on the Internet need to be
tempered by the growing body of empirical research which demonstrates that the
digital divide (Norris, 2001) and/or digital inequalities (DiMaggio and Hargittai,
2001) are shaped by class, ethnicity, gender and location (see also Korupp and
Szydlik, 2005; Wilson et al., 2003; James, 2005). Furthermore, when we speak of the
digital divide, it is worth remembering that the majority of citizens in poorer parts of
the world are concerned with basic survival and that access to what many people in
the Northern hemisphere would consider to be very basic (and outdated) media
technologies such as the fixed line telephone, television or radio is limited.

BOX 2.5 'THE MOSQUE AND THE SATELLITE: MEDIA AND ADOLESCENCE IN A MOROCCAN TOWN' (DAVIS AND DAVIS, 1995)

'We were struck by the pervasiveness and manifest similarity of adolescents' media experience across developing countries. English speaking Inuit (Eskimo) youth 300 miles north of the Arctic circle were sitting with their Inuktitut speaking parents watching the *Love Boat* or southern Canadian hockey; young men in an Aboriginal settlement in northern Australia were dressing like Afro-American teens and listening to reggae; and Moroccans were discovering Dolly Parton and arguing over who shot J.R. Ewing.' (1995: 578)

CRITICAL QUESTIONS 2.2   THE GLOBALIZATION OF NEWS

1   It has become commonplace for many transnational news and other media organizations to use symbols of globalization – usually symbolic representations of the globe itself – to suggest that their news coverage is truly global in its scope. Write a brief report on this evening's news bulletin in terms of how it prioritizes certain kinds of stories as news items.

2   In doing this exercise it might be interesting to compare a national news broadcast with one from CNN or BBC World.

3   Of the total number of news items broadcast, what proportion are concerned with local/national issues as opposed to international/global issues?

4   In what order are the stories broadcast?

5   How significant is proximity in determining the news value of the story?

6   If stories dealing with international/global issues are broadcast, to what extent are they told from an elite nation's perspective?

7   Compare your findings with those of your fellow students and discuss the extent to which the 'spectre of the global' is truly evident in television news.

Globalization and media audiences

See Chapter 7 for an elaboration of reception analysis

The Cultural Imperialism and Political Economy perspectives, referred to earlier, have many merits, especially in terms of how they have critically examined the dominant global market position of media conglomerates. However, insufficient attention has been paid by both perspectives to the diverse experiences of globalized media audiences in their day-to-day lives as users and consumers of local, globalized and 'glocalized' media texts. The hermeneutic dimension which focuses on the meanings derived in the context of consuming globally circulated media texts has been largely ignored (Oliveira, 1993; Thompson, 1995; Tomlinson, 1999; Machin and Van Leeuwen, 2004). Media globalization resulting from the dominant position and the activities of media conglomerates using new technologies has radically transformed the media landscape in which audiences exist, but it is not a one-way process. Developments within ICT have created space for audiences to exercise agency and to be the creators of counter-hegemonic media texts, and, as we note below, the recent focus by researchers on diasporic media audiences highlights the extent to which media audiences (both diasporic and non-diasporic) now experience an increasingly complex globalized media environment.

Recognizing this, the pluralist perspective holds that audiences shape and are shaped by media globalization (see, for example, Lull, 1995). This position argues that while media audiences now exist in an unalterably changed media environment, they continue to possess considerable agency. They possess the power to appropriate, localize and hybridize globally distributed media messages, resulting in 'glocalization' (see, for example, Husband, 1998). In this context Silverstone reminds us that globalization is an active dynamic process, stressing that 'cultures form and reform around the different stimuli that global communications enable' (1999: 111–12). In everyday life 'the topic may be global, but it becomes a resource for the expression of local particular interests and identities' (1999: 112).

Media globalization has resulted in globalized diffusion of media texts but it has also resulted in local appropriation and hybridization (see, for example, Liebes and Katz, 1993; Sreberny-Mohammadi and Mohammadi, 1994). In a fascinating anthropological study of media use amongst Moroccan adolescents, Davis and Davis argue that:

> much of the content of Western media images is hard to reconcile with traditional Moroccan values rooted in Islam and a strong extended family. While the young people we interviewed and observed often seemed acutely aware of the apparent contradictions between traditional and modern ways – between the Mosque and the satellite – they did not typically see these contradictions as irreconcilable and most seemed eager to preserve core traditional values while hoping to reap the benefits of the affluent and exciting society promised by the media. (1995: 578–9)

And they also note that 'for television viewing, about half of both boys and girls said they preferred both Arab and Western programs. Many of both sexes seem to want to see what is going on all over the world. The visual character of television makes language differences less important' (1995: 590) (see also Box 2.5). There is also some evidence to suggest that, in the face of media globalization and the threat of cultural homogenization, other forms of local identities actually intensify. Localization, however, is not just restricted to media audiences. As our outline of

Time Warner's activities demonstrates, (see Boxes 2.4a and b), the global media giants localize many of their products to ensure global market domination and profits (see Herman and McChesney, 1999; Machin and van Leewen, 2003).

While media globalization is a powerful process, it is not a one-dimensional homogenizing force. The reception or hermeneutic model would suggest that audiences retain considerable power in terms of how globalized media texts are received, consumed, interpreted and even resisted – a phenomenon recognized in the emergence of a distinct strand of media analysis focused on diasporic media audiences.

Diasporic media audiences

Earlier in this chapter we noted that the movement of people (as asylum seekers, refugees or as migrant workers) is an intrinsic part of the overall process of globalization. The flow of people raises important questions concerning identity formation and belonging and integration or segregation, especially in the context of the existence of discourses which either 'other', racialize, or problematize the migrant within mainstream media content or render them invisible.

The recent emergence of diasporic media audience research brings a number of important questions into focus (see Karim, 2003). In acknowledging the complexities involved in being part of the diaspora, this research has concentrated on four key issues which have developed within these new 'mediascapes' (Appadurai, 1996):

1 The consumption and reception of transnational media (such as satellite television, radio and film genres such as 'Bollywood').
2 The consumption and reception of mainstream media content that is available to both diasporic and non-diasporic audiences in the so-called 'host' country.
3 The production and consumption of locally based media such as newspapers, magazines and newsletters.
4 The use of media technologies such as the VCR or DVD and ICT-based media such as websites, discussion boards and blogs.

There has been a particular focus on the degree to which diasporic audience members exercise agency in their media lives and on the emergence of glocalized hybrid identities, given that many of the diaspora live somewhere 'between' the host society and their homeland.

The technological developments that are responsible for media globalization have created new contexts in which the diaspora can consume media texts emanating from their countries of origin (see Naficy, 2003). In addition to media content produced and/or disseminated by mass media conglomerates (such as Telemundo in the USA), diasporic satellite and cable-based television and radio channels allow for immediate contact with media content from the 'homeland' (also referred to as 'home' or the 'motherland'). A growing number of satellite and cable-based radio and television channels produced within the host society (many of which are based upon very modest budgets and of variable quality in terms of production values) are also available. Since 9/11, for example, Al Jazeera (now broadcasting in both Arabic and English) is arguably the best-known satellite television channel broadcast to the transnational Arabic world and has a viewership of 50 million (see Georgiou, 2005). Zee TV, similarly, is consumed by a growing number of the Asian diaspora (see Box 2.6). The significance of Bollywood films amongst the latter in places such as the UK and Australia has also been examined in terms of their construction of Indian identities within an epic romance genre (see Ray, 2003; Dudrah, 2002b, 2006).

BOX 2.6 ZEE TV AND DIASPORIC MEDIA AUDIENCES

The BBC is arguably the best-known public service broadcasting organization that is also a global player in terms of the dissemination of media content through satellite television (BBC World, BBC 24), radio (BBC Radio World Service; BBC Russian; BBC Mundo; BBC Persian) and a growing number of digital radio channels such as Asian Radio). In the context of a changing and multicultural Britain, the state broadcaster has been accused of articulating both monolithic and hegemonic discourses about nationhood and identity. In 2001 its own Director General described the BBC as being 'hideously white' (Helen, 2001 cited in Creeber, 2004: 32) and it was conceded that the organization was not accurately reflecting the increasing ethnic diversity within British society.

One particular response to this issue has been the rise of new satellite and cable-based television stations which are aimed at diasporic media audiences. Creeber (2004) reports that there are approximately 12 such stations operating in the UK. Zee UK and Europe is perhaps the best known. Owned by the Mumbai (formerly Bombay) based Zee Telefilms India, Zee TV has a potential audience of 2 million in the UK and a further 8 million in continental Europe. Creeber argues that:

> For many Asian viewers, this channel provides their main source of non-English programming, broadcasting in languages such as Hindi, Urdu, Punjabi, Bengali and Tamil. As well as screening Bollywood films, the channel provides several movie quiz shows and celebrity gossip about film stars and directors. It also transmits 'high quality' Pakistani dramas while making its own 'lifestyle' and children's programs. . . . This sort of TV clearly plays an important role in cementing relations between Asian families and communities, providing a 'common culture' for those viewers who do not fit easily into any neat definition of British citizenship. (2004: 33)

(Continued)

> Channels like Zee TV attract diasporic audiences because they reflect more accurately the particularities of being Asian in a British context. Commenting, for example, on the hybridity evident within a children's television programme aired on Zee TV, one viewer stated that:
>
> > It's a guy sitting there, and he's talking in Urdu and then he changes to English . . . Like a lot of us if we were sort of talking amongst each other, we wouldn't be talking pure English. We would be talking English and Urdu and Punjabi, sort of everything mixed, you know. That is what he does. (Qureshi and Moores, 2000: 133, cited in Creeber, 2004: 33)
>
> The larger Zee TV network broadcasts to a potential Asian audience in eighty-four countries using a combination of free and pay television. May argues that Zee TV has positioned itself as 'a halfway house between the transnational (Asian) Star TV brand and traditional Hindi film, creating a hybrid genre that refers strongly to Western-style music and dance' (2003: 29) (see also Dudrah, 2002a, 2002b, 2005). See also www.zeetv.com.

As was noted earlier in this chapter, the consumption and reception of media texts that are more widely available, such as globally circulated television and film, has been explored in terms of the emergence of new hybrid identities (see Punathambekar, 2005). Hybridity is also in evidence in the way in which the diaspora communicate with one another on-line. Tsaliki (2003: 167) has demonstrated how some members of the Greek diaspora make use of a hybrid language which she terms 'Greenglish' in communicating with one another. Gillespie's (1995) research on young Punjabi youth in South London also notes the ways in which diasporic audience members appropriate and hybridize elements of widely circulated popular culture such as soap operas (see Box 2.7; see also Ray, 2003; Kraidy 1999; Davis and Davis, 1995). The production of newspapers, magazines and newsletters by and for diasporas is another a feature. In addition to this, use is made of new media spaces such as blogs, websites and discussion forums.

Media research concerned with the diaspora reminds us that in spite of (and sometimes because of) media globalization, audiences have more possibilities in terms of communicating with one another and countering the dominant or hegemonic discourses which are part of the overall globalization process. Media technologies that are central to the spread of a homogenizing (Western) culture also enable the circulation of other cultural forms, which often results in the cementing of other cultural identities and/or the creation of newer hybrid forms.

BOX 2.7   DIASPORIC MEDIA AUDIENCES: GILLESPIE'S (1995) *TELEVISION, ETHNICITY AND CULTURAL CHANGE*

Marie Gillespie's work (1989, 1993, 1995, 2002) has examined the interplay between the globalization and the localization of culture. She has focused on the first-generation Indian diaspora in terms of their media use and the 'television talk' of Punjabi teenagers.

Globalization has resulted in the movement of people and the circulation of media texts on a transnational basis. But what are its implications for local cultures? Gillespie contends that while the consumption of a growing number of transnational television programmes and films has affected cultural change among London Punjabi families, she argues that 'Punjabi cultural "traditions" are just as likely to be reaffirmed and reinvented as to be challenged and subverted by television and video viewing experiences' (1995: 76).

Her earlier research on the importance of the video-cassette recorder in Indian homes in the United Kingdom stressed:

how the VCR enables families to maintain strong cultural ties with their countries of origin through the consumption of popular film and television exported from the Indian sub-continent. It pointed to the ways in which a 'new' communications technology is being mobilized for the purposes of maintaining and reinventing traditions, showing how it is implicated in the construction of 'ethnic' identities in the Indian diaspora. (1995: 49)

In *Television, Ethnicity and Cultural Change* (1995), Gillespie uses an ethnographic approach (see Chapter 5 for a discussion of this methodological framework) in analysis of ethnicity and identity among Punjabi teenagers in Southall, south London. Gillespie is interested in the formation of British Asian identity in an era of media globalization. The research focuses on the media consumption and the 'television talk' of some members of the Punjabi diaspora. Gillespie argues that young Punjabis are 'shaped by but at the same time reshaping the images and meanings circulated in the media and in the market' (1995: 2). She argues that in Southall 'the redefinition of ethnicity is enacted in young people's collective reception and appropriation of television. Transnational and diasporic media representing several cultures are available in Southall homes, offering a range of choices of symbolic identification' (1995: 206).

Gillespie observes that in Southall, 'a transnational media product is locally appropriated in ways [that] encourage people to refine their conceptions of their own local culture, and at the same time redefine their collective identity in relation to representations

(Continued)

of "others"' (1995: 207). 'Gossip' is singled out by Gillespie's informants as that which characterizes the culture of the Southall Punjabi diasporic community. The ethnography reveals that the Punjabi teenagers have appropriated the main gossip character of the Australian soap *Neighbours* (broadcast on BBC), 'Mrs Mangel'. According to Gillespie, 'Among young people the term "Mangel" has entered everyday usage as a term of abuse for anyone who gossips: "Oh! She's a right Mangel!" can be heard commonly' 152). Gillespie underscores the need to understand media audiences as cultural actors, a theme to which we still return in more detail in Chapter 7.

BOX 2.8   GLOCALIZATION: THE CASE OF CANTOPOP

As we have already noted, globalization is not a one-way street (see Grixti, 2006). Cultural and economic globalization as exemplified by the activities of the decreasing number of multimedia conglomerates has resulted in developments and changes not all of which are negative in the production of popular culture. Ho's (2003) research on the Hong Kong popular music industry is a powerful example. The music industry in Hong Kong was for a long time on the receiving end of Western globalizing forces. The emergence (and popularity) of pop music sung in Cantonese (as opposed to English or Mandarin) is shown to be a concrete example of cultural hybridization or glocalization. Many local singers who previously sang in English or Mandarin now record and perform in Cantonese only. Localization of global popular culture is however far from being seamless. Ho notes, for example, that 'five cover versions of Wham's [*sic*] "Careless Whisper" were released simultaneously, each with different Cantonese lyrics' (2003: 149). Globalizing forces – in the shape of the global recording industry as well the availability of cheaper forms of technology (synthesizers, samplers etc.) have all helped in the growth and development of a vibrant local music scene. He concludes that:

> Despite movements of popular artists, capital and technologies across national boundaries, nation-states still constitute the nexus of [the] global–local exchange. Global localization involves the adaptation of global products to suit the local Hong Kong conditions. Whilst the development of Hong Kong pop has been enabled by the development of multinational media industries such as EMI, Warner and Sony, the growth of the local Emperor Entertainment Group (EEG) Limited has injected new energy into the Hong Kong music business. Nonetheless, the 'international success' of Hong Kong artists is still almost exclusively within the

Chinese diaspora in Southeast Asia, Canada and the USA and the UK, with more modest success in Japan, and very little inroad into mainstream English-speaking markets in the West (although top local popular artists have performed there). (2003: 154–5)

You should now read EXTRACTED READING 2.3, *Media Glocalization* (Kraidy, 1999) and consider the following issues:

1   In Kraidy's account of this example of glocalization how does 'hybridity' manifest itself?

2   Discuss how Kraidy's respondents exhibit varying degrees of agency in their encounters with globalized media texts.

CASE STUDY

Print media coverage of Third World crises

A great deal of our knowledge about what is happening elsewhere in the world is as a result of mass-mediatization. The latter determines what people are informed about, how they are informed and indeed when they are informed. This case study of *The Irish Times* newspaper examines how a global issue is interpreted and dealt with at a local level: how a famine in Sudan is viewed from Ireland. Both Sudan and Ireland exhibit a high level of dependence on the global media industries; they rely on foreign news agencies in order to frame the 'story' of famine crises. Nevertheless, the local media appropriate these global issues through their own routines of news production (see Devereux, 2000; Devereux and Haynes, 2000).

The 1998 Sudanese famine crisis

In the middle of 1998 it was estimated that between 350,000 and 700,000 people were at starvation point in the war zone in Bahr el Ghazal province in southern Sudan. The Sudanese crisis presented an interesting challenge to the Irish media, not least because of the complexities involved in the 15-year-old civil war raging between the Muslim north and the Christian and animist south. *The Irish Times* provided detailed and analytical coverage of the story. Its commitment to covering such issues

(Continued)

was evident at both editorial and resource levels. A range of ideological positions is evident in the newspaper's coverage of the issues involved. While dominant understandings of Third World famine – drought, crop failure, food shortages, civil war and local political corruption – can be easily identified in *The Irish Times'* coverage, there is also in evidence a range of explanations which either counter the accepted reasons for the Sudanese crisis or are at the very least critical in their orientation.

The cycle of the Sudanese story in *The Irish Times* began on 6 April 1998 with the initial warnings from aid agencies about the need for assistance in the form of food, seeds and tools. From the beginning it was stated that the Sudanese crisis could be resolved only through a combination of humanitarian aid and the political pressure needed to resolve the civil war. By 18 April the newspaper warned that people were beginning to die from famine in southern Sudan; 350,000 people were said to be at risk. The report noted the logistical problems caused by the refusal of the Khartoum government to give permission for humanitarian flights to drop food and supplies to southern Sudan. The civil war was cited as the key reason for the famine.

Bob Geldof's appearance on the BBC's *Six O'Clock News* served to guarantee further coverage of the Sudanese crisis by the Irish print media. The follow-up report in *The Irish Times* (25 April 1998) conformed to the argument that much of what we learn about the Third World is in terms of the activities or utterances of elite white Western figures. The fact that a heroic (and Irish) figure had made a statement about the potential crisis in Sudan increased the possibility that the BBC story would be picked up by the Irish print media. As a piece of journalism, it is illustrative of the dependence of the Irish media on others in reporting on the Third World. The story is of interest in that it both draws upon the BBC report of the previous evening and uses additional material from the Guardian Service news agency.

The month of May witnessed a number of shifts in terms of how the story was being told to *The Irish Times'* readership. On 4 May the original estimation of those at risk from famine was doubled to 700,000. The international pressure being brought to bear on both sides of the conflict resulted in the resumption of peace talks, although the logistical problems in delivering aid continued. *The Irish Times* then began to concentrate on reporting on Irish aid efforts – how the Irish government and aid agencies were responding to the crisis.

The coverage of the crisis then switched to a more critical discourse as the Khartoum government began to allow a limited number of flights into southern Sudan. The *Irish Times* began to concentrate on how the Khartoum government was attempting to use hunger as a weapon in the civil war. The newspaper also reflected upon the dilemmas facing aid agencies.

The aid agencies realized that the timing of their appeals to their respective publics via the media in the West had to be strategic. If they raised money and the

Khartoum government continued to restrict or refuse flights of mercy to the region, there was a possibility that the public might lose interest or stop donating. The collection and distribution of aid was therefore determined not by the immediate needs of the famine victims in southern Sudan, but rather by the way in which the media could best be managed. The response of the public in Ireland and elsewhere was determined by the flow of media coverage – not by real time, but by media time – within the global media industries.

The newspaper's development correspondent went to Sudan in late May. The immediate result was an obvious increase in the extent of detailed reporting and analysis. His reports described the conditions facing the southern Sudanese and attempted to assess whether they constituted a famine or the threat of famine. The coverage extended to examining the underlying reasons for the crises in Africa and made specific reference to colonialism. Some of the themes of the earlier coverage – the heroic Irish aid worker, the manipulation and misuse of humanitarian aid by the Khartoum government, repeated warnings about the imminence of famine – were central to how the story was told in June. One of the more notable pieces of reporting on the Sudanese crisis occurred on 6 June when the newspaper's development correspondent criticized the role of the Western media in their reporting (or failure to report) on African issues.

The coverage ended in August. For *The Irish Times* and other media organizations, the newsworthiness of the story ceased when international humanitarian flights began to get through to the Sudanese and famine was averted. The problems inherent in alerting the public to the crisis without the political dimension being resolved meant that many journalists felt that there was nothing more to add to the famine story. It had lost its newsworthiness.

The local and the global

Tomlinson (1994) has placed particular emphasis on the question of the mediation of experience (see also Extracted Reading 2.1). While globalization stretches the relations between the distant and the local, he argues that the concept of mediation implies the experience of passing though an 'intermediary'. He is referring to the role of the mass media in linking distant events with the everyday experience of those living in late modernity and is questioning the true extent to which the world has become more 'open'.

The mass media are clearly responsible for the increased amount of information that some social actors are now offered. We are not, however, living in an egalitarian global village where information and knowledge flow freely between continents. The global media industry has immense power in terms of how it covers events outside the developed world. Global news agencies and major broadcasting organizations are primarily responsible for the selection and packaging of news from the Third World. Third World countries have an obvious dependence on the global media industry, and especially in times of crisis when news has to travel fast. In this light, media coverage of Third World issues sustains the unequal relations of power that exist between the West and the Third World.

Global issues such as famine or poverty, although experienced through the mass media, are nonetheless appropriated through a local prism. Media audiences are exposed to stories about faraway places and events, but these stories have a heavy emphasis on local involvement. Thus many of the stories about the Sudanese famine crisis focused on the Irish response, both voluntary and statutory, and celebrated the heroic role of the Irish aid worker. The process of globalization now at work links, in a rather direct way, locales with large structures and occurrences. But the reverse also holds true: local factors play a strong role in the way global processes are experienced. The latter have to make themselves local in order to become effective.

CRITICAL QUESTIONS 2.3

We have already noted that powerful economic and political interests construct globalization in an unproblematic way.

1   How would critics of globalization such as environmentalists or green activists, for example, interpret the globalization process?
2   In your experience how are critics of globalization portrayed in a media setting?

Conclusion

While we cannot deny the reality of media globalization, we need to approach this complex issue with some caution. By this we mean that students of the mass media should be critical of the way in which the agents of globalization and of media globalization in particular describe their project. Globalization has resulted in the creation of a series of interconnected but unequal global villages. While the global has become more prominent in people's local lives, other forms of identity – the ethnic, the local, the regional, the national, the subcultural – clearly remain potent. They are especially powerful in determining how audiences read media texts. The restructuring of the media industry along global lines has resulted in the creation of a very small number of transnational conglomerates with immense power and control whose *raison d'être* is profit. So far, media globalization has proved itself to be more amenable to particular forms of mass media such as television, film and popular music recordings. While the almost insatiable demands of television have resulted in a diet of reruns and copycat programming – of what the influential late French sociologist Pierre Bourdieu refers to as 'cultural fast food' – we cannot take the arguments about cultural homogenization for granted. Audiences, as we will discuss in greater detail in Chapter 7, possess considerable agency when encountering either locally or globally produced media texts.

Extracted readings

2.1   A window on the world?

John Tomlinson, 'A phenomenology of globalization? Giddens on global modernity', *European Journal of Communication* 9 (1994): 149–72

The point of maintaining this distinction between modes of experience is that it qualifies the claim about distanciated events being 'integrated into the frameworks of personal experience'. While the mass media provide the most obvious access to 'the world' for the majority of people, this experience is always, in a sense, contained within the lifeworld as 'mass-mediated experience'. To compare this with [Anthony] Giddens's claim about the 'provisional' sense in which we experience localities, we might think of mass-mediated experience as a very provisional sense of the global: instantly and ubiquitously accessible, but 'insulated' from the local quotidian by virtue of its very form. If this is so, it has implications for the idea that the world becomes 'open' to us via the mass media. Zygmunt Bauman is sceptical of the idea that television overcomes cultural distance by giving us insight into the lives of 'institutionally separated' others:

> Contrary to widespread opinion, the advent of television, this huge and easily accessible peephole through which the unfamiliar ways may be routinely glimpsed, has neither eliminated the institutional separation nor diminished its effectivity. McLuhan's 'global village' has failed to materialize. The frame of a cinema or television screen staves off the danger of spillage more effectively than tourist hotels and fenced off camping sites; the one-sidedness of communication further entrenches the unfamiliars on the screen as essentially incommunicado. (Bauman, 1990: 149)

. . . local exigencies maintain a certain priority even in a lifeworld opened up to the global. This derives from the sheer material demands of local routines tied to the satisfaction of basic needs. But it also derives from the distinctions people routinely make between an 'immediate' local world and the mass-mediated experience of the global which is, for most people, the commonest way in which the world is opened to them. Clearly the mass media represent a highly significant linkage between local and global experience, and there is a lot of work to be done investigating the phenomenology of this linkage: the precise sense in which, for example, television can be said to bring the world into our living rooms. What I have tried to suggest is that this problematizing of mass-mediated experience is a necessary qualification for Giddens's claims about the 'intrusion of distant events into everyday consciousness'. (p. 160)

2.2   'Culture jammers and semiotic resistance'

Owen Worth and Carmen Kuhling, 'Counter-hegemony and anti-globalisation', *Capital and Class* 84 (2005): 31–42

Klein's book *No Logo* (2001) focuses on the emergence of what she calls a new type of anti-consumerist activism, which challenges the intrusion of the commodity form into all avenues of public and private space. Some aspects of this anti-consumerist movement can be understood as subcultures of resistance to neoliberal globalisation, in the tradition of the Birmingham School of Cultural Studies. . . .

Klein's 'culture jammers' express a 'semiotic resistance' to the hegemony of neoliberal globalisation, through a variety of strategies designed to transform and subvert advertising messages and, therefore, the ideological foundation of consumer society. 'Ad-busting', 'ad-bashing' and the other strategies of anti-globalisationists identified by Klein subvert the messages purveyed by advertisers, by exposing the various contradictions underlying advertising messages. For instance, the cynical targeting of vulnerable populations is exposed through the practice of 'skulling' or drawing skeletons, or writing 'Feed Me' on billboard models, in order to highlight the connection between advertising and eating disorders in teenage populations; the false equation of consumer 'choice' with agency is exposed by, for example, changing the Nike billboard slogan 'Just Do It' to 'Just Screw It'; the vacuousness of advertising messages is exposed through similar subversive interventions: for example, changing Absolut Vodka slogans to 'Absolut Nonsense'.

While anti-consumerist activists engage in a wide variety of strategies of resistance at a micro-political level, many are members of 'virtual communities' with networks at local, regional, national and transnational levels. As Klein argues, the accessibility of new technologies makes the circulation of ad parodies much easier, and has facilitated the sharing of a variety of media technologies that have been used in such parodies. . . .

These groups practice 'subvertising', combining adbusting with the publication of 'alternative' magazines, pirate radio broadcasts and the creation of independent videos, all with anticonsumerist messages. These jammers are joined by a global network of 'hacktivists', who break into corporate websites and leave their own messages behind.

2.3   Media glocalization

Marwan M. Kraidy, 'The global, the local, and the hybrid: a native ethnography of glocalization', *Critical Studies in Mass Communication* 16 (1999): 456–76

Young Maronites articulated the discourse of individual freedom primarily with American television programs, with *The Cosby Show* and *Beverly Hills 90210* mentioned the most. Young Maronites liked *90210* because they connected their personal lives with the characters. Maha and Karine emphasized that the television series showed a higher degree of freedom and openness in intimate relationships than they had personally experienced, and Peter and Antoun told me that they used the program in their daily lives, drawing on its events to articulate their social identity. *The Cosby Show*, broadcast in Lebanon in the eighties and early nineties, also emerged as a major text. Interlocutors indicated that they watched it with their families. Marianne told me how she 'exploited' *The Cosby Show* to gain more freedom from her parents: She would discuss the relationship between the parents on *The Cosby Show* and their daughters, arguing that although the parents were socially conservative, they allowed their daughters to go out on dates because they trusted them. Marianne strongly believed that the show helped her reduce parental restrictions.

In contrast to that favourable reading of *The Cosby Show*, most interlocutors criticized 'many' American movies and television programs for containing 'cheap, purely commercial, sexual scenes' (Elham, Maha), or to portray 'excessive promiscuity between teenagers' (Serge, Rima). Whereas Adib argued that such scenes were 'OK because, to an extent, they [reflected] real life,' Antoun and Peter recognized that some movies, such as *Basic Instinct*, effectively used sexuality for dramatic and aesthetic values. When I probed them about their own social and sexual freedom, interlocutors pointed out that they enjoyed less freedom than American youth, but believed that they endured less restrictions than Arab Muslim youth, thus positioning themselves, again, between the contrapuntal 'Western' and 'Arab' discourses.

Television emerged as my interlocutors' medium of choice. They adopted and rejected elements from both Arab and Western programs, underscoring symbolic leakage between the two worldviews, and speaking at their point of contact. As a general strategy, this hybrid enunciative posture harnessed three everyday life tactics: a propinquity towards consuming ostensibly hybrid texts, quotidian acts of mimicry, and nomadic reading strategies. Consumption, mimicry and nomadism thus enacted hybridity as the daily condition of Maronite youth identity. (pp. 466–7)

Exercise 2.1

Exploring media globalization through the use of focus groups

In this chapter we emphasized the importance of recognizing the role of the audience to see how media globalization works in practice. This exercise is an example of how a combination of basic quantitative and qualitative research methods may be used to learn more about audiences and the process of media globalization (see Hansen et al., 1998). Think critically about how the phenomena of media globalization are experienced by audience members in their everyday lives. Pay particular attention to the social and cultural factors that might possibly explain differences in how media globalization is experienced among your selected audience groups.

Focus groups

Focus groups help capture real-life data in a social environment: they are flexible and have high face validity. Such groups often bring to the fore aspects of the topic that might not otherwise be anticipated by the researcher. In this exercise the use of audience groups offers a real-life simulation of a typical audience situation, where interpersonal factors play a significant role in terms of content effects.

The exercise

Depending upon local circumstances, the course lecturer or tutor divides the class or tutorial group into a number of research teams. The research teams select audience groups that are defined – individually or in combination – by such characteristics as age, gender, class, ethnicity or membership of subcultural groupings. Some basic data about the selected individuals should be gathered through the use of a short questionnaire. The remaining data should be collected through the facilitation of audience groups whereby the researchers make use of a schedule of questions. It's best to use a semi-structured interview schedule, as this will allow for some flexibility in taking account of the participants' experiences and viewpoints.

With the permission of the participants, their responses should be recorded and transcribed. The research team then analyses the findings of both the questionnaire and the responses of the informants. At this stage the researchers should be endeavouring to identify key patterns in the data according to the make-up of the audience group. They should then tease out the implications that their empirical research findings have for the theories of media globalization that they have read about in this chapter.

Research or discussion themes

1 Access to and use of new media technologies.
2 Television news and its coverage of famine and other crises in the Third World.
3 Consumption of and meanings derived from globally versus locally produced media genres such as soap operas, radio programmes, television news or films.
4 The experience of living in a mass-mediated world.
5 'Zappers' or 'grazers'? Audiences in the context of increased fragmentation of mass-media content in an age of media globalization.

Questions for consideration and discussion

1 Does a global village exist?
2 For local audiences media globalization does not necessarily mean a window on the world. Discuss.
3 The global media industry is primarily concerned with profit, not media content. Discuss.
4 What do you now understand by the term 'glocalization' and where might you find examples of the glocalization processes at work in your immediate environment?
5 Having read all three extracted readings, outline and discuss the key issues concerning audiences in an age of media globalization.

——————— References ———————

Appadurai, A. (1996) *Modernity at Large: Cultural Dimensions of Globalisation.* Minneapolis: University of Minnesota Press.
Bagdikian, B.H. (2004) *The New Media Monopoly.* Boston, MA: Beacon Press.
Bauman, Z. (1990) 'Modernity and ambivalence' in M. Featherstone (ed.) *Global Culture: Nationalism, Globalization and Modernity.* London: Sage.

Burnett, R. (1996) *The Global Jukebox: The International Music Industry*. London and New York: Routledge.

Campbell, P.B. (2003) 'Mind the gap: the tarnishing of a transcendent technology' in M. Breen, E. Conway and B. McMillan (eds) *Technology and Transcendence*. Dublin: Columba Press, pp. 44–59.

Campbell, P.B. and M.J. Breen (2001) 'The Net, its gatekeeper, their bait and its victims: ethical issues relating to the Internet' in E. Cassidy and A.G. McGrady (eds) *Media and the Marketplace: Ethical Perspectives*. Dublin: Institute of Public Administration.

Chandler, D. and M. Griffiths (2004) 'Who is the fairest of them all? Gendered readings of *Big Brother 2* (UK)' in E. Mathijs and J. Jones (eds) *Big Brother International: Format, Critics and Publics*. London: Wallflower Press.

Couldry, N. (2002) 'Playing for celebrity: Big Brother as ritual event', *Television and New Media* 3(3): 283–93.

Creeber, G. (2004) '"Hideously white": British television, glocalization and national identity', *Television and New Media* 5(1): 27–39.

Cullen, P. (2000) 'Global capitalism comes to the rescue as rattling the tin cup doesn't do it any more', *Irish Times*, 22 January 2000.

Cullen, R. (2001) 'Addressing the digital divide', *Online Information Review* 25(5): 311–20.

Davis, S.S. and D.A. Davis (1995) '"The mosque and the satellite": media and adolescence in a Moroccan town', *Journal of Youth and Adolescence* 24 (5): 577–93.

Devereux, E. (2000) 'A media famine' in E. Slater and M. Peillon (eds) *Memories of the Present*. Dublin: Institute of Public Administration.

Devereux, E. and A. Haynes (2000) 'Irish print media coverage of the 1998 Sudanese crisis: the case of the *Irish Times*', *Media Development* 1: 20–3.

van Dijk, J.A.G.M. (2005) *The Deepening Divide: Inequality in the Information Society*. Sage: London.

DiMaggio, P. and E. Hargittai (2001) 'From the 'Digital Divide' to 'Digital Inequality': studying internet use as penetration increases', Center for Arts and Culture and Policy Studies, Princeton, Working Paper No. 15, Summer.

DiMaggio, P., E. Hargittai, W.R. Neuman and J.P. Robinson (2001) 'Social implications of the Internet', *Annual Review of Sociology* 27: 307–36.

Dudrah, R.K. (2002a) 'Zee TV in Europe: non-terrestrial television and the construction of a pan-South Asian identity', *Contemporary South Asia* 11 (1): 163–81.

Dudrah, R.K. (2002b) 'Vilayati Bollywood: popular Hindi cinema going and diasporic South Asian identity', *Javnost: The Public* 9(1): 9–36.

Dudrah, R.K. (2005) 'Zee TV: diasporic non-terrestrial television in Europe', South *Asian Popular Culture* 3(1): 33–47.

Dudrah, R.K. (2006) *Bollywood: Sociology Goes to the Movies*. London: Sage.

Dutta-Bergman, M.J. (2005) 'Access to the Internet in the context of community participation and community satisfaction', *New Media and Society* 7(1): 89–109.

Frau-Miggs, D. (2006) '*Big Brother* and reality TV in Europe: towards a theory of situated acculturation by the media', *European Journal of Communication* 21(1): 33–56.

Georgiou, M. (2005) 'Diasporic Media Across Europe: Multicultural Societies and the Universalism–Particularism Continuum', *Journal of Ethnic and Migration Studies* 31(3): 481–98.

Giddens, A. (1999) *Runaway World: How Globalization Is Reshaping Our Lives*. London: Profile Books.

Gillespie, M. (1989) 'Technology and tradition: audio-visual culture among South Asian families in west London', *Cultural Studies* 3 (2): 226–39.

Gillespie, M. (1993) 'The Mahabharata. From Sanskrit to sacred soap; a case study of the reception of two contemporary televisual versions' in D. Buckingham (ed.) *Reading Audiences: Young People and the Media*. Manchester: Manchester University Press.

Gillespie, M. (1995) *Television, Ethnicity and Cultural Change*. London: Routledge.

Gillespie, M. (2002) 'Dynamics of diasporas: South Asian media and transnational cultural politics' in G. Stald and T. Tufte (eds) *Global Encounters: Media and Cultural Transformations*. Luton: University of Luton Press, pp. 151–73.

Griffen-Foley, B. (2004) 'From *Tit-Bits* to *Big Brother*: a century of audience participation in the Media', *Media, Culture and Society* 26(4): 533–48.

Grixti, J. (2006) 'Symbiotic transformations: youth, global media and indigenous culture in Malta', *Media, culture and Society* 28(1): 105–22.

Hansen, A., S. Cottle, R. Negrine and C. Newbold (1998) 'Media audiences: focus group interviewing' in *Mass Communication Research Methods*. London: Macmillan.

Helen, N. (2001) 'Dyke attacks "hideously white" BBC', *The Sunday Times*, 7 January, p. 3.

Herman, E. and R. McChesney (1999) 'The global media in the late 1990s' in H. Mackay and T. O'Sullivan (eds) *The Media Reader: Continuity and Transformation*. London: Sage.

Hesmondhalgh, D. (1999) 'Indie: the institutional politics and aesthetics of a popular music genre', *Cultural Studies* 13(1): 34–61.

Hill, A. (2002) '*Big Brother*: the real audience', *Television and New Media* 3(3): 323–40.

Ho, W.C. (2003) 'Between globalization and localization: a study of Hong Kong popular music', *Popular Music* 22(2).

Husband, C. (1998) 'Globalisation, media infrastructures and identities in a diasporic community', *Javnost: The Public* 5 (4): 19–33.

James, J. (2005) 'The global digital divide in the Internet: developed world constructs and Third World realities', *Journal of Information Science* 31 (2): 114–23.

Karim, K.H. (ed.) (2003) *The Media of Diaspora*. London: Routledge.

Kit-Wai Ma, E. (2000) 'Re-thinking media studies: the case of China', in J. Curran and M-J. Park (eds) *De-Westernising Media Studies*. London: Routledge.

Klein, N. (2001) *No Logo*. London: Flamingo Books.

Korupp, S.E. and M. Szydlik (2005) 'Causes and trends of the digital divide', *European Sociological Review* 21(4): 409–22.

Kraidy, M.M. (1999) 'The global, the local, and the hybrid: a native ethnography of glocalization', *Critical Studies in Mass Communication* 16: 456–76.

Liebes, T. and E. Katz (1993) *The Export of Meaning: Cross-cultural Readings of 'Dallas'*, 2nd edn. Cambridge: Polity Press.

Lull, J. (1995) *Media, Communication, Culture: A Global Approach*. Cambridge: Polity Press.

Machin, D. and T. van Leeuwen (2003) 'Global schemas and local discourses in *Cosmopolitan*', *Journal of Sociolinguistics* 7(4): 493–512.

Machin, D. and T. van Leeuwen (2004) 'Global media: generic homogeneity and discursive diversity', *Continuum: Journal of Media and Cultural Studies* 18(1): 99–120.

Mathijs, E. (2002) '*Big Brother* and critical discourse: the reception of *Big Brother* Belgium', *Television and New Media*, 3(3): 311–22.

Mirchandani, K. (2004) 'Practices of Global Capital: Gaps, Cracks and Ironies in Transnational Call Centres in India', *Global Networks* 4(4): 355–73.

Nacifiy, H. (1993) The Making of Exile Cultures: Iranian Television in Los Angeles. Minneapolis: University of Minnesota Press.

Negroponte, N. (1995) *Being Digital*. London: Hodder & Stoughton.

Norris, P. (2001) *Digital Divide*. Cambridge: Cambridge University Press.

Oliveira, O.S. (1993) 'Brazilian soaps outshine Hollywood: Is cultural imperialism fading out?' in K. Nordenstreng and H.I. Schiller (eds) *Beyond National Sovereignty: International Communication in the 1990s*. Norwood, NJ: Ablex.

Pecora, V.P. (2002) 'The culture of surveillance', *Qualitative Sociology* 25 (3).

Peters, S. and T. Peters (2005) 'What is globalization?', www.topics-mag.com.

Pilger, J. (1999) *Hidden Agendas*. London: Verso.

Pilger, J. (2002) *The New Rulers of the World*. London: Verso.

Punathambekar, A. (2005) 'Bollywood in the Indian-American diaspora', *International Journal of Cultural Studies* 8(2): 151–73.

Quereshi, K. and S. Moores (2000) 'Identity, tradition and translation' in S. Moores (ed.) *Media and Everyday Life in Modern Society*. Edinburgh: Edinburgh University Press.

Ray, M. (2003) 'Nation, nostalgia and Bollywood' in K.H. Karim (ed) *The Media of Diaspora*. London: Routledge.

Ritzer, G. (2000) *The McDonaldization of Society*. Thousand Oaks, CA: Pine Forge Press.

Robertson, R. (1992) *Globalization, Social Theory and Global Culture*. London: Sage.

Sabbagh, D. (2006) 'No Tibet or Tiananmen on Google's Chinese site', 25 January, www.timesonline.co.uk.

Scannell, P. (2002) '*Big Brother* as a Television Event', *Television and New Media* 3 (3): 271–82.

Scholte, J.A. (2000) *Globalization: A Critical Introduction*. London: Palgrave.

Silverstone, R. (1999) *Why Study the Media?* London: Sage.

Sklair, L. (1999) 'Globalization' in S. Taylor (ed.) *Sociology: Issues and Debates*. London: Macmillan.

Sreberny-Mohammadi, A. and A. Mohammadi (1994) *Small Media, Big Revolution: Communication, Culture and the Iranian Revolution*. Minneapolis, MN: University of Minnesota Press.

Thompson, J.B. (1995) *The Media and Modernity: A Social Theory of the Media*. Cambridge: Polity Press.

Tomlinson, J. (1994) 'A phenomenology of globalization? Giddens on global modernity', *European Journal of Communication* 9: 149–72.

Tomlinson, J. (1997) 'Internationalism, globalization and cultural imperialism' in K. Thompson (ed.) *Media and Cultural Regulation*. London: Sage; Milton Keynes: Open University Press.

Tomlinson, J. (1999) 'Cultural globalization: placing and displacing the West' in H. Mackay and T. O'Sullivan (eds) *The Media Reader: Continuity and Transformation*. London: Sage.

Tsaliki, L. (2003) 'Globalization and hybridity: the construction of Greekness on the Internet' in K.H. Karim (ed) *The Media of Diaspora*. London: Routledge, pp. 162–76.

Van Zoonen, L. (2001) 'Desire and resistance: *Big Brother* and the recognition of everyday life', *Media, Culture and Society* 23(5): 669–77.

Van Zoonen, L. and M. Aslama (2006) 'Understanding *Big Brother*: an analysis of current research', *Javnost/The Public* 13(2): 85–96.

Webb, D. (2005) 'On mosques and malls: understanding Khomeinism as a source of counter-hegemonic resistance to the spread of global consumer culture', *Journal of Political Ideologies* 10(1) 95–119.

Wilson, K.R., J.S. Wallin and C. Reiser (2003) 'Social stratification and the digital divide', *Social Science Computer Review* 2 (2): 133–43.

Woltz, A. (1999) 'Surrogaat voor het leven', *NRC Handelsblad*, 2 December.

--- **Going further** ---

Collins, R. (2002) *Media and Identity in Contemporary Europe: Consequences of Global Convergence*. Intellect Books: Bristol, UK. A critical examination of the European media landscape in the face of the global dominance of the US media industry.

Cunningham, S. and J. Sinclair (eds.) (2002) *Floating Lives: The Media and Asian Diasporas*. St Lucia, Queensland: Queensland University Press and Lanham, MD: Rowman & Littlefield Publishers. A critical examination of the Asian diaspora in an Australian context combining political economy, reception and content analysis approaches.

van Dijk, J.A.G.M. (2005) *The Deepening Divide: Inequality in the Information Society*. Sage: London. This text situates the digital divide in its social and political contexts and goes beyond technocentric accounts of the issues involved in information inequalities.

von Feilitzen C. and U. Carlsson (eds) (2002) *Children, Young People and Media Globalisation*. The Unesco/Nordicom/Goteburg University. This collection of essays examines, amongst other themes, the reception and appropriation by children and young people of globally circulated media texts such as animation (Pikachu) and on-line games.

Mirchandani, K. (2004) 'Practices of global capital: gaps, cracks and ironies in transnational call centres in India', *Global Networks* (4): 355–73. This is a fascinating study of the resistive practices employed by Indian call-centre workers in New Delhi who work for many of the global giants such as AOL, British Airways and Dell Computers.

Rantanen, T. (2004) *The Media and Globalization*. London: Sage. An accessible, student-friendly introduction to the complexities of media globalization.

Thomas, P.N. and Z. Nain (eds.) (2004) *Who Owns the Media? Global Trends and Local Resistance*. London: Zed Books. The essays in this book examine recent trends in the political economy of mass communication.

3

MEDIA OWNERSHIP: CONCENTRATION AND CONGLOMERATION

Summary

The ownership and control of the mainstream media are the focus of this chapter. Our discussion concentrates on the following issues:

- Changing patterns of media ownership and control in an age of media globalization.
- The explanatory power of the political economy perspective in terms of understanding these changes.
- The social, cultural and political implications of the increased concentration of media ownership and control.
- The increasingly powerful role of media conglomerates and media moguls in the global media industry.
- The implications for media content and media audiences arising from the increased concentration of media ownership.

Key concepts

- Ownership and control
- Vertical integration
- Horizontal integration
- Conglomeration
- Media moguls

- Synergies
- The public sphere
- Deregulation
- Public service broadcasting

In this chapter we examine the question of media ownership. We begin by outlining the shift towards concentration and conglomeration evident within the overall structure of the media industries. The political economy perspective is explained in detail. In the context of examining whether the increased concentration of media ownership has in fact resulted in a narrowing of the range of voices heard in a media setting, we outline the concept of the public sphere and apply it to the Internet. In addition to a number of short exercises on media ownership, this chapter contains three extracted readings, two of which deal with the political economy of the Internet.

In recent years a number of global media conglomerates have attempted to monopolize the ownership and distribution of cultural events, many of which were once freely available to media audiences. A common thread in the strategies employed by media moguls is the purchase and control of sporting events and sports clubs or teams and we examine this recent trend. It is particularly striking that since the first edition of this textbook was published in 2003, the pace of change amongst the mass media conglomerates in terms of both corporate structure and areas of concentration has further hastened. The Big Six have become the Big Five. Several of the mass media conglomerates have radically restructured themselves and have shifted away from older forms of media activities such as book publishing and the more traditional means of distributing popular music. The further colonization of everyday media experience by private commercial interests continues unabated, adding to concerns raised by some about the continued debasement of media content as well as the ideological significance of a narrowing ownership base, especially at a time of renewed ideological (and military) conflict between the West and the Islamic world.

Media ownership matters

Structures of ownership, whether non-profit, public or private, are seen to have a direct bearing upon media content. Interest in the issue of the changing structure of media ownership and its relationship to media content has focused upon a number of critically important questions concerning:

1 The progressively more concentrated nature of mass media ownership by a small number of transnational multimedia conglomerates.
2 The fact that many of these transnational conglomerates own, control or have substantial interests in both media and non-media companies.
3 The continued shrinkage of the mass media's public sphere role arising from greater concentration and conglomeration.
4 The consequences for news, current affairs and investigative journalism, given the macro shift towards entertainment, populism and 'infotainment'.
5 The redefinition of audiences as consumers rather than citizens.

6   Unequal access to both media content and media technologies.
7   The political and economic power of individual media moguls.

At the heart of the debate about media ownership are concerns about diversity. Both liberal and Marxist commentators have expressed fears in relation to the threat that increased concentration poses for democratic dialogue and debate in society. Concentration of ownership and conglomeration, it is argued by proponents of political economy theory and others, mean less pluralism within media content and closer links and involvement with the larger project of global capitalism. While media saturation and the convergence of media ownership are taking place simultaneously, more media does not necessarily mean more choice for audiences. As we noted in Chapter 2, significant information inequalities persist in an age of media globalization. All human societies continue to be divided into 'media haves' and 'media have-nots' (van Dijk, 2005).

You should now read EXTRACTED READING 3.1, 'The Big Five' (Bagdikian, 2004) and consider the following issues:

1   What are the dangers inherent in conglomeration and concentration?
2   The Big Five: competitors or cartel?
3   What implications does conglomeration and concentration have for news production in particular and by extension for democracy?

CRITICAL QUESTION 3.1

In an era of mass media saturation, does more media in our daily lives really mean less?

Media ownership

Along the continuum of media ownership patterns, we can differentiate between community/not-for-profit media, public or state-owned media and privately owned (and increasingly transnational) media organizations.

Community-based media such as local radio (whether licensed or pirate), e-zines, blogs or newsletters are usually organized on a non-profit basis by specific interest groups such as a women's collective or an ethnic minority group, for example. Attracting relatively small audiences, they are typically run on a modest budget and

Not-for-profit media organizations	Public/state owned media organizations	Privately owned media organizations: • Owned by individuals • Owned by families • Owned by mass media conglomerates

FIGURE 3.1 Media ownership

aim to serve the needs and interests of a clearly defined community such as the students in a university or the inhabitants of a small town. While many community-based media depend upon small amounts of advertising and sponsorship from commercial interests, they are relatively independent of such interests. Depending upon specific circumstances, such media may have greater editorial freedom in terms of content and style.

State ownership and control of newspapers, television and radio were – and remain – a key aspect of communist societies such as the former USSR, Romania, China and Cuba. State control has an obvious ideological role to play in attempting to secure hegemony among citizens. In spite of trends towards liberalization and deregulation in liberal democratic political systems, the state continues to have an involvement in the regulation of media such as radio and television. In the Republic of Ireland, for example, radio and television broadcasting (whether public, private or community owned) is controlled by the Broadcasting Commission of Ireland. The commission regulates radio, for example, in a number of key ways. It controls the issuing of broadcast licences; it determines how much air time should be given over to 'public interest' broadcasting; and it regulates how much air time can be expended on advertising or sponsorship. This pattern is repeated elsewhere. In Sweden, local and neighbourhood radio is licensed by the Radio and Television Authority, whilst programming content is controlled by the Swedish Broadcasting Commission. Similarly, in the Netherlands the Commission for the Media controls the public system of television and radio broadcasting.

In liberal democratic political systems such as those of Western Europe or Australia, public ownership of television and radio has long been a feature of the social landscape, although one that is now under real threat from both deregulation and the rise of transnational multimedia conglomerates. Publicly owned media may be funded from direct and indirect taxation, a licence fee, revenue generated from advertising, sponsorship or other commercial activities, such as the production and selling of content to other media organizations. These publicly owned media organizations operate in a mixed public–private marketplace and many are involved in co-production work with privately owned media companies in the film, radio and television sectors, for example. Public service broadcasters such as ABC (Australia), the BBC (United Kingdom) or RTE (Ireland), for example, have traditionally had a strong focus on news, current affairs and documentaries in their overall mix of programming content. While not wishing to over-idealize the public sphere role of public service media, many have had a distinguished history of catering for a wide range of audience (and some minority) interests and tastes. In this regard we can find many examples of programming targeted at linguistic or ethnic minorities but other minorities (gays, lesbians, bisexuals or transgendered, for example) are often ignored.

Media may be privately owned by companies controlled by individuals, families, shareholders or holding companies. Historically, many newspapers were owned, controlled and even edited by individual media entrepreneurs. In the nineteenth century, for example, many of the so-called press barons wielded considerable editorial power and allied themselves with the interests of the capitalist class. The vast majority of privately owned media companies are now owned and controlled by multimedia conglomerates. These organizations have immense economic and political power. They generate vast revenues for their owners and shareholders. While conglomeration is by no means risk-free – as evidenced in the collapse of several media companies – the fact is that more and more cultural production and distribution are controlled by a small number of privately owned players. One of the most telling aspects of this change is that entertainment is prioritized over information and knowledge. Critical journalism, while not by any means moribund, is under increased pressure in a world where, in Postman's (1986) words, we are 'Amusing Ourselves to Death'.

CRITICAL QUESTIONS 3.2

1   What sorts of constraints do you think exist for media professionals who work for privately owned media organizations, given their dependence on advertising and sponsorship?
2   How do you think these might compare with the experiences of media professionals who work within publicly or community owned media organizations?

Conglomeration, concentration and content

As a result of mergers, takeovers, deregulation, privatization, globalization and technological change, a substantial amount of mainstream media ownership increasingly rests in fewer hands. The growing concentration of media ownership, the formation of alliances and the merging of media and other companies into larger (and increasingly global) conglomerates raises serious concerns for many media scholars. Increased concentration, it is believed, has important implications for the media industry, media workers, media content and media audiences. There are additional worries concerning the power wielded by individual media moguls to influence editorial decisions: to shape overall media output and to exert considerable political power.

> ∞
> *See Chapter 2 for discussion of media globalization.*

Those who are critical of these changes in the structure of media ownership are concerned, in the main, about the ideological implications of such developments. They see a clear link between increased media ownership concentration and the narrowing, as they perceive it, of the range of voices heard within a media setting. The contraction of the public sphere, the rise of 'infotainment', the decline of critical investigative journalism, the casualization of much media work, the homogenizing tendencies inherent in media globalization, and the so-called 'dumbing down' of much media content (and of news and current affairs in particular) are all seen as resulting directly from this increased concentration.

In this new era of concentrated media ownership, O'Sullivan et al. (1994: 191) argue that 'The search for profit is seen as the key arbiter of what is produced in the media, first in the economic sense of achieving surplus revenue and secondly in the ideological sense of the values and beliefs which support capitalism.' As we will see shortly in this chapter, the radical political economy perspective has been to the fore in raising these and other important issues.

Much media ownership is now increasingly characterized by both concentration and conglomeration. Individual media companies may be owned and controlled by conglomerates that concentrate exclusively on media activities or by conglomerates that have a wider range of commercial activities within their specific portfolios (see Boxes 3.1a and 3.1b). Conglomerations operate at the local, regional, national and increasingly at the transnational levels. There has been a particular focus on how media conglomerates are controlled. Murdock (1982) has suggested that the control of media conglomerates is best understood in terms of a distinction between 'allocative control' and 'operational control'. The owners and those in senior management possess allocative control in that they determine the overall direction of the media organization(s) in question. They decide whether to concentrate on particular forms of programming over others, for example. Decisions are taken in terms of how much money will be allocated to news and current affairs programming as opposed to 'reality' or entertainment-based shows. Those with allocative control may decide to invest in other media companies who are in the business of producing or distributing media content through the use of new media technology, for example. Operational control exists on a much lower level in the media organization. An editor or a series producer may exert operational control in the making of a particular television or radio programme. She will decide on content and on how a budget is spent during production. Operational control is constrained by the allocative control exerted by those at a more senior level in the media organization.

BOX 3.1(A)   VIVENDI UNIVERSAL

Vivendi Universal is an example of a transnational conglomerate that has had interests in both media and non-media sectors. Its parent company, Compagnie Générale des Eaux, was originally established to supply water in Lyons (France) in 1853. In recent years Vivendi Universal has retreated from its activities in the non-media sectors and instead has chosen to concentrate on music (recording, publishing and distribution), telephony and telecommunications, and gaming and interactive entertainment. It owns the formerly independent company mp3.com. Such rationalization has also meant that it has disengaged from more traditional mass media activities such as book publishing. In 2001, for example, the conglomerate sold the publishing house Houghton Mifflin. It fully owns Universal Music Group, Vivendi Universal Games and the Canal+ Group. It owns a 56 per cent share of the telecommunications group SFR and 28 per cent of Neuf Cegetel. Vivendi Universal has a controlling interest (51 per cent) in Maroc Telecom (Morocco). The conglomerate is also a part owner (20 per cent) with General Electric of NBC Universal, which has interests in theme parks and film and television production and distribution. For a detailed account see: www.vivendiuniversal.com.

BOX 3.1(B)   GENERAL ELECTRIC

Vivendi Universal's dominant partner in NBC Universal is General Electric (GE). The GE conglomerate comprises six divisions that have interests in commercial and consumer finance; healthcare; industrial and domestic appliances; as well as mass media production and distribution. It owns the film company Universal Pictures and a range of television news and entertainment channels such as Bravo, NBC News and Telemundo. The latter channel is aimed at the Hispanic community. NBC Universal's recent successes include the films *Brokeback Mountain* (2005) and *Nanny McPhee* (2005) as well as the US version of the hit BBC series *The Office*. For a detailed account, see www.ge.com.

--- Exercise 3.1 ---

The scale and scope of conglomerate activities

Do an Internet search on any of the following media giants in order to establish the range of companies that they own and control. Choose from Disney, General Electric, Bertelsmann, Sony,

(Continued)

Liberty and AT&T. Is your selected media conglomerate engaged exclusively in media activities or does it also have other economic interests? To what extent is it intertwined with other media conglomerates? Would you characterize it as being either horizontally or vertically integrated?

You should now read EXTRACTED READING 3.2, *Will the Internet set us free?* (McChesney, 1999) and consider the following issues:

1   Where the Internet is concerned, why is 'David' not really favoured over 'Goliath'?

2   Why is McChesney pessimistic about the possibility of creating an Internet-based public sphere?

Vertical and horizontal integration

Concentration is usually described as being either vertical or horizontal. (For a variation on these definitions see Doyle, 2002.) According to Croteau and Hoynes (2003: 40), 'vertical integration refers to the process by which one owner acquires all aspects of production and distribution of a single type of media product'. Horizontal integration, conversely, 'refers to the process by which one company buys different kinds of media, concentrating ownership across differing types of media rather than "up and down" through one industry'. Media conglomerates that engage in horizontal integration own and control a diverse range of media companies involved in the print, broadcast and ICT sectors, for example.

Vertically integrated media conglomerates usually own and control a number of companies, all of which are involved in various stages in the production and distribution of a specific kind of media product. Vertical integration or concentration occurs when, for example, a conglomerate owns and controls the companies that print, publish, distribute and sell a women's magazine. A vertically integrated conglomerate in the field of television involved in making a drama serial might, in turn, own and control the production company, the television station and the cable network that broadcasts the programme in question.

A growing number of media conglomerates are horizontal in structure. Global media conglomerates such as Bertelsmann, Vivendi Universal or Time Warner own and control a wide variety of media companies in the 'old' and 'new' media sectors. Their horizontal character may extend to owning companies that produce and sell merchandise associated with their media products.

There are clear strategic reasons why media (and other) firms engage in both horizontal and vertical integration. Doyle notes that horizontal expansion allows for greater economies of scale. In the case of a conglomerate involved in the television sector, for example, its ability to produce, sell or distribute a television programme in more than one territory means that once production costs have been met, in the United States, for example, they increase the likelihood of generating even greater profits in other territories.

Furthermore, Doyle writes that:

> Vertically integrated media firms may have activities that span the creation of media output (which brings ownership of copyright) through to distribution or retail of that output in various guises. Vertical expansion generally results in reduced transaction costs for the enlarged firm. Another benefit, which may be of great significance for media players, is that vertical integration gives firms some control over their operating environment and it can help them to avoid losing market access in important 'upstream' or 'downstream' phases. (2002: 4)

The term 'synergy' has become the watchword of media conglomerates and a core part of their strategy in maintaining a position of power or dominance. Turow (1992: 683) defines synergy as: 'the co-ordination of parts of a company so that the whole actually turns out to be worth more than the sum of its parts acting alone, without helping one another'. In the face of increasing audience and media fragmentation, conglomerates have used synergies in their endless search for profits.

The rationale for such an approach is quite clear. Turow (1992: 688) remarks that from the perspective of those who own and control media conglomerates, 'Power would accrue to those who could use them synergistically to play out materials across a gamut of holdings for the most value possible'. Playing as they do on a global stage, media conglomerates try to maximize profits on the cultural products that they produce. The latest Hollywood movie, for example, produced by one of the studios owned and controlled by one of the global players, will maximize profits through the film itself and its subsequent release on DVD and video. In many instances the studios that make the film also own the distribution companies and cinemas where the movies are shown. This form of vertical integration gives the larger media organizations considerable leverage. Their considerable power is manifest in their ability to keep smaller players out of the mainstream (and more profitable) market. Their influence goes further, however. There may be a wide range of promotional 'tie-ins' at the local McDonald's. 'Happy Meals' will come with a cheaply produced toy associated with the film. Toy shops will sell toys produced in a Third World country made under licence from the media conglomerate. More profits may be generated in the form of merchandising such as hats, t-shirts, folders, pencil cases and posters, for example. There may be further promotion across the range of media owned by the conglomerate in question. The blurring of the distinction between the ownership and control of the culture industries and other

MEDIA OWNERSHIP

types of economic production raises a number of important issues. Do the ownership and control of the media by conglomerates have a direct bearing on media content? How objective can a news organization be in reporting on the armaments industry if its parent company has a vested interest in the latter? Have concentration and conglomeration created new kinds of constraints for media professionals?

BOX 3.2(A)   THE BREAK-UP OF VIACOM

As Boxes 3.2(b) and (c) demonstrate, multimedia conglomerates are subject to a significant amount of ongoing change. While many conglomerates are focused on synergistic development and ownership concentration, the Viacom group (which came about as a merger of CBS and Viacom in 1999) disaggregated into two separate, publicly traded companies in 2006. In a somewhat confusing move, Viacom would now trade as CBS Corporation (a name previously used in CBS's long history as a media company) and the remaining companies would trade under the name Viacom. The 'new' Viacom concentrates on cable and digital media in addition to the production and distribution of filmed entertainment and music publishing. The CBS Corporation is more focused on older forms of media such as TV, radio, book publishing and outdoor advertising and continues to make use of the Viacom name in its outdoor advertising business in Europe. The break-up of the 'old' Viacom was seen by many analysts as an attempt to improve the overall trading value of the conglomerates on the US stock exchange.

BOX 3.2(B)   VIACOM INC.'S KEY BRANDS

Cable and digital platforms

BET	Neopets
CMT: Country Music Television	Nick at Nite
Comedy Central	Nickelodeon
game trailers.com	Noggin
Ifilm	Spike TV
Logo	The N
MTV2	TV Land
MTV Digital Networks Suite	VH1
MTV: Music Television	
MTV Networks International	
MTV Networks Online	
MTVU	

Filmed entertainment production & distribution

Dreamworks SKG
Paramount Home Entertainment
Paramount Pictures

Music publishing

Famous Music

Source: Viacom Inc.'s corporate website. See www.viacom.com

BOX 3.2(C)   CBS CORPORATION'S KEY BRANDS

Television (stations, networks, production and distribution)

CBS Television Network
CBS Television Stations (39 in total)
UPN

CBS Paramount television:

- CBS Paramount Domestic Television
- CBS Paramount International Television
- CBS Paramount Worldwide Distribution

Showtime (Television Networks)
King World (Syndication)

CSTV Networks:

- CSTV-College Sports TV
- cstv.com
- CSTV All Access

Digital platforms

CBS Digital:
- cbs.com
- upn.com

(Continued)

- cbsnews.com
- cbssportsline.com

Publishing

Simon & Schuster Media:

- Simon & Schuster Adult Publishing
- Simon & Schuster Audio
- Simon & Schuster Children's Publishing
- Simon & Schuster Online

Theme parks

Paramount Parks own 5 theme parks and they operate a further 3.

Outdoor advertising

- CBS Outdoor (North America)
- Viacom Outdoor International (Europe)
- Magic (China) (70 per cent)

Radio

CBS Radio runs 179 radio stations as well as holding the franchise for 29 American Football teams. The company also provides news and other talk-based programming (such as weather and sports coverage) to over 1,500 radio stations in the US.

CBS consumer products

Various. Licenses a wide range of products such as DVDs, clothing and games that tie in with syndicated programming such as *Star Trek* and *Survivor*.

CRITICAL QUESTION 3.3

A standard criticism levelled at media conglomerates is that they engage in cross-promotion of their various media products. What are the implications for media professionals and for audiences of this practice?

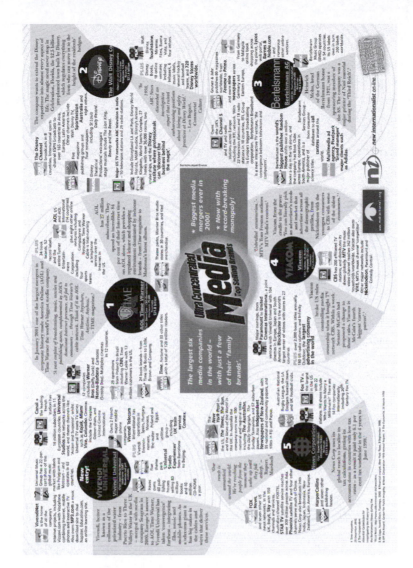

Plate 3.1 Ultra Concentrated Media. Reproduced by kind permission, New Internationalist Publications, Mediachannel.org & Granville Williams © 2001.

BOX 3.3   SYNERGIES AND CONGLOMERATION: A MEDIA INDUSTRY PERSPECTIVE

'A media company that intended to compete successfully in this environment would have to be big enough to be heard and big enough to hold consumer attention It

(Continued)

99

would have to propose products and synergies that only a large, versatile organization could offer. It'd have to be able to move its products through the emerging global marketplace and amortize its costs over as many distribution networks as possible. Advertisers would be demanding more speed, responsiveness, flexibility and teamwork. Time Inc. was big and strong and successful, but not big enough or strong enough for the challenges we saw on the fast approaching horizon. Long-term, we saw the world accommodating perhaps a half-dozen global media companies. And we intended to be one of them. Bigness for bigness's sake didn't interest us very much. We certainly didn't want to be caught up in an old Gulf & Western or ITT type of diversified conglomerate where the core business can get lost along the way. What we wanted was solid vertical integration so we could offer synergies that would bring together magazines, publishing ventures, studios, cable channels and other activities into a coherent operation. We wanted to be able to offer more than the Murdochs and Maxwells of the world.'

Source: D. Elliman, Jr, executive at Time Magazines, speaking on Time Inc.'s decision to merge with Warner Communications, quoted in Turow, 1992: 688–9.

You should now read EXTRACTED READING 3.3, *Mapping Internet Inequalities* (Patelis, 2000) and consider the following issues:

1 Having considered Patelis's findings, do you think that we all share equally in the global village?

2 What determines access to the Internet?

The political economy perspective

Political economy theory has been to the fore in attempting to understand and critique the implications of media concentration and conglomeration. There are a variety of strands of political economy theory, which have been influenced by both Marxism and critical theory (see, for example, McChesney, 1999; Bagdikian, 2004). The political economy perspective is concerned with investigating how the capitalist class promote and ensure their dominant or hegemonic position. It is first and foremost a theory about unequal power relations (see, for example, Mosco, 1996). In its more recent formulation it has been preoccupied with explaining the media's central role in the rise of global capitalism and the consequences of concentration and conglomeration for the public sphere.

In terms of its application in a media setting, McQuail provides us with a useful definition of political economy theory:

> [It is] a socially critical approach that focuses primarily on the relation between the economic structure and dynamics of media industries and the ideological content of media. It directs research attention to the empirical analysis of the structure of ownership and control of media and to the way media market forces operate. From this point of view, the media institution has to be considered as part of the economic system, with close links to the political system. The predominant character of what the media produce can largely be accounted for by the exchange value of different kinds of content, under conditions of pressure to expand markets and by the underlying economic interests of owners and decision makers (Garnham, 1979). These interests relate to the need for profit from media operations and to the relative profitability of other branches of commerce as a result of monopolistic tendencies and processes of vertical and horizontal integration (such as into or from oil, paper, telecommunications, leisure, tourism and property. (2000: 82)

McQuail summarizes the implications of changes in the ownership structures of the media industries from a political economy perspective as being a:

> reduction in independent media sources, concentration on the largest markets, avoidance of risks, and reduced investment in less profitable media tasks (such as investigative reporting and documentary film-making). We also find neglect of smaller and poorer sections of the potential audience and often a politically unbalanced range of news media. (2000: 82)

Concentration and conglomeration, according to this perspective, have serious implications for media content (especially factual genres such as news, current affairs and documentaries) and media audiences. Audiences are constructed primarily as consumers rather than as citizens who have a right to be informed. Concentration and conglomeration also have implications for media workers. Casualization of media work has increased and the greater economies of scale demanded by the media oligopolies have also resulted in job losses.

BOX 3.4   WHO OWNS WHAT?

Media ownership patterns are intricate and subject to regular change. *The Columbia Journalism Review* maintains a regularly updated website on media ownership patterns. This invaluable resource is available at www.cjr.org/owners/.

Further guidance on investigating media ownership patterns may be obtained in Deacon et al. (1999). In a subsection of their chapter entitled 'Dealing with documentation' (pp. 34–8) the authors outline how you might map the complex web of ownership and control of the media industries. The website thenation.com also carries interesting up-to-date research on this theme. See, for example, Mark Crispin Miller's article 'What's wrong with this picture?' (2002) and Maurice Hinchey's article 'More media owners' (2006). Other useful websites which keep track of media ownership patterns include mediachannel.org and freepress.net.

The political economy perspective holds that if we wish to understand media content, and especially its ideological character, then we must begin by examining the ownership and control of the media industries. We need to examine both the ownership structure of the media industries and their relationship to other political and economic elite groups in society. If cultural production is driven predominantly by the relentless search for profit and is increasingly undertaken by media organizations that have a wide range of economic interests, then the political economy perspective would lead us to conclude that one of the first casualties tends to be media content that directly challenges the prevailing capitalist interests.

'Follow the money . . .'

In a world where an increasing amount of media activity (production, distribution and access) is being privatized, the political economy perspective is of critical importance. In attempting to understand the relationship between media ownership and media content, the political economy perspective demands that we critically examine the profit-driven motives of media organizations that commodify both cultural production and audiences (McQuail, 2000). Media products, be they cartoons, DVDs or computer software, are primarily commodities produced to generate maximum profit. McQuail (2000: 82) notes that one strand of political economy theory holds that in age of media globalization, it is audiences that are being commodified. We can see evidence of this, for example, in the radio industry, where some media conglomerates speak of 'delivering key demographic groups' to advertisers and sponsors. Further evidence may be found in the practice of cross-promotion (of other media products, goods and services) between the various media companies owned and controlled by media oligopolies.

The political economy perspective illuminates our understanding of the media both historically and contemporaneously. Changes within the media industry would seem to add further weight to the political economy thesis. McQuail (2000) cites the work of Golding and Murdock (1996), who argue for the continued relevance of this theoretical perspective. They hold that the political economy perspective has two key tasks, namely the examination of cultural production and cultural consumption.

First, it must examine the relationship between structures of ownership (both private and public) and cultural production. As we will see in the next part of this chapter, political economists (and others) argue that the rise of the media oligopolies has resulted in a significant change in media content and a consequent contraction in the media's public sphere role. This perspective helps us to understand why there is now a greater concentration on entertainment and infotainment within media content. Entertainment sells. In the USA, for example, changes in the ownership structure of local television stations resulting in the creation of 'duopolies' – whereby a media conglomerate such as GE owns more than one television station – has been shown to have had a negative impact in terms of the overall level of educationally based programming aimed at younger viewers. The Children Now organization found that in Los Angeles there was a significant reduction in the amount and diversity of children's programming between 1998 and 2003 – a fact explained by the shrinkage in ownership terms of the local television networks (Children Now, 2003).

Second, access to the growing number of cultural products in daily life is being increasingly privatized. Access to the array of cultural products and media technologies now available is not equal, thus creating media haves and have-nots. Media conglomerates define their (potential) audiences primarily as consumers. Accessing much of the media is predicated upon one's ability to pay. Media conglomerates have managed to privatize a wide range of media activities by charging, for example, for cable television, selling pay-per-view movies, and accessing the Internet.

BOX 3.5(A)   TWO MEDIA MOGULS AT A GLANCE . . .

Silvio Berlusconi

- Born in Italy in 1936.
- Estimated to be worth US$13 billion.
- A highly controversial politician, he served as Italian Prime Minister in 1994 (for nine months) and from 2001–2006.
- Owner of the Italian Fininvest media empire – which controls in excess of 50 companies.

(Continued)

- Media interests include commercial television (Canale 5, Italy 1, Rete 4 which claim a combined 45 per cent share of the Italian television audience), advertising sales, publishing (Mondadori) and the print media (the daily newspaper *Il Giornale* and the current affairs magazine *Panorama*). Berlusconi's television stations attract over 45 per cent of the Italian viewing public.
- Has other financial interests in the insurance and banking sectors as well as construction, food production and a department store – Standa.
- Founder of the political party Forza Italia (Go Italy).
- Also owns the Italian soccer club AC Milan.
- Has been criticized by many because of his direct and indirect control of the Italian mass media – a factor which his critics say has helped his rise to political power.

For further details see: 'Silvio Berlusconi' by G. Murdock at www.museum.tv

Rupert Murdoch

- Born in Australia in 1931 (has held US citizenship since 1985).
- Estimated to be worth US$5.3 billion.
- Owner of 40 per cent of global media giant News Corporation.
- Has referred to his media empire as 'freedom's greatest messenger'.
- Media interests lie in film, television, broadcasting delivery systems (cable, digital and satellite), print media (newspapers and magazines in the US, Australasia and the UK), book publishing and Internet-based services. Buying sports teams as well as controlling the broadcasting rights to key sporting events has been a key part of his overall strategy in the USA, Australasia, the UK and India for example.
- Key media brands include Fox News, Twentieth Television, Sky television, Star television (China), myspace.com, HarperCollins, a range of tabloid and broadsheet newspapers including *The News of The World*, *The Sun*, and *The Times* (UK); *The Daily Telegraph* (Australia) and *The New York Post* (USA). News Corporation print in excess of 40 million newspapers each week.
- Like Berlusconi, Murdoch has been controversial in political terms. Avowedly anti-trades union, his newspapers have openly supported political parties in favour of deregulation and liberalization. In the UK, for example, he has openly supported both the Conservatives and (New) Labour. Despite his own ideological commitment to free market capitalism, he has managed to hammer out an arrangement with state communist China in order to facilitate the spread of his Star TV network. He removed the BBC World Service TV from that network when Chinese authorities expressed alarm at the critical tone of the public service broadcaster's coverage of world (and Chinese) affairs. (See Wheen, 2004: 231–3; and Pilger, 1999.)

For further details see: 'Rupert Murdoch' by D. Gunzerath at www.museum.tv

BOX 3.5(B)   NEWS CORPORATION

Print Newspapers	Television and filmed entertainment	Other

Print Newspapers

UK
News International
News of the World
The Sun
The Sunday Times
The Times
Times Literary Supplement

USA
New York Post

Australasia
Daily Telegraph
Fiji Times
Gold Coast Bulletin
Herald Sun
Newsphotos
Newspix
Newstext
NT News
Post-Courier
Sunday Herald
Sun
Sunday Mail
Sunday Tasmanian
Sunday Territorian
Sunday Times
The Advertiser
The Australian
The Courier-Mail
The Mercury
The Sunday Mail
The Sunday Telegraph
Weekly Times

Magazines
Big League
Inside Out
donna hay
Alpha
News America
Marketing
Gemstar TV Guide

Book Publishing
HarperCollins Publishers
(HC) Australia
(HC) Canada
(HC) Children's Books
(HC) United States
(HC) United Kingdom
Regan Books
Zondervan

Television and filmed entertainment

Filmed entertainment
20th Century Fox
20th Century Fox Español
20th Century Fox Home Entertainment
20th Century Fox International
20th Century Fox Television
Blue Sky Studios
Fox Searchlight Pictures
Fox Studios Australia
Fox Studios Baja
Fox Studios LA
Fox Television Studios

Television
Fox Broadcasting Company
Fox Sports Australia
Fox Television Studios
Foxtel
Star

Cable
Fox Movie Channel
Fox News Channel
Fox College Sports
Fox Sports Enterprises
Fox Sports En Español
Fox Sports Net
Fox Soccer Channel
Fox Reality
Fuel TV
FX
National Geographic USA
National Geographic Worldwide
Speed
STATS, Inc.

Other

Other
Broadsystem
Classic FM
ign.com
Intermix
myspace.com
National Rugby League
NDS
News Interactive
News Optimus
News Outdoor
Radio Veronica
Scout.com

Jürgen Habermas and the public sphere

The concept of the public sphere as developed by the German sociologist Jürgen Habermas (1962) has been the subject of much debate and criticism (see, for example, Benhabib, 1992). Although not without its conceptual difficulties, it continues to inform thinking on how media organizations should operate. In his original study *Strukturwandel der Öffentlichkeit* (translated as *The Structural Transformation of the Public Sphere*), Habermas (1962) distinguishes between three types of sphere in society. These are the private sphere (consisting of family and economy), the sphere of public authority (consisting of state and judiciary) and the bourgeois public sphere.

For Habermas the coffee houses and salons of Enlightenment Europe represent the beginnings of a bourgeois public sphere. Within this sphere (bourgeois) citizens could debate matters of political importance. The development of the print media (newspapers, books, journals and pamphlets, etc.) allowed further growth in the public sphere. In Habermas's account the decline of the public sphere begins in the late nineteenth and early twentieth centuries once the print media become commercialized mass media. There is less room for the mass media to operate as a public sphere facilitating political discourse. In a critical essay, Verstraeten (1996: 348) identifies three key dimensions to Habermas's conceptualization of the public sphere:

1 The public sphere requires a 'forum' that is accessible to as many people as possible and where a large variety of social experiences can be expressed and exchanged.
2 In the public sphere, the various arguments and views are confronted through rational discussion. This implies that 'rational' political choice is possible only if the public sphere first offers a clear insight into the alternatives from which one can choose. At the same time, the media should offer the widest possible range of interpretation frames so that the citizen is also aware of what he did not choose (Murdock, 1992: 17–41).
3 Systematically and critically checking on government policies is the primary task of this public sphere.

While recognizing the continuing importance of the concept, Verstraeten (1996) argues against the interpretation (held by Habermas and many others) that the public sphere has undergone a rise and subsequent fall. He suggests that, in practice, the public sphere has yet to be achieved. Furthermore, in examining the contemporary mass media, a focus on political economy remains necessary. As Verstraeten states:

When studying the public sphere, especially as it is more and more mediatized, one should always bear in mind the following question: whose public sphere are we talking about and whose political or socio-economic interest is it? For it would be extremely naïve to assume that in our conflict-laden and dual society, an ideal-typical neutral public sphere, belonging as it were to everyone, would emerge. It is therefore necessary always to examine and re-examine critically whose public sphere we are dealing with. (1996: 357–8)

While they recognize its limitations, the Goldsmiths Media Group are also supportive of the retention of Habermas's idea of the public sphere. Stressing its ethical significance, they argue that: 'It provides an indispensable perspective on the operations of media organisations, since it insists that we continually evaluate the media for what they contribute to our lives as citizens, as active participants in the public sphere' (2000: 43).

In summary, then, Habermas's notion of the public sphere stresses the importance of political discourse among citizens. Ideally, a public sphere has a crucial role to play in ensuring the continuation of a civic and democratic society. It allows rational discussion, debate and the exchange of information. Its key function is to facilitate debate and argument about the behaviour and performance of the powerful in society.

The proposition that the contemporary mass media operate as a public sphere is difficult to sustain. It is problematic because of increased ownership concentration and conglomeration. A major constraint on the mass media realizing their public sphere role arises from the fact that a growing amount of cultural production is in the hands of powerful media organizations whose sole *raison d'être* is profit. While certain kinds of media genres may have a public sphere dimension (talk radio, letters to the editor or Internet bulletin boards, for example) there is now, arguably, less scope for a broadly based public sphere to be realized. In the context of greater media complexity, it may be more appropriate to think in terms of a range of public spheres that appeal to different kinds of audience members rather than a single public sphere. Such public spheres may operate within and without the dominant discourse. From a neo-Marxist position, one could argue that the public sphere is a new opiate for the people, allowing them the illusion of democracy in a capitalist-controlled society.

BOX 3.6   KEY THINKER: JÜRGEN HABERMAS (1929–)

Born in Düsseldorf in 1929, Jürgen Habermas has contributed hugely to how we understand modernity, democracy, power relationships and the role of the mass media in particular. A major figure within Critical Theory, Habermas is best described as eclectic in terms of the range of disciplinary influences he has drawn upon in his many writings. He mixes ideas and concepts from philosophy, political science and sociology in order to understand and explain modern civil society. As noted in this chapter, his most important (and most contentious) contribution rests in the ideas he has developed around the concept of the *public sphere*.

As a major intellectual figure he has been embroiled in many controversies. As a graduate student, Habermas's supervisors (Horkheimer and Adorno of the Frankfurt

(Continued)

School,) vehemently disagreed over the direction his PhD research was taking. Later in his career Habermas himself was to have a very public row with the French theorist Derrida. As a public intellectual he has argued against attempts by some revisionist historians to lessen the significance of the Nazi regime in Germany. His concept of the public sphere has as many detractors as it has supporters, yet it remains an important lens through which we can evaluate whether or not the mass media contributes to the further development of civil society.

See Chapter 6 for more on the Frankfurt School.

The Internet as public sphere

The Internet has been heralded by many as having major potential as a media-based public sphere. One can search for information or engage in on-line discussions about a seemingly endless list of topics, many of which are critical of the status quo. On-line discussion forums and blogs are examples of where democratic dialogue and debate can take place. On the face of it, the Internet seems to offer almost utopian possibilities. However, if we examine the workings of the Internet more closely, we can find significant differences between its promise and its reality. Users of the Internet are more likely to be searching for pornography than for matters of public concern.

The Internet is now dominated by mass-media conglomerates or oligopolies. As we have already noted in Chapter 2, access to this potential public sphere is not equal. The persistence of the global North–South information divide is in clear evidence in the data compiled by Campbell and Breen (2001) and Campbell (2003) listed in Table 3.1.

Powerful commercial interests have colonized the Internet. The colonization and commercialization of Internet space are evident every time you log on to the Internet via one of the major Internet Service Providers (ISPs). The multimedia conglomerates or oligopolies own and control the most widely used ISPs. In examining the flow of Internet traffic in March 1999 and 2003, Campbell and Breen (2001) and Campbell (2003) forcefully illustrate the hegemony of the 'top ten' ISPs (see Table 3.2). ISPs operate as portals in terms of access to the World Wide Web. Campbell and Breen argue that:

The issue of portals has become important because whichever company gains dominance will have a huge 'captive' audience for on-screen advertising and various forms of direct and indirect marketing. The portals also make sure that when their users look for particular services (e.g. on-line bookstores), they are first directed to those companies who have paid the portals' owners to promote them. (2001: 230)

TABLE 3.1 Million Internet users by continent, 1996, 1997, 1999, 2002 and 2007

	1996	1997	1999 March	2002 September	2007 January
Africa	–	1.0	1.14	6.31	33
Asia	6	14.0	26.55	187.24	389
Europe	9	20.0	36.11	190.91	313
Middle East	–	0.5	0.78	5.12	19
US/Canada	30	64.0	94.2	182.67	232
South America	–	1.3	4.5	33.35	89

Sources: Campbell and Breen (2001: 223) and Campbell (2003: 46) based on data generated by NUA. Reproduced courtesy of the authors and the Institute of Public Administration, Dublin and the Columba Press, Dublin. The 2007 data was generated by www.worldinternetstats.com © Minitell.

TABLE 3.2 The top ten Internet Service Providers, 1999 and 2003

Rank	1999	2003
1	Yahoo	Yahoo
2	AOL	Google
3	Microsoft	MSN
4	Netscape	AOL
5	Geocities	AskJeeves
6	Excite	Overture
7	Lycos	Infospace
8	MSN.com	Netscape
9	Infoseek	Altavista
10	Altavista	Lycos

Sources: Campbell and Breen (2001: 223) and Campbell (2003: 50) based on data generated by NUA. Reproduced courtesy of the authors and the Institute of Public Administration, Dublin and the Columba Press, Dublin.

The Internet retains the potential to operate as a public sphere. It has not, as of yet, realized that role. It cannot realistically be seen as a democratic space because access to the Internet is not equal. Extracted readings 3.2–3 by McChesney (1999) and Patelis (2000) confirm that we must be very cautious in engaging with those who uncritically celebrate the Internet as public sphere.

CRITICAL QUESTION 3.4

Why do some commentators argue that the public sphere has not yet been realized?

CASE STUDY

It's all in the game: monopoly, football and satellite television

Williams (1994) gives a critical analysis of the role of sport, and of soccer in particular, in the spread of satellite television in the United Kingdom. As part of a larger
examination of citizenship and the commercialization of sport, Williams explains
how Rupert Murdoch's BSkyB achieved a position of dominance through brokering
an exclusive deal with the Football Association's Premier League. His study raises several important questions about access to sporting events in a media setting.

The merging of British Satellite Broadcasting (BSB) with Murdoch's Sky television
in 1990 to form BSkyB initially resulted in major losses for the global conglomerate
News Corporation. This was to be short-lived, however. Williams (1994) argues that
international sport played a highly significant role in changing the fortunes of BSkyB.
He says: 'The major reason for this apparent upturn in the fortunes of BSkyB is clear.
BSkyB has emphasized coverage of international sport. More especially, exclusive
'live' coverage of Premier League soccer from England has been the key cultural
product in establishing BSkyB as a major European-wide pay-to-view satellite channel' (1994: 383). This emphasis on sport replaced an earlier combined emphasis on
movies and sport as a key reason for audiences to subscribe to BSkyB.

In a deal hammered out in 1992 between BSkyB and the recently formed Football
Association Premier League, Murdoch's organization bought the sole rights to broadcast
live English football on a pay-to-view basis. Williams (1994) estimates that the deal cost
BSkyB £304 million. While this represents a significant (and risky) investment for BSkyB,
there is ample evidence to suggest that the strategy has worked well in the battle for ratings and subscriptions in the United Kingdom and elsewhere. Williams notes, for example, that in the mid-1990s, Murdoch's Fox TV bought the exclusive rights to NFL football
in the United States. The strategic role of soccer in the game plans of global and other
media organizations is stressed by Williams. While he concedes that variations exist in
other European countries where soccer is a popular sport, he notes that:

> France now seems most like the English case these days. Canal Plus, a subscription
> only commercial channel, has monopolized live coverage of soccer since 1984,
> showing twenty-two matches a season costing an estimated £20 million per year.
> In Germany, the private SAT 1 cable channel agreed to a new five-year deal in
> 1992/93 costing DM 700 million (about £245 million); 75 per cent of German
> households expect soon to be cabled. In Spain, a joint deal worth about £300 mil-
> lion between local region channels and Canal Plus produces two live matches a
> week for eight years (from 1989), while in Italy, the state-funded RAI and Silvio
> Berlusconi's Fininvest network shared extensive highlights-only coverage of Serie A

soccer matches up until 1993/4, when weekly coverage of one live match was introduced. (1994: 387)

Williams underlines the emergence of a two-tier system within the world of soccer and among audience members who would wish to view Premier League matches. The formation of the Premier League divided English soccer in two, with the wealthier clubs benefiting from the BSkyB deal. Access to the live Premier League matches is now restricted to those who can afford the pay-to-view or subscription channels on Sky Sports.

The commodification of sport (and of soccer, rugby, cricket and boxing in particular) has been a key part of the market domination strategies engaged in by media conglomerates such as BSkyB. In their attempts at market domination, the possibility of viewing the main sporting events live is heavily emphasized. There is evidence to suggest, however, that some audience members (and sports fans in particular) are critical of this strategy. Audience viewing patterns may also be changing as a direct result of pay-per-view. Soccer, in particular, is watched in bars or public houses rather than in a domestic setting.

Conclusion

This chapter has stressed the importance of understanding the changing patterns of media ownership. It has examined the main trends involved in concentration and conglomeration now evident within the globalized media industries. As an antidote to the emphasis placed by the cultural studies approach on both media texts and media reception, researchers interested in the economics of the media industry argue that we must begin our analysis with a thorough appreciation of the ownership structures within which cultural production initially takes place.

Perhaps the most critical change within the structure of media ownership patterns, identified in this chapter, is the growing overlap, in ownership terms, of companies involved in cultural as well as other forms of production such as car manufacturing, nuclear power, or the armaments industry, for example. We can speculate as to the implications for media content that might arise from such cross-ownership. A majority of media organs in the nineteenth century were allied with the interests of the capitalist class. In the twenty-first century a growing number of media organizations are part of more general media conglomerates that have a wide range of media and other economic interests. A number of questions you should consider:

- What are the overall implications for media content?
- How real is the pressure on media professionals to cross-promote products, goods or services owned and controlled by the larger conglomerate to which their media organization belongs?
- Does it mean that there is now a greater likelihood of interference in the daily work of media professionals?
- What sorts of tensions emerge between those who have allocative control and those who exercise managerial control in a media setting?

That the orientation of mainstream media content is changing as a result of greater concentration and conglomeration cannot be disputed. There is clear evidence that media genres of a more critical orientation (such as news, current affairs or documentary programmes) are coming under increasing pressure in the battle for resources and audiences. The shift towards 'reality' television and infotainment generally has to be understood in terms of the decisions taken by media companies to maximize audiences (and profits). In many respects this chapter has painted a bleak scenario – especially in its discussion of the political economy perspective and the likelihood (or not) of a public sphere emerging in the current context of largely privatized media ownership.

Within public discourse there is a tendency to personalize the complex state of affairs regarding contemporary media ownership in terms of the activities of individual media moguls. While these well-known individuals have significant amounts of economic and political clout, the reality is that the key players in terms of the restructuring of media ownership are large-scale transnational conglomerates. Their dominant position has clear implications for stand-alone media organizations, for the practice of journalism and even for individual nation states. The increased concentration and conglomeration evident within the media industries are of major ideological significance. This restructuring has a direct bearing on the macro changes evident in both media content and in terms of how unequal relationships of power are portrayed – themes that we will discuss further in Chapters 5 and 6. The increase in conglomeration means that media space is being further colonized by commercial interests. We can see this within everyday media content where in addition to advertising, sponsorship, product placement and cross-promotion are becoming even more significant features.

Extracted readings

3.1　'The Big Five'

Ben H. Bagdikian, in *The New Media Monopoly*, 7th edn. Boston, MA: Beacon Press, 2004, pp. 3–6

Five global-dimension firms, operating with many of the characteristics of a cartel, own most of the newspapers, magazines, book publishers, motion picture studios, and radio and television stations in the United States. Each medium they own, whether magazines or broadcast stations, covers the entire country, and owners prefer stories and programs that can be used everywhere and anywhere. Their media products reflect this. The programs broadcast in the six empty stations in Minot, N. Dak., were simultaneously being broadcast in New York City.

These five conglomerates are Time Warner, by 2003 the largest media firm in the world; The Walt Disney Company; Murdoch's News Corporation, based in Australia; Viacom; and Bertelsmann, based in Germany. Today, none of the dominant media companies bother with dominance merely in a single medium. Their strategy has been to have major holdings in all the media, from newspapers to movie studios. This gives each of the five corporations and their leaders more communications power than was exercised by any despot or dictatorship in history. . . .

No imperial ruler in past history had multiple media channels that included television and satellite channels that can permeate entire societies with controlled sights and sounds. The leaders of the Big Five are not Hitlers and Stalins. They are American and foreign entrepreneurs whose corporate empires control every means by which the population learns of its society. And like any close-knit hierarchy, they find ways to cooperate so that all five can work together, to expand their power, a power that has become a major force in shaping contemporary American life. . . .

The Big Five 'competitors' engage in numerous such cartel-like relations. News Corporation, for example, has a joint venture with the European operations of Paramount Pictures, which belongs to Viacom, another of its 'competitors' in the Big Five. According to American securities agencies, Vivendi, the disintegrating French media conglomerate, had agreed to place $25 million worth of advertising in AOL media in return for AOL giving the French firm a share of one of its operations in France. Some competition is never totally absent among the Big Five media conglomerates. The desire to be the first among many is as true for linked corporations as it is for politicians and nations. It was true two decades ago when most big media companies aspired to command market control in only one medium, for example, Gannett in newspapers; Time Incorporated in magazines; Simon & Schuster in books; the three TV networks in radio; CBS in television; Paramount in motion pictures. But the completion of that process fed an appetite for expansion toward a new and more powerful goal, a small group of interlocked corporations that now have effective control over all the media on which the American public says it depends.

3.2   Will the Internet set us free?

Robert W. McChesney, *Rich Media, Poor Democracy*. Champaign, IL: University of Illinois Press, 1999, pp. 182–3

By 1999 notions of the Internet providing a new golden age of competitive capitalism were quickly fading from view in the business press. *The New York* Times argued that the lesson of the Internet was 'The big get bigger and the small fade away.' Indeed, as the newspaper noted, the Internet, rather than having a competitive bias, may in fact stimulate monopoly and oligopoly:

> At first glance, the Internet seems to favor David over Goliath, as any upstart can open an on-line store or an electronic publication. But it appears that the first capable pipsqueak to shoot a slingshot in any given area may grow to a giant size so quickly tha[t] any new challengers have been kept at bay.

The prospect for new giants emerging was even more remote in the area of 'content.' Despite its much ballyhooed 'openness', to the extent that it becomes a visible mass medium, it will likely be dominated by the usual corporate suspects. Certainly a few new commercial content players will emerge, but the evidence suggests that the content of the digital communication world will appear quite similar to the content of the pre-digital commercial media world. In some ways the Web has even extended commercial synergies and the role of advertising and selling writ large to new dimensions. This does not mean that the Internet will not be a major part in reconfiguring the way we lead our lives; it almost certainly will. Some aspects of these changes will probably be beneficial whereas others may be detrimental. Nor does this mean that there will not be a vibrant, exciting and important noncommercial citizen sector in cyberspace open to all who veer off the beaten path. For activists of all political stripes, the Web increasingly plays a central role in organizing and educational activities. But from its once lofty perch, this nonprofit and civic sector has been relegated to the distant margins of cyberspace; it is nowhere near the heart of the operating logic of the dominant commercial sector. In a less dubious political environment, the Internet could be put to far greater democratic use than it is or likely will be in the foreseeable future. But the key point is simply that those who think the technology can produce a viable democratic public sphere by itself where policy has failed to do so are deluding themselves.

3.3   Mapping Internet inequalities

Korinna Patelis, 'Political economy of the Internet', in James Curran (ed.) *Media Organisations in Society*. London: Arnold, 2000, pp. 92–3

In 1997 Network Wizards figures showed only fifteen countries in the world with more than 100,000 hosts registered under their own domain name. . . . All of those are in the West, which leaves 128 countries with fewer than 100 computers connected. Similarly the OECD *Communication Outlook* places 92 per cent of all Internet hosts in the OECD area. From Network Wizard statistics one can deduce that at least 60 per cent of these hosts are in the US. . . . There were no host computers in the Honduras in 1995 and merely 400 in 1997. Today there are 45,000 users in Jamaica. . . . There are 500 hosts in Morocco, none in some central African countries. Basic indicators also show that Europe is far behind in cyberspace. There were a total of 4.38 million hosts in the EU at the end of 1997, an increase of 140 per cent from the previous years, but still very low if one considers the total estimated number of hosts worldwide.

Discrepancies between EU countries are dramatic. There were 2.7 hosts per 1000 habitants in Greece and only 0.2 domain names; 17.0 per 1000 in the UK – both countries being far from Finland's 95 per 1000. . . . Such discrepancies show the exact opposite of what Internetphilac claims: the geo-economic periphery is not centred in the virtual world.

Profiles of the average user reconfirm these inequalities. CommerceNet Nielsen found that Internet access in the US and Canada was up by 50 per cent, from 23 million users in August–September 1996 to 34 million by April 1997. A Find/SVP and Jupiter Communication survey found that 14.7 million households were on-line (a figure that had doubled from previous years), while International Data Corp. estimated that 20 per cent of American households in the US were on-line. . . . Jupiter estimates that 3.7 million households are on the Net in Europe and 3.4 in the Asia Pacific Rim... The Internet is like a tree out of whose trunk branches keep growing all the time. The way this tree grows is not accidental; it is dictated by international economico-political structures. . . . There is a main Internet backbone, a central intercontinental network to which smaller networks are connected. The US is at the centre of the majority of these connections.

Exercise 3.2

Who owns your favourite television programme?

Record an episode of any one of your favourite television series broadcast on a privately owned station. From the rolling credits at the end of the programme, try to establish which company owns and controls the production and distribution of your selected programme. Use the Internet to establish who owns and controls the company in question and to identify whether there are linkages between it and other media and non-media organizations. Compare your findings with those of your fellow students. What overall patterns emerge?

Exercise 3.3

Media ownership and control

In the light of what you have read in this chapter about changing styles of media ownership, map out who owns the key media organizations in your country then answer the following questions:

1   What sorts of media organizations predominate?
2   Would you describe the ownership patterns as being mainly public, private or a mixture of both?
3   To what extent are individual media organizations engaged in horizontal or vertical integration?
4   Does the predominance of either media conglomerates or state-controlled media organizations have implications in terms of the contents of media coverage and for news coverage in particular?

Media moguls

Selecting any one of the better-known media moguls, try to establish the range and extent of their media ownership and control around the globe. In terms of either the print or the broadcast media organizations owned or controlled by your selected mogul, do these media organizations, in your opinion, share a common ideological view of the world?

Questions for consideration and discussion

1 Profits, not content, matter most to media conglomerates.
2 Is the Internet a public sphere?
3 In an age of concentration and conglomeration, critical and pioneering journalism is increasingly difficult to sustain.

References

Bagdikian, B.H. (2004) *The New Media Monopoly*, 7th edn. Boston, MA: Beacon Press.

Benhabib, S. (1992) 'Models of public space: Hannah Arendt, the liberal tradition and Jürgen Habermas' in C. Calhoun (ed.) *Habermas and the Public Sphere*. Cambridge, MA: MIT Press.

Bettig, R.V. (1997) 'The enclosure of cyberspace', *Critical Studies in Mass Communication* 14: 138–57.

Campbell, P.B. (2003) 'Mind the gap' in M. Breen, E. Conway and B. McMillan (eds) *Technology and Transcendence*. Dublin: The Columba Press.

Campbell, P.B. and M.J. Breen (2001) 'The Net, its gatekeeper, their bait and its victims: ethical issues relating to the Internet' in E. Cassidy and A.G. McGrady (eds) *Media and the Marketplace: Ethical Perspectives*. Dublin: Institute of Public Administration.

Children Now (2003) *Big Media, Little Kids: Media Consolidation and Children's Television Programming*. www.childrennow.org/publications.

Croteau, D. and W. Hoynes (2003) *Media Society: Industries, Images and Audiences*, 3rd edn. Thousand Oaks, CA: Pine Forge Press.

Deacon, D., M. Pickering, P. Golding and G. Murdock (1999) 'Dealing with documentation' in D. Deacon et al. *Researching Communications*. London: Arnold.

Van Dijk, J.A.G.M (2005) *The Deepening Divide: Inequality in the Information Society*. London: Sage.

Doyle, G. (2002) *Media Ownership*. London: Sage.

Garnham, N. (1979) 'Contribution to a political economy of mass communication', *Media, Culture and Society* 1 (2): 123–46.

Golding, P. and G. Murdock (1996) 'Culture, communications and political economy' in J. Curran and M. Gurevitch (eds) *Mass Media and Society*. London: Arnold.

Goldsmiths Media Group (2000) 'Media organisations in society: central issues' in James Curran (ed.) *Media Organisations in Society*. London: Arnold.

Habermas, J. (1962) *Strukturwandel der Öffentlichkeit*. Frankfurt: Luchterhand Verlag.

Habermas, J. (1992) 'Further reflections on the public sphere' in C. Calhoun (ed.) *Habermas and the Public Sphere*. Cambridge, MA: MIT Press.

McChesney, R.W. (1999) *Rich Media, Poor Democracy: Communication Politics in Dubious Times*. Champaign, IL: University of Illinois Press.

McQuail, D. (2000) *McQuail's Mass Communication Theory*. London: Sage.

Miller, M. (2002) 'What's wrong with this picture?' www.thenation.com

Mosco, V. (1996) *The Political Economy of Communication*. London: Sage.

Murdock, G. (1982) 'Large corporations and the control of the communications industries' in M. Gurevitch, T. Bennett, J. Curran and J. Woollacott (eds) *Culture, Society and the Media*. London and New York: Methuen.

Murdock, G. (1992) 'Citizens, consumers and public culture' in M. Skovmand and K.C. Schroder (eds) *Media Cultures: Reappraising Transnational Media*. London and New York: Routledge.

O'Sullivan, T., B. Dutton and P. Rayner (1994) *Studying the Media: An Introduction*. London: Arnold.

Patelis, K. (2000) 'The political economy of the Internet' in James Curran (ed.) *Media Organisations in Society*. London: Arnold.

Pilger, J. (1999) *Hidden Agendas*. London: Verso.

Postman, N. (1986) *Amusing Ourselves to Death*. London: Viking Penguin.

Tunstall, J. and M. Palmer (1991) *Media Moguls*. London: Routledge.

Turow, J. (1992) 'The organizational underpinnings of contemporary media conglomerates', *Communication Research* 19(6): 682–704.

Verstraeten, H. (1996) 'The media and the transformation of the public sphere: a contribution for a critical political economy of the public sphere', *European Journal of Communication* 11 (3): 347–70.

Wheen, F. (2004) *How Mumbo-Jumbo Conquered the World*. London: Harper-Perennial.

Williams, J. (1994) 'The local and the global in English soccer and the rise of satellite television', *Sociology of Sport Journal* 11: 376–97.

Going further

Bagdikian, B.H. (2004) *The New Media Monopoly*, 7th edn. Boston, MA: Beacon Press. This classic text has been radically revised and updated. It is a 'must' for all students who wish to understand the implications of the recent consolidation of media ownership.

Croteau, D. and W. Hoynes (2006) *The Business of Media: Corporate Media and the Public Interest*, 2nd edn. Thousand Oaks, CA: Pine Forge Press. An accessible text that demystifies the complexities of media ownership with reference to public sphere and market models of the media industry. See chapter 5 'How business strategy shapes media content' and chapter 7 'Choosing the future: citizens, policy and the public interest' in particular.

Hartgittai, E. (2004) 'Internet access and use in context', *New Media and Society*, 6 (1): 137–43. This is a succinct review essay on the question of media 'haves' and 'have-nots.'

Thomas, P.N. and Z. Nain (2004) (eds) *Who Owns the Media? Global Trends and Local Resistance*. London: Zed Books. Fifteen essays on the political economy of contemporary mass media ownership in a wide range of settings including Africa, Asia, Latin America and China.

4

MEDIA PRODUCTION AND MEDIA PROFESSIONALS

Summary

This chapter introduces you to the following:

- The production research approach.
- The rationale for and research methodologies employed in doing research on media production and media professionals.
- The significance of understanding the contexts in which media professionals operate and in which media texts are initially created.
- The concepts of structure and agency in understanding media professionals and media production.
- The emergence of new forms of independent media production where alternative or counter-hegemonic voices may be heard.

Key concepts

- Production research
- Media professionals
- Encoding and decoding
- Qualitative media analysis
- Structure and agency

- Ethnography
- Participant observation
- Media professionals and constructing audiences
- Indymedia

Media globalization and the restructuring of media ownership have, as we have already seen in Chapters 2 and 3, very real implications for media audiences, media content, media organizations and the day-to-day working lives of media professionals. In this chapter we turn our attention towards understanding the media at a micro level by examining the organizational or institutional contexts in which media professionals operate in the initial 'making' of media texts.

Research on media professionals has been traditionally orientated towards understanding news journalism (see Ekstrom, 2002; Esser, 1998) and most recently the spotlight has been thrown upon the many challenges (and opportunities) that technological changes and convergence present (see Dupagne and Garrison, 2006; Huang et al., 2006; Deuze, 2004). While genuine concerns have been raised about the contraction of the mainstream media's public sphere role, as we will see in this chapter, technological developments have resulted in the emergence of hopeful signs in the shape of alternative media such as Indymedia, Freespeech and SourceCode. As a counterbalance to the kinds of changes already discussed in Chapters 2 and 3 (such as homogenization and the decline of critical journalism), media production engaged in by activists of all kinds represents a critically important development (see Box 4.5).

Production research

Consider for a moment any mainstream media text that you may have encountered in the last few days. The text, in all likelihood, has come about as a result of the interaction of a large number of media professionals working within a specific organizational context. The front page of this morning's newspaper will, in all likelihood, have involved the interaction of the editor, journalists, sub-editors, advertising copywriters, photographers and printers, to name but a few. Media professionals such as those involved in bringing you the main stories on last night's main news bulletin will have engaged in a certain amount of agency or creativity in attempting to tell audience members a particular story about the world. The media texts that they created will have been based upon agreed and invariably unspoken notions of 'newsworthiness' and audience interest.

Their activities, however, are also shaped and constrained by a large range of forces both within and without their individual media organization. They are in direct competition with other media organizations for the eyes and ears of audience members and may be dependent on other media organizations such as one of the international news agencies like Reuters, the Press Association or Agence France-Presse in order to bring the news story to your television screen. Depending upon particular circumstances, media professionals may or may not reproduce dominant ideological discourses within their media texts. The interplay between the agency or creativity of media professionals and the structures or constraints under which they operate lies at the heart of what production research is all about (see Box 4.1). These tensions, however, are not confined to those working in the media industry but are also evident in other forms of media production produced by members of the alternative or counter-hegemonic media.

As you will discover in this chapter, in spite of the recent dominance within media studies of textual and reception analysis, there is in fact a long-standing research tradition of investigating the culture of media organizations and the activities, experiences and ideologies of media professionals. Researchers have examined news media organizations with a view to understanding more about the workings of agenda setting, the use of particular sources in writing news stories, and the increasing importance of other media professionals such as PR experts who attempt to generate a 'Spin' on specific stories (see, for example, Davis, 2000; Iyengar and Kinder, 1987). Interest in the cultural industries is once again attracting the attention of media scholars. This is both timely and necessary given the radical changes that are occurring within the media industries. (See, for example, Hesmondhalgh (2006, 2007), who successfully combines a political economy and cultural studies approach in his attempt to understand the cultural industries.) Bourdieu's (1996) writings on journalism, in which he applies the concept of 'field' in order to understand more about the world of the journalist has resulted in a further revival of research interest in the media professional (see, for example, ITO, 2006).

Production research has the potential to reveal much about the experiences of media professionals, the constraints within which they operate, and the intended meanings that they encode into media texts. A legitimate stand-alone research strategy in its own right, production research may be used on its own, or as a constituent part of a wider approach that seeks to understand media production, content, reception and effects in one or other combination (see, for example, Deacon et al., 1999).

BOX 4.1   CREATIVITY AND CONSTRAINT: EXPLAINING STRUCTURE AND AGENCY

Our behaviour as human beings takes place in a social context. All of us are influenced by the dynamic generated between what sociologists term structure and agency. As members of society, our viewpoints, attitudes, opinions and ultimately our behaviour are shaped by both structure and agency. The tension between both is at the core of what sociology is all about and is of vital importance in terms of understanding the workings of the mass media. Bilton et al. define structures as 'constructed frameworks and patterns of organization which in some way, constrain or

(Continued)

121

direct human behaviour' (1997: 8) and agency on the other hand 'implies that actors have the freedom to create, change and influence events' (1997: 13).

We are constrained by the social context in which we find ourselves but we are also capable of independent action as a result of reflection and growing self-awareness. Family, schooling and the mass media have undoubtedly shaped your understanding of gender roles, for example. You are not, however, a prisoner to the kinds of roles laid out for you in the social context in which you find yourself. You can exercise agency when you resist or reject the 'script' as laid out in the patriarchal view of the social world. Our task is to recognize the duality of both structure and agency in human behaviour. While we are constrained by social structures, we are also clearly capable of transcending these constraints through independent agency or action.

Within mass media analysis the relationship between structure and agency is especially important when we come to examine media professionals and media audiences. Media professionals such as print or broadcast journalists work in specific organizational contexts, each of which has its own constraints in terms of shaping media work. Audiences in turn may be influenced by media content but are well capable of exercising considerable agency in their interpretation of media texts.

In this chapter we begin by tracing the theoretical and methodological roots of production research. We outline the main methodological choices facing researchers interested in understanding more about media professionals and media production. Hall's (1974) seminal Encoding/Decoding model is described. Its significance lies in the fact that it stresses the need to understand the media message or text in terms of both production and reception. We discuss how this model has been applied towards understanding media coverage of false-memory syndrome and cloning. Two case studies from Irish and North American television are then used as illustrations of how the production research model has been utilized to learn more about the media.

The production research approach underlines for you once again the significance of understanding context as much as text in undertaking even rudimentary media analysis.

By examining the production context of media texts, their contents and how audiences subsequently read media texts, we have the potential to understand more fully the dynamics involved both in media production as a result of the activities of media professionals and in the production of meaning through audience interpretation. An appreciation of the production research approach will also be of significance when we come to examine the media and the reproduction of dominant and other ideologies in Chapter 5. The approach suggests that we place our investigative gaze on the kinds of discourses employed by media professionals in their efforts to communicate with audiences in an increasingly diverse range of regional and cultural settings.

CRITICAL QUESTION 4.1   HOW DO MEDIA PROFESSIONALS 'KNOW' THEIR AUDIENCES?

The era of media globalization poses new questions about the relationship(s) between media professionals and media audiences. Other than ratings or sales figures, or perhaps audience response through email or interactive satellite television, how do media professionals who produce globally distributed media texts gauge audience interest and response to their texts?

Two traditions

We can identify two main and often overlapping strands of production research. The first concentrates on the media professional in terms of constraints, professional ideologies and work practices. The second is of a more textual orientation in that it attempts to combine an understanding of the former concerns with an in-depth analysis of a specific media text or texts. Thus, in many instances, researchers have 'worked backwards' from the 'finished media product' or text to investigate the internal and external forces on the media professional that may have shaped its content (see, for example, Devereux, 1998; Elliot, 1979; Shoemaker and Reese, 1996).

The production research approach is primarily concerned with understanding more about how the creativity or agency of the media professional is constrained by both organizational and external factors. The organizational factors might be, for example, the specific routines of production, ownership structure, editorial line, culture or ethos of a particular media organization. External factors might be, for example, the economic power of advertisers or sponsors, the laws and regulations imposed by the nation state concerning libel or defamation, the willingness (or not) of the politically or economically powerful to co-operate in the production of certain kinds of media texts such as news reports, investigative documentaries or current affairs programmes. Negative audience response might also be considered to be a possible constraint. In the production research tradition that is more textual in orientation, there are strong echoes of the 'author–text' tradition in literary criticism and the attempts within media studies to understand the relationship between the media professional and his or her text.

Theoretical underpinnings of production research

Production research aims to understand more about media production and media professionals. Four main theoretical perspectives have predominated in the field, namely political economy, critical theory/neo-Marxism, feminism and liberal pluralism. All four inform our understanding of media production in different but complementary ways.

The *political economy approach* emphasizes the extent to which media production and media professionals are constrained by powerful political and economic forces. As you saw in Chapters 2 and 3, an increasing amount of media production is now undertaken in media organizations that are owned and controlled by global media conglomerates. While the globalization of media production may have a direct impact on the autonomy of individual media professionals, the qualitative shift evident in much media content and its commercialization has created new kinds of pressures and constraints. In the context of increased competition for audiences in the television sector, for example, one concrete example might be the pressure on media professionals to 'dumb down' the content of (or indeed replace altogether with lighter entertainment-focused programming) programme areas that might traditionally have been more critical or investigative in orientation. The practice of doing the 'And finally . . .' story at the end of news bulletins means that even news bulletins on more 'serious' networks have embraced news values that emphasize the importance of celebrity, at the expense presumably of harder news.

Increased competition and the need to deliver larger audiences in order to satisfy commercial interests are among the key underlying reasons for the increased amount of 'infotainment' and 'newzak' evident on mainstream television (see Franklin, 1997). Those within the political economy camp have also raised concerns about the restructuring of media production in terms of the day-to-day working conditions of media professionals. Changes in the way in which media organizations are owned and controlled, and an increase in the casualization of media work, have created a less stable environment for media workers. Technological changes and convergences have also radically altered the way in which day-to-day media work is undertaken.

The *critical theory* or neo-Marxist approach to production research has a related set of concerns. The emphasis here is on the extent to which media professionals knowingly (or otherwise) engage in the production of dominant ideology in support of the ruling class or other dominant social groups. As you will see in Chapter 5, while there has been some degree of slippage in the traditional critical theory perspective – conceding that both media professionals and audiences can exercise some amount of agency in the production and reception of media texts – there remains a strong sense that, while alternative ideologies are evident within some media texts, the mainstream mass

See Chapter 5 for more on the critical theory perspective.

Plate 4.1   The production research approach invites us to go behind the scenes in order to understand more fully the tension between 'structure' and 'agency' evident in the creation of media texts such as news programming. Photograph reproduced by kind permission of Sky News (London) 2006 ©.

media tend to reproduce ideologies that are favourable to the politically and economically powerful in society. One way in which media professionals might do this is by giving certain ideological positions privileged space within specific media texts, thus according them greater legitimacy. While audiences and media professionals are clearly capable of agency, the question of how and why dominant ideologies and discourses such as patriarchy, racism or homophobia continue to surface in many media texts – and the role of media professionals in sustaining or challenging these ideologies – remains a central issue worthy of further study and debate.

The last quarter of the twentieth century witnessed a growing amount of production research written from a *feminist* perspective. In a large range of geographical territories, feminist media researchers have examined the experiences of female journalists working in the print and broadcast news media (van Zoonen, 1998; Chambers et al., 2004). A starting point for this research has been how female journalists cope with working in what has traditionally been a male-dominated environment. Although an increasing number of women are working in the print and broadcast news media, for example, there remains anxiety about the extent to which news values are still driven by what are perceived to be male concerns. Drawing upon the Dutch experience, van Zoonen (1998) notes that more women are ending up in news journalism because the genre itself is changing in orientation, having a stronger 'human interest' focus. Feminist research has restated the importance of examining the socialization of media professionals, their work practices and ideological positions.

The *liberal pluralist* perspective, in contrast to both political economy and critical/Marxist approaches, argues that media professionals are evidently not slaves to the demands of the ruling class or other dominant social groups. What we see in media content is a vast array of media messages some of which are supportive of the status quo while others question it directly. The liberal pluralist point of view recognizes the complexity of media organizations and the agency or creativity of the media professionals who work in such organizations.

You should now read EXTRACTED READING 4.1, *Alienation and Exclusion Mechanisms in Production* (Kim, 2006) and answer the following questions:

1 According to Kim (2006), what sorts of factors work to exclude women working in the field of journalism?

2 Kim's (2006) work is focused on Korea. To what extent would her arguments apply to female journalists working in your home country?

BOX 4.2   MAIN METHODOLOGIES EMPLOYED IN PRODUCTION RESEARCH

When researchers engage in production research they usually make use of a number of qualitative research methodologies. It is fair to describe the production research model as being a hybrid. The terms 'participant observation' and 'ethnography' are the ones most likely to be used in reference to this kind of research strategy (see Deacon et al., 1999). In reality, production research typically involves the use of a wide range of research methodologies such as observation, participant observation, interviews, case studies, archival research and detailed analyses of public and private documents. This research model is reliant upon achieving access to and co-operation from media professionals and media organizations. Depending on the research question, media professionals and media organizations can sometimes be reticent in allowing themselves to be observed or questioned by academic or student researchers. So in line with other kinds of ethnographic research, once access is achieved, the building of trust between the researcher and those researched is crucial.

The greatest strengths of production research are its flexibility and the potential it holds for shedding light on an otherwise hidden world. Production research may be demanding in terms of the amount of time spent doing fieldwork, but it can be one of the most rewarding kinds of mass media research. Those following this research path have, for example, observed television and news reporters in their everyday work situations; they have undertaken participant observation through working as junior reporters themselves; they have used formal, informal and retrospective interviewing techniques in order to see the world from the point of view of the media professional and especially as a means of gaining further insights into the content of 'finished' media products. Production research can be illuminating in that it can reveal much about the day-to-day realities of media production. Because it situates the media professional in an organizational context, it can shed light on the internal and external pressures and constraints that prevail upon media production. It can be useful in explaining why certain decisions were made and why certain production values pertain.

Methodological basis

In terms of its methodological basis, the production research approach is predominantly qualitative, and as Box 4.2 indicates, it has borrowed much from social anthropology, the sociology of organizations, the sociology of occupations and the sociology of art in seeking to understand more about the realities of media production. To date, researchers have largely concentrated upon the experiences of media professionals in the shape of journalists and reporters engaged in the making of news for the broadcast and print media. A smaller body of work – but by no means of any less significance – has examined the making of other types of television programmes such as drama and documentary series (see, for example, Newcomb, 1991).

CRITICAL QUESTION 4.2   NEWS JOURNALISTS AND 'OBJECTIVITY'

News journalists often describe their professional activities as being 'objective' and 'neutral' in terms of how they report on events in the world. In your own experience of print and broadcast news journalism, are these realistic assessments?

MEDIA PRODUCTION AND PROFESSIONALS

> You should now read EXTRACTED READING 4.2, *From Buerk to Band Aid* (Philo, 1993) and consider the following issues:
>
> 1   Is inter and intra-media competitiveness the key to understanding whether a story may be considered newsworthy or not?
>
> 2   In your opinion is the Third World less newsworthy?

BOX 4.3   KEY THINKER: STUART HALL (1932–)

Stuart Hall was born in Kingston, Jamaica in 1932 and emigrated to Britain in 1951. He has made a major contribution to intellectual and public life in Britain and beyond. Hall served as Director of the now defunct Centre for Contemporary Cultural Studies at the University of Birmingham and as Professor of Sociology at the Open University. More recently, Hall has been involved with the Runnymede Trust which is concerned with examining the shape of a multi-ethnic Britain. His professional life has been characterized by serious engagement with questions surrounding unequal power relationships in terms of class, ethnicity/race and gender. Renowned as the person who coined the phrase 'Thatcherism', as a neo-Marxist Hall has been equally critical of the British Conservative Party and Blair's 'New' Labour project.

Hall's scholarly output has been voluminous. His writings on media and ideology, ethnicity, race and racism, multiculturalism as well as the concept of 'moral panic' have been highly influential. His most cited work within media and cultural studies is his famous essay 'Encoding and decoding in the media discourse' (1973). As we note in this chapter, Hall's work reminds us that the mass media do not simply *reflect* 'reality', they are actively involved in *constructing* it. Such construction is never neutral, reflecting as it does the ideas of the dominant social class or group. Foremost in Hall's work is the contention that ideological struggle is real and in evidence within media discourse. Hall's key publications include *The Hard Road to Renewal* (1988) and *Resistance through Rituals* (with T. Jefferson) (1976). See also Proctor (2004), Davis (2004) and McRobbie (2005).

Hall's encoding/decoding model

Stuart Hall's (1974) celebrated and highly influential essay 'The television discourse: encoding and decoding' suggests that we examine both the production and the reception of media messages. The encoding/decoding model as described by Hall argues that in the communicative exchange we need to pay attention to the production of media message(s) by media professionals and examine the subsequent readings that audiences place upon such messages. For as Hall says: 'the symbolic form of the message has a privileged position in the communicative exchange: and that the moments of "encoding" and "decoding", though "relatively autonomous" in relation to the communicative process as a whole, are determinate moments' (1974: 8).

Hall's model runs counter to both effects and content analysis models of media research and instead situates the communicative exchange in a broader set of cultural, economic, historical, ideological, organizational, political and social contexts. If we wish to understand, for example, how a media message works or doesn't work at an ideological or at a discursive level, we have to explore the codes and conventions employed by media professionals in the initial making of the media message and its subsequent decoding by audience members.

Hall's model allows for a certain amount of 'openness' in the media message. However, the reading or decoding of the message takes place in a social context where individual audience members occupy unequal positions of power and have the capacity to accept, adapt or reject media messages.

The encoding/decoding model outlines four main codes that are utilized in the production of meaning by media professionals and media audiences. These are the *dominant/ hegemonic* code, the *professional* code, the *negotiated* code and the *oppositional* code.

Media professionals encode a preferred or intended meaning into a media message such as a television news report or current affairs programme. If audience members interpret or decode the message in accordance with the intended or preferred meaning, they are said in Hall's terms to be 'operating inside the dominant code' (1974: 10). The professional code refers to the conventions that media professionals use in order to encode meaning within the media message. Hall is referring here to the production techniques that are employed to tell a story in a particular way whilst remaining within the confines of the dominant code. Typically, audience members use a negotiated code when making sense of media messages. According to Hall:

> Decoding within the negotiated version contains a mixture of adaptive and oppositional elements: it acknowledges the legitimacy of the hegemonic definitions to make grand significations, while, at a more restricted level, it makes its own ground-rules, it operates with 'exceptions' to the rule. It accords the privileged position to the dominant definition of events, whilst reserving the right to make a more negotiated application to 'local conditions', to its own more corporate situation. (1974: 14)

An audience member operating within the negotiated code might accept the broad thrust of a specific media message and yet either adapt or reject elements of the overall message because it does not fit with their own immediate experience of the world. Finally, the oppositional code refers to the capacity of audience members to reject outright the preferred or intended meaning of a media message. Audience members

MEDIA PRODUCTION AND PROFESSIONALS

who engage in an oppositional decoding recognize but ultimately reject the preferred or intended meaning as signified through the use of the dominant or hegemonic code.

Exercise 4.1

Television texts and encoding

Choosing either a series of television adverts or a recent current affairs television documentary, see if you can identify Hall's (1974) dominant, professional, negotiated and oppositional codes within the text(s).

Research on media production and media professionals

Devils and Angels by Eoin Devereux

In *Devils and Angels*, Devereux (1998) examines how the Irish radio and television public service broadcasting organization Radio Telefís Éireann (RTÉ) portrays poverty on its two television networks. Drawing upon a neo-Marxist theoretical position, the study uses a combination of qualitative content analysis and an ethnography – undertaken over a period of two years – in investigating how RTÉ's news, current affairs, serialized drama and telethon programmes construct poverty stories. In addition to content analysis, the study makes extensive use of the views, opinions and perspectives of media professionals involved in the production of television texts about Irish poverty. Observation, participant observation and a variety of interviewing styles are used to gain insights into the thinking of media professionals and the constraints both within and without the media organization under which they operate. The study uses a range of explanations – biographical, economic, ideological, organizational and production value-oriented – in arguing that the television coverage in question reproduces a dominant ideological account of poverty.

BOX 4.4(A)   ENCODING AND DECODING
RESEARCH IN PRACTICE (1)

'From inception to reception: the natural history of a news item' by David Deacon, Natalie Fenton and Alan Bryman (1999a) is an important example of media research that seeks to combine the analysis of production and reception. Restating the significance of Hall's (1974) Encoding/Decoding model of media analysis, the

---

authors examine the 'natural history' of a British broadsheet newspaper article concerning the phenomenon of 'false memory' in cases of sexual and other forms of abuse (*Guardian*, 13 January 1995, 'Psychologists guarded on "false memory" of abuse'). This research project is a telling example 'of the benefits that can accrue from a research focus that isn't solely fixated with the distinctiveness of decoding and which retains the holism of the original encoding/decoding formulation' (Deacon et al., 1991a: 6). The case study examines the production, content and reception of the newspaper article. It begins by investigating the inception and production of the article, focusing on the interactions that took place between a range of individual and institutional sources with news professionals. The authors discuss the article's content as well as its decoding by a wide range of social groups. The author of the article in question was interviewed and audience reception was examined by means of holding fourteen focus group interviews. The audience groups discussed a wide range of news items as well as the specific article.

The authors argue that the 'preferred reading' of the text 'wasn't created by the journalist, but constituted by the source given most privileged access' (i.e. the British Psychological Society) (1999a: 25). Furthermore, they argue that their research:

> adds further support to those who argue that there are dangers in overstating the interpretative freedom of the audience from textual confines (see, for example, Murdock, 1989). The details reveal a marked consistency between intended meaning at the point of production and audience understanding and interpretation of the text. This is not to say that audience members passively deferred to the text – on the contrary, we found substantial evidence of independent thought and scepticism. However, the 'distinctiveness of decoding' in this instance occurred at the evaluative rather than interpretative level. Resistance to the message did not lead to a renegotiation of it. It was interrogated not expanded. (Deacon et al., 1999a: 26)

BOX 4.4(B)   ENCODING AND DECODING RESEARCH IN PRACTICE (2): 'DOLLY THE SHEEP' AND HUMAN CLONING

In February 1997 the print and broadcast media in Britain reported that the Scottish-based Roslin Institute had successfully cloned a Finn Dorset sheep from a somatic cell. Reputedly called after the country and western singer Dolly Parton, 'Dolly the Sheep' became the focus of intense news media coverage in which specific concerns were

(Continued)

raised about the implications this development might have for human cloning. The Dolly story was one of a number of instances of cloning which attracted media interest in the late 1990s and represents an important example of media coverage of scientific and ethical matters.

In an exemplary study, Holliman (2004) examines the production, content and reception of media coverage of cloning. His research is governed by three interrelated questions:

- How was cloning represented within media coverage?
- What sources were used?
- What memories and understandings do audience members have of the coverage?

Holliman's detailed study combines quantitative and qualitative content analysis of print and broadcast media; semi-structured interviews with media professionals and a representative of the Roslin Institute; as well as focus group interviews with audience members. His detailed content analysis is based upon a sample from television news and broadsheet, tabloid and 'mid-market' newspapers over a two-year period. The media professionals involved in covering the story were identified and interviewed. In addition to exploring how scientific issues were covered by individual media professionals, the interviews focused specifically on their use of sources. A representative from the Roslin Institute was also interviewed in order to understand more about the organization's own media strategy in attracting media interest in the issue of cloning.

The reception analysis was based upon six group interviews which were subdivided in terms of gender, geographical region and knowledge of science. The group interviews used a combination of research strategies in order to understand more about the participants and their memory of media coverage of cloning. The participants were asked to complete a short questionnaire and to write headlines in order to demonstrate how they thought the media represented cloning. They then took part in the News Game exercise in which they were asked to write a news bulletin. The focus groups concluded with a semi-structured discussion and a second questionnaire.

See Chapter 7 for more on the News Game exercise.

Holliman's (2004) findings show how cloning was represented by the media through the use of specific frames and templates. (See Chapter 6 for an elaboration on media framing and templates.) He notes that 'the coverage made regular use of science fiction references, associating Aldous Huxley's novel *Brave New World*, Mary Shelley's *Frankenstein* and the film *The Boys from Brazil* with cloning experiments. As previous researchers have sugested, . . . by drawing on these dystopian visions, these cultural references framed the coverage in a negative light' (2004: 118).

Holliman's reception analysis demonstrates a clear link between media coverage of cloning and audience understandings of the issues. Furthermore, he provides a convincing example of how analyses of production, content and reception can be usefully combined in order to reach a more thorough understanding of the mass media's role in the social construction of reality.

In Devereux's research, access to the media organization and to individual departments had to be negotiated and trust had to be established with those being studied. The researcher was given permission to observe all the weekly planning meetings in current affairs and the daily planning meetings in news as well as being allowed to actively participate in the television station's biannual fund-raising telethon programme. Semi-structured and informal interviews were undertaken with media professionals at all levels of the production process. Devereux recalls:

> In my observation and unstructured interviews I had discovered evidence of intraorganizational conflict over the content of particular poverty stories. The semistructured interviews were used to gain further information on these disputes and to compare the accounts of individual informants. These interviews helped in constructing a deeper understanding of the production processes which surrounded the making of poverty texts. They helped in validation and clarification of data gathered through both observation and participant observation. (1998: 153)

The participant observation dimension of the ethnography proved to be particularly fruitful. Covert participant observation was used in order to understand the background production processes of the *People in Need* telethon. The researcher worked as a volunteer (along with approximately 100 other volunteers) for the station's Variety Department, which was responsible for the programme's production. He adopted two potentially conflicting roles in undertaking participant observation. Devereux states that:

> From past knowledge of previous Telethons I correctly anticipated that there would be protests from an unemployment action group at the gates of RTÉ. During a two-hour break from my role as a runner on the Telethon programme, I managed to join the protestors to hear about their perspective on the event. As a protester, I witnessed how the police treated those on the picket line as well as gathering first hand information about their views. My main role however was that of runner for the event itself. This task involved the collection and delivery of faxes donating money to the programme's fund. It allowed me direct access to the broadcast and production studios. Even in the context of a busy fourteen-hour programme I found that this type of covert observation was useful in terms of furthering my understanding of the making of the Telethon programme. (1998: 154)

The close critical reading of specific media texts undertaken in the qualitative content analysis was strengthened further through regular contact with those who created the texts in the first place. The production research approach allowed the author to ask questions about the many constraints involved in covering what is potentially a controversial social and political issue. It provided insights into the use of particular kinds of production values and it shed light on how the media professionals in question viewed audience perceptions of poverty and other social problems. The study highlights the interplay between structure and agency in the creation of media texts from a variety of television genres. Ethnography of this kind allows the media professional to explain his or her intentions and may tell us much about how they perceive the media audience. One of the interviewees in the study who produced a contentious television documentary about Irish poverty argued that his documentary was: 'designed to do something dangerous . . . it was designed to make people uncomfortable' (1998: 58). In the producer's words: 'The intention was to fling it at the audience and say, "You, there! Are you sitting comfortably? And if so, should you be thinking about what is going on around you, and why are you sitting comfortably when others aren't?"' (1998: 58).

As an illustration of the production research approach, Devereux's (1998) study attempts to explain ideological content by reference to how media professionals structure meaning. The study is quite traditional in its orientation in that it does not consider how television audiences variously decode stories about poverty.

Inside Prime Time by Todd Gitlin

The controversial decision by the CBS television network to axe the critically acclaimed *Lou Grant* series in 1982 is the starting point for Gitlin's (1994) classic production research study *Inside Prime Time*. CBS's decision typified for Gitlin the interplay between power, politics and decision making within primetime network entertainment television. Gitlin tells us that he embarked upon this ambitious project with:

> a question – or rather a curiosity – about how much a show's commercial success depended on its 'fit' with social trends abroad in the land. I also started with the notion that what sometimes gives commercial television its weird vitality, perhaps even its profitability, is its ability to borrow, transform – and deform – the energy of social and psychological conflict. Sometimes network television seemed to succeed in packaging images that drew upon unresolved tensions in the society. Cramming these tensions into the domesticated frame of the sitcom and the action-adventure, television whether 'realist' or 'escapist' clearly bore some relation to the real world of popular desire and fear. (1994: 12)

Gitlin starts out with the intention of examining closely how American primetime network television fares in its treatment of social issues. Although some media analysts might question the wisdom of concentrating on popular television and its representation of social reality, Gitlin defends his decision by arguing that:

> Network television did seem to track some version of social reality. But whose? It began to dawn on me that I could not hope to understand why network television was what it was unless I understood who put the images on the small screen and for what reasons. (1994: 13)

What follows is a hugely detailed analysis of the ideological role of the television entertainment industry in capitalist society. The work has been hailed by many as one of the most comprehensive production research studies ever undertaken (Newcomb, 1991). Gitlin combines detailed textual analysis of primetime entertainment television with secondary data in the form of television ratings alongside extensive primary data drawn from hundreds of interviews with network executives, producers, writers, agents, actors and others.

Given his interest in the ideological aspects of popular media representations of social reality, Gitlin tells us that he 'wanted to see whether the industry "knew" what "it" was doing when it came up with these images' (1994: 13). How do media professionals and media organizations come to agree on what is an 'acceptable' representation of race, class or poverty issues, for example, in a television series like *Hill Street Blues*? What happens when there are disagreements? What sorts of commercial and other pressures are brought to bear on scriptwriters, producers and directors? Gitlin's decision to take a production research approach allows him the opportunity to attempt to answer these questions and at the very least it allows him to document the kinds of tensions involved in the making of primetime television.

Gitlin's fieldwork was based upon creating an opportunity sample among a wide range of media professionals. He was allowed to observe the production of specific series on the set and he witnessed at first hand how scripts changed and developed in response to industry and other pressures. Gitlin reports that those interviewed spoke freely to him and a majority of his interviewees spoke 'on the record'. It was his intention to give a detailed ethnography of the media industry 'as it is lived' by media professionals. At an early stage of his fieldwork he quickly realized that it was a mistake to compartmentalize how media professionals treat 'social issues', as their views on these questions are inseparable from how they see anything else.

At a methodological level the strength of this study is its sheer depth of analysis. By choosing the ethnographic path, Gitlin was able to check for consistencies and inconsistencies in his interview data. It allowed him to witness events as they happened on set and to have a fuller picture of the outcomes of specific controversies concerning programme content.

In three parts, *Inside Prime Time* begins by examining how the television industry attempts to control both the supply of and the demand for its products. Part one examines how networks try to achieve a maximum audience through an

MEDIA PRODUCTION AND PROFESSIONALS

investigation of programme testing, audience ratings, demographic and schedule calculations, and self-imitation. Part two examines how the networks depend on major suppliers and agents for products. Gitlin describes the activities of networks and producers in the creation of television 'docudrama' movies and he focuses specifically on how they deal with political controversy. Part three illustrates how network decision making about primetime television series is shaped by politics. Here, Gitlin considers 'national political trends (both badly and well understood), the crusade of the fundamentalist right, and the normal political weight of advertisers' (1994: 15).

In the light of these concerns, *Inside Prime Time* concludes with a thorough analysis of the hit television series *Hill Street Blues*. We get an extraordinarily detailed account of the creation of the series. Gitlin documents the tensions between those involved in the conception and actual making of the series with the NBC television network. As if to contradict the television industry's 'rational system of production' approach as described in the study's first section, *Hill Street Blues* bucked the usual trends in terms of primetime television programme structure. It had a larger number than usual of central characters and its script structure was atypical. Gitlin recalls the many pressures that were brought to bear on the programme's creators, such as the attempts to curtail the sex scenes between two of the principal characters (1994: 299). The internal constraints on the programme makers are amply demonstrated. Gitlin writes that:

Sometimes, for example, someone in NBC's Current Programming department might object to something in the rough cut, which is the first stage of the assembled film. The producers could finesse such objections by counting on the inefficiency of the organization. 'It's amazing how much they don't know about film,' said Michael Kozoll. 'You say to them, you know, "That's just the rough cut; it will be smoothed and fixed." By the time they see the [late-stage] answer print, they don't remember any more.' There were simply too many shows and not enough time to police them. The network's desire to control the show was defeated by organizational overload, by inefficiency, and also by ignorance. 'They didn't know what they wanted,' said a delighted and relieved Kozoll. 'You'd go to meetings and say, Yeah, yeah, yeah, and go off and do what you want. If you did everything they wanted you'd end up in Cedars of Sinai – do they have a psychiatric ward?' (1994: 304)

Gitlin's conclusions are quite bleak. At best, one witnesses the prevalence of a liberal rather than a critical ideological framework within the content of popular television entertainment series such as *Hill Street Blues*. Many of his informants believe that there are no easy solutions to social problems and this viewpoint is shown to be reproduced within media content. As Newcomb comments: 'For Gitlin, television entertainment is a debased form of expression growing from, and contributing to, a social and political world already debased by consumer capitalism. The result in the television industry is a non-critical, indeed celebratory acceptance of "recombinative" art suggesting "cultural exhaustion"' (1991: 97).

BOX 4.5   A DAY IN THE LIFE OF THE FT

07.00 – News editors and reporters begin assessing likely news stories and review the morning's newspapers.

07.30 – First news conference of the day. From this time onwards and throughout the day the FT's integrated writing teams file stories for FT.com.

10.30 – Main news conference – discussion of likely news stories for FT.com and the newspaper for tomorrow's editions.

11.30 – Leader conference – discussion of subjects for editorial comment.

13.00 – Shift of focus from FT.com stories to newspaper articles.

17.00 – Final news conference – front-page story lists and illustrations agreed for all editions. Night editors are briefed on possible late developments.

20.15 – Last pages for first edition sent to print sites in Asia and the United States.

20.35 – Last pages for first edition sent to print sites in Europe.

21.15 – Last pages for first UK edition sent to print sites. New York first edition updated to include US stock market close.

23.30 – Second UK edition sent to print sites.

00.00 – Asia-based correspondents begin their working day and file stories on early developments in markets for late editions.

00.50 – Second US edition sent to print sites.

01.30 – Final UK edition sent to print sites.

03.00 – Optional fourth UK edition, depending on news developments.

Source: © *The Financial Times* (2002), reproduced with permission.

You should now read **EXTRACTED READING 4.3**, *Media Organization Roles* (Shoemaker and Reese, 1996) and consider the following issues:

1   In your opinion how do ownership structures relate to media content?

2   What do Shoemaker and Reese understand by the relationship between organizational roles and views or perspectives?

CASE STUDY

Structure and agency in media production: Alan Parker's film *Angela's Ashes*

Alan Parker directed the film version of Frank McCourt's memoir *Angela's Ashes*. Released in 2000, the film had varied fortunes, attracting mixed critical reviews and

(Continued)

a limited amount of box-office success. Directed by Parker and released through the Hollywood-based Universal Paramount Studios, the film is a good example of the operation of structure and agency within mass media production.

We can see agency or creativity on a number of fronts. Parker himself exercises considerable agency in interpreting both McCourt's original work and the film script that had been developed previously by the Australian writer Laura Jones. He states:

> Scott Rudin and David Brown [the film's producers] developed the script with Laura Jones and she was able to take what was a very difficult and complex book and pare it down to the very bare minimum. I thought she'd probably been too strict with paring it down, and I tried to flesh it out. One of the things I did was to go back to the book because there's always so much more in the book than you could possibly put in a film. (Parker, 2000)

Parker's agency as a film director is also seen in the production values he chooses to use to retell McCourt's story. The most obvious example is Parker's metaphorical use of rain throughout the movie. The original text makes continual reference to 'the damp', and the dampness in Limerick is seen as being one of the main reasons why some of the McCourt children suffer from illnesses and die. In shooting the film, Parker replaces the dampness experienced by the memoir's main protagonist with rain, primarily because it is relatively easier to film. The rain is intended to act as a signifier of dampness for the audience. We can also identify a humorous encoding by the director. In many of his films, Parker himself appears in a minor role. In *Angela's Ashes* he plays the part of a doctor who breaks wind whilst attending to a young Frank McCourt. In a previous Parker film – *The Commitments* – we can see an encoding of an intertextual reference when a number of the films characters walk past a cardboard cut-out display in a record store advertising Parker's movie based on Pink Floyd's *The Wall*.

Audiences themselves, of course, have also got the capacity to engage in creativity or agency. The film version of *Angela's Ashes* is interesting in this regard in that audience agency in interpreting the film may have been based, for example, upon their own personal experiences of poverty, on their reading of the original text by McCourt, or on discussions they may have had with others prior to seeing the movie version.

On the constraint side of the equation, we can identify a number of important factors. The fact that the original text had been a commercial and critical success with audiences produced a constraint of its own for the film's director. Given that a significant number of the film's potential audience had read the memoir (either in English or in translation) prior to seeing the film version, it was realized that this created a certain difficulty around audience expectations. The fact that Universal Paramount studios funded the film created a further constraint in that the makers of the film were presumably expected to create a film that would be a commercial as well as a critical success. From a working-class British background, Alan Parker's previous film work demonstrates a firm commitment to documenting working-class lives in a gritty and realistic way. Parker's commitment to telling a story about poverty is, however, constrained by the demands of making a movie that would have a mass audience appeal.

Exercise 4.2

Warner Brothers, which is part of the Time Warner multimedia conglomerate, own the film rights to the Harry Potter series. Do a Wikipedia search on Harry Potter and apply the concepts of structure and agency to the film versions of J.K. Rowling's works:

1   What sorts of constraints do you think would shape the production of these films?
2   How might audience members (and the films' directors) exercise agency in their interpretation of J.K. Rowling's original work?

Power to the people? Citizens as producers: the case of Indymedia

Indymedia is the best-known recent example of citizen journalism. (For an elaboration of citizen journalism see Atton, 2002; Downing, 1988, 2001; Rodriguez, 2001.) It follows in the footsteps of a much longer tradition of counter-hegemonic or radical journalism (Atton, 2002) and is best understood in terms of the wider context of what Carroll and Hackett (2006) refer to as 'democratic media activism'.

Founded in Seattle in 1999, as a global network of independent media centres, Indymedia was comprised of 190 affiliated groups by 2006. Coyer describes Indymedia as a 'global online network' made up of 'local autonomous Indymedia organisations around the world offering "grassroots non-corporate coverage" of major protests and issues relevant to the anti-capitalist, peace and social justice movements' (2005: 34).

It is no accident that Indymedia is most prevalent in the USA, where many community-based activists have raised concerns about the ideological orientation of media content produced by the mainstream multimedia conglomerates. The core philosophy of Indymedia is one of participatory democracy, whereby activists and ordinary citizens can themselves become the producers of media content that is freely available. Constituent media organizations should ideally be democratic and non-hierarchical in structure (Platon and Deuze, 2003: 345).

The independent media centres that make up this global network are involved in the production of audio, video, print and web-based content (see www.indymedia.org). Independently produced content is disseminated via public access television and radio networks, through video, newsletters as well as the Internet. Indymedia use an open publishing system whereby activists and ordinary citizens can contribute and/or edit content. Blogs, email and discussion forums are also used to highlight particular events or issues.

Indymedia has been a phenomenal success with many elements of the mainstream media relying upon it for information during the various G8 summits held since its foundation in 1999. Indymedia has had a particular interest in monitoring the World Trade Organization as well as the (non) implementation of the Kyoto Protocol concerning emissions that are damaging to the environment. As an indication of its success, Platon and Deuze note that 'During the 1999 protests, the IMC site in Seattle had an average of two and a half million viewers every two hours. This high figure doubled during the protests in Genoa in 2002' (2003: 339).

Indymedia has understandably attracted an amount of attention from media scholars. Following in the path of previous researchers interested in media production, Coyer (2005) interviewed participants in a community-based media project. She also drew upon her own involvement with an Indymedia project. Eliasoph (1988) similarly engaged in participant observation in a US-based radio station that produced counter-hegemonic content, a research strategy replicated by Platon and Deuze (2003) who participated in the generation of web-based news content for an alternative news organization.

Two key issues come to mind when considering Indymedia. Given its commitment to open publishing, how is content controlled? What editorial guidelines are in place and how are these administered? What happens, for example, if racist, homophobic or sexist content is posted to the Indymedia open-source newswire site? Is Indymedia any different from the mainstream in terms of how content is controlled?

Platon and Deuze's (2003) ethnographic study of Indymedia suggests that clear tensions exist between the network's technical personnel and its editorial team. One of their informants stated:

in the beginning there was a kind of editorial group . . . . Although the word 'editorial' was kind of forbidden [laughs, coughs]. But it is simply an editorial team. Because the big shameful secret now about IMC is that the tech guys are running the show. And we have these editorial boards and these editorial practices and shit. And very few tech guys actually know what the editorial team has decided, and feels . . . feels like implementing it. (Cited in Platon and Deuze, 2003: 347)

Indymedia's editorial guidelines disallow any postings to its newswire that incite hatred or which are fascist, racist, sexist or homophobic in orientation. Platon and Deuze's (2003) account of Indymedia's editorial practices suggests that content propagating hate against specific individuals or groups is discussed by the editorial team and 'hidden'. Content is hidden by removing it from Indymedia's newswire service and placing it on another part of the Indymedia website with an editorial disclaimer.

Exercise 4.3

Log on to the Indymedia website (www.indymedia.org) and address the following issues:

1   Summarize what the main stories on its newswire are concerned with. How does Indymedia's coverage of global affairs differ to that of the mainstream media?
2   In your opinion what sorts of production values predominate in Indymedia's video-based reports? Are they dominated by first-person eyewitness accounts? To what extent are these reports 'balanced' in terms of the sources used and opinions expressed?

BOX 4.6   FREE SPEECH TV

Based in Boulder, Colorado, Free Speech TV is an interesting example of independent media production focused on the coverage of issues that are considered 'alternative' by the mainstream media. Founded in 1995, Free Speech TV broadcasts to a potential audience of 25 million homes. It is available on satellite (on the Dish Network) and via cable in a total of 34 states in the USA. Its programming content deals with a variety of issues concerning the war in Iraq, AIDS/HIV; the gay/lesbian/bisexual/transgendered community; immigrant workers' and women's rights etc. While production values can be variable, the channel's programming content serves as a powerful example of counter-hegemonic media activism. It is worth noting that the decision to allow community groups access to between 4 and 7 per cent of airtime on satellite channels was as a result of a ruling by the state body the Federal Communications Commission. See www.freespeech.org and www.SourceCode.org.

Conclusion

Although not as prominent in recent times as reception or content analyses of the mass media, production research remains a dynamic, exciting and essential area of

Plate 4.2 Free Speech TV: An Example of Alternative Media Production. Reproduced with kind permission, Free Speech TV © 2006.

mass media research. The emergence of new forms of media production whereby activists (and, theoretically, ordinary audience members) become media producers in their own right raises interesting questions for production research. What sorts of constraints operate within the alternative media movement? To what extent do independent producers have greater agency than their counterparts who typically work full-time in the media industry (see Platon and Deuze, 2003)? While it has been noted in this chapter that this research approach has focused heavily on journalists as a discrete category of media professionals – and by extension the research literature has been dominated by analyses of news production – the approach retains the potential to reveal a great deal about media professionals and media production in general. By adopting, as we do, an approach that examines the totality of the communicative exchange, we need to pay sufficient attention to the production context of media texts. The production research approach, with its emphasis on the tensions between the creativity of media professionals and the constraints under which they operate, is an important first step in this regard. Analyses of the content and reception of a wide range of media genres informed by a production research approach hold the potential for a more truly holistic and critical understanding of the media.

4.1 Alienation and exclusion mechanisms in production

Kyung-Hee Kim, 'Obstacles to the Success of Female Journalists in Korea', *Media, Culture and Society* (2006), 28 (1): 126–7, 130

The alienation of female journalists can be investigated either at the level of the news organization or at the personal level. First, when investigating it from the organizational level, the marginalization of female journalists is the best example to show how they are alienated in a patriarchal and capitalist society. This . . . defines the marginalization of females as the state in which they are put at the margin, far away from the power that decides on the strategic direction of an organization, while men are put at the centre of the organization. Generally, power is defined as an agent's potential influence over the attitudes and behavior of one or more designated target persons (Yukl, 1994). When considering the social meaning of the news, the most important power in the newsroom is the power to decide editorial direction, and to influence the course of editorial direction. . . .

At the personal level, the alienation of females appears as a form of dissatisfaction with their work, or a low level of the sense of belonging to their organization. The most fundamental reason for the alienated state of females is the capitalist patriarchal structure. That is, the capitalist patriarchies make the mechanisms of exclusion work, which cause the alienation of females in the news production process. . . .

The exclusion mechanisms within the news organization are those that alienate female journalists from the organization they belong to, that is, the mechanisms that derive from working in a male-centred system within the newsroom. The exclusion mechanisms in news gathering are external, and reject females in contexts outside the newsroom. Communication occurs through social networks and there is a tendency to ignore females in Korean society, so that some areas are not so easy for female journalists to report on as for male reporters. The exclusion mechanisms in the private area are those deriving from family issues which prevent females from living the life of a journalist. These exclusion mechanisms can function as the source of alienation of female journalists from the public area. . . .

Informal communication is defined as communication that takes place between journalists and sources in an informal setting. In Korea, much important information is shared in a bar or a public bath rather than in an office. Since most of the news sources are male, it is difficult for female journalists to participate in male public baths or late night meetings in bars in order to obtain information. Informal communication, therefore, plays a central role as a mechanism that excludes females from the news production process.

4.2 From Buerk to Band Aid

Greg Philo, 'From Buerk to Band Aid' in John Eldridge (ed.) *Getting the Message*, London: Routledge (1993), pp. 113–14

News organizations. A good reason for covering a story is that someone else might do it before you. There were strong suggestions in 1984 that such concerns had influenced the BBC's decision to go into Ethiopia. . . . Competition between channels can mean that they will all suddenly pursue a story if it is judged to be sufficiently important, or in different circumstances it can mean that some organizations will reject the story if they decide that it has already been covered by their competitors. Television is so competitive that even bulletins on the same channel compete with each other over the treatment of specific stories. Michael Buerk told us how this had affected the treatment of his second report from Ethiopia. The *Six O'Clock News* on the BBC had led with the story as a six-minute piece, giving it maximum impact. By contrast, the *Nine O'Clock News* had downgraded the story to fourth position and led with a story on the continuing British miners' strike, which was then in its seventh month. Buerk commented to us that:

> The *Nine O'Clock* News began on some minor accretion in the miners' strike of no consequence and [the Ethiopian report] was the fourth story on the *Nine O'Clock News*. The *Six O'Clock News* was intended to be a programme rather than simply a bulletin – so their instinct was that if they had a big story, to go to town on it. There are rivalries between the bulletins and possibly [the *Nine O'Clock News* editor] thought that he had better be different.

Even with the *Six O'Clock News*, the decision to use the Buerk/Amin piece first was not immediate. By chance, it was a slack news day, but even then there was a discussion about whether to use other possible lead stories. John Simpson of the BBC . . . commented that 'We could have led with any of a handful of fairly substantial stories . . . in the end it was decided to try an imaginative lead' . . . Mike Wooldridge's radio report fared worse. He had filed it while the team was still in Ethiopia. It was a strong report but was not even given peak time exposure as it did not receive the necessary support in London.

4.3   Media organization roles

Pamela J. Shoemaker and Stephen D. Reese, *Mediating the Message: Theories of Influences on Mass Media Content*, Boston, MA: Longman, 1996, pp. 151–3

Institutional position greatly determines the power vested in a role, although this power does not stem entirely from one's position in the organization chart. Lower ranking employees may have special expertise or other means to thwart directives from the top, often making negotiation and compromise necessary.

Media organization structure. Given this basic outline, there are any number of variations in the ways these roles can be combined and structured with organizations. The power associated with organization roles and the relationships between them vary both across and within media. Organization structure has a pervasive, if not readily identifiable, effect on media content.

In a typical newspaper organization a publisher runs the entire organization, which comprises the news, editorial, advertising, circulation and production departments. A glance at the masthead of most papers reveals their top management. At the *New York Times*, for example,

Publisher Arthur Ochs Sulzberger oversees the editor of the paper and the president, who in turn oversees the vice-presidents in charge of operations, production, advertising, finance/human resources, systems, and circulation. . . .

Regardless of the medium, the ultimate power lies in ownership. In most companies, stock ownership entitles one to vote for directors on the board that runs the company. Top management is either part of the board or accountable to it. That stock may be broadly owned or controlled by one family or a few large investors. The *New York Times* is a good example of how ownership can be structured to ensure the autonomy and control of a media organization. *The Times* is part of the *New York Times* Company, a $1.7 billion enterprise, which also owns other newspapers, magazines and broadcasting companies. The paper has remained in the hands of descendants of Adolph S. Ochs, who purchased the paper in 1891, earning for itself a strong reputation as an independent and leading voice among the news media. Recognizing the importance of ownership, Ochs distributed company stock such that voting rights and control remain within the family (the Sulzbergers), and thus management is not subject to pressures from outside stockholders and threat of corporate takeovers. Furthermore, a stockholders' agreement among the trustees prevents them from selling, merging or giving up control of the company.

--- **Exercise 4.3** ---

Researching media professionals and media production

In this chapter you have read about the world of the media professional. Drawing from what you have discovered about the production research approach, either (1) organize an interview with a media professional of your choice or (2) invite a media professional to come and speak to your class about their day-to-day working lives.

Issues for consideration

1 Ask your interviewee/speaker to describe their media organization in terms of its organizational, ownership and management structures.
2 Encourage your interviewee/speaker to describe fully the kinds of media production that their organization is involved in.
3 Drawing from what you have read in this chapter about professional autonomy and the various constraints which pertain to media production, ask your interviewee/speaker to describe their day-to-day working life.
4 Technological changes and media globalization have had a profound effect on media professionals. Ask your interviewee/speaker to elaborate on the impact of both of these on their professional life.
5 If your speaker/interviewee is engaged in the production of factual media content, such as news or current affairs, encourage him/her to speak about the sources that they typically use in researching or writing a story.

6 One useful strategy in doing research work of this kind is to ask your interviewee/speaker about a recent example of their work. This 'retrospection' may be used as a way of encouraging the media professional to talk about the background to the text in question, its intended message or meaning, the constraints involved in creating the text and its intended audience.
7 Ask your interviewee/speaker about the significance of audience reaction to their media work. In their everyday media activities how conscious are they of audience reaction? Why? How does your interviewee construct the audience in his/her mind?

Questions for consideration and discussion

1 The tension between 'structure' and 'agency' lies at the heart of understanding the world of the media professional. Discuss.
2 For all its merits, production research is quite limited in its scope.
3 The 'Encoding/Decoding' model suggests that we need to go beyond the media professional in examining the production of meaning.

References

Atton, C. (2002) 'News cultures and new social movements: radical journalism and the main-stream media', *Journalism Studies* 3 (4): 491–505.

Bilton, T., K. Bonnett, P. Jones, D. Skinner, M. Stanworth and A. Webster (1997) *Introductory Sociology*. London: Macmillan.

Bourdieu, P. (1996) *Sur la télévision: suivi de l'emprise du journalism*. Paris: Raisons d'Agir Editions.

Carroll, W.K. and R.A. Hackett (2006) 'Democratic media activism through the lens of social movement theory', *Media, Culture and Society* 28 (1): 83–104.

Chambers, D., L. Steiner and C. Fleming (2004) *Women and Journalism*. London: Routledge.

Cottle, S. (1993) 'Behind the headlines: the sociology of news' in M. O'Donnell (ed.) *New Introductory Reader in Sociology*. Walton on Thames: Nelson.

Coyer, K. (2005) 'Where the "hyper local" and the "hyper global" meet: case study of Indymedia radio', *Westminster Papers in Communication and Culture*. London: University of Westminster.

Davis, A. (2000) 'Public relations, news production and changing patterns of source access in the British national media', *Media, Culture and Society* 22 (1): 39–59.

Davis, H. (2004) *Understanding Stuart Hall*. London: Sage.

Deacon, D., N. Fenton and A. Bryman (1999a) 'From inception to reception: the natural history of a news item', *Media, Culture and Society* 21: 5–31.

Deacon, D., M. Pickering, P. Golding and G. Murdock (1999b) 'Being an observer' in *Researching Communications*. London: Arnold.

Deuze, M. (2004) 'What is multimedia journalism?', *Journalism Studies* 5 (2): 139–52.

Devereux, E. (1998) *Devils and Angels: Television, Ideology and the Coverage of Poverty*. Luton: University of Luton Press/John Libbey Media.

Downing, J. (1988) 'The alternative public realm: the organization of the 1980s anti-nuclear press in West Germany and Britain', *Media, Culture and Society* 10: 163–81.

Downing, J. (2001) *Radical Media: Rebellious Communication and Social Movements*. Thousand Oaks, CA: Sage.

Dupagne, M. and B. Garrison (2006) 'The meaning and influence of convergence: a qualitative case study of newsroom work at the Tampa News Center', *Journalism Studies* 7: 237–55.

Ekstrom, M. (2002) 'Epistemologies of TV journalism', *Journalism* 3 (3): 259–82.

Eliasoph, N. (1988) 'Routines and the making of oppositional news', *Critical Studies in Mass Communication* 5 (4): 313–34.

Elliot, Philip (1979) *The Making of a Television Series*, 2nd edn. London: Constable and Sage.

Esser, F. (1998) 'Editorial structures and work principles in British and German newsrooms', *European Journal of Communication* 13 (3): 375–405.

Franklin, B. (1997) *Newszak and News Media*. London: Arnold.

Gitlin, T. (1994) *Inside Prime Time*. London: Routledge.

Goldsmiths Media Group (2000) 'Media organisations in society: central issues' in J. Curran (ed.) *Media Organisations in Society*. London: Arnold.

Hall, S. (1974) 'The television discourse: encoding and decoding', *Education and Culture* 25: 8–14.

Hall, S. (1988) *The Hard Road to Renewal*. London: Verso.

Hall, S and T. Jefferson (eds) (1976) *Resistance through Rituals: Youth Subcultures in Postwar Britain*. London: Hutchinson.

Hansen, A., S. Cottle, R. Negrine and C. Newbold (1998) 'Participant observation: researching news production' in A. Hansen et al. (eds) *Mass Communication Research Methods*. London: Macmillan.

Harrison, P. and R. Palmer (1986) *News out of Africa: From Biafra to Band Aid*. London: Shipman.

Hesmondhalgh, D. (2006) 'Inside media organizations: production, autonomy and power', in D. Hesmondhalgh (ed.) *Media Production*: Maidenhead and Milton Keynes: The Open University Press/The Open University, pp. 49–90.

Hesmondhalgh, D. (2007) *The Cultural Industries*. 2nd edn. London: Sage.

Holliman, R. (2004) 'Media coverage of cloning: a study of media content, production and reception', *Public Understanding of Science*, 13: 107–30.

Huang, E.K. Davison, T. Davis, E. Betterdorf, S. Shieve and A. Nair (2006) 'Facing the challenges of convergence: media professionals' concerns of working across media platforms', *Convergence* 12 (1): 83–98.

Ito, T. (2006) 'Journalism in power relations and Pierre Bourdieu's concept of "field": a case study of the coverage of the 1999 group bullying case in Tochigi Prefecture', *Keio Communications Review* 28: 71–86.

Iyengar S. and D.R. Kinder (1987) *News That Matters: Television and American Opinion*. Chicago: University of Chicago Press.

Kim, K.H. (2006) 'Obstacles to the success of female journalists in Korea', *Media, Culture and Society* 28 (1): 123–41.

McRobbie, H. The Uses of Cultural Studies. London: Sage.

Newcomb, H. (1991) 'The creation of television drama news' in K. Bruhn Jensen and N.W. Jankowski (eds) *A Handbook of Qualitative Methodologies for Mass Communication Research*. London: Routledge.

Parker, A. (2000) 'Alan Parker interviewed by Barry Norman', *The Guardian interview* www. filmunlimited.co.uk.

Philo, G. (1993) 'From Buerk to Band Aid' in J. Eldridge (ed.) *Getting the Message*. London: Routledge.

Platon, S. and M. Deuze (2003) 'Indymedia journalism: a radical way of making, selecting and sharing news?' *Journalism* 4 (3): 336–55.

Proctor, J. (2004) *Stuart Hall*. London: Routledge.

Rodriguez, C. (2001) *Fissures in the Mediascape*. Cresskill, NJ: Hampton Press.

Shoemaker, P.J. and S.D. Reese (1996) *Mediating the Message: Theories of Influences on Mass Media Content*, 2nd edn. Boston, MA: Longman.

Tuchman, G. (1991) 'Qualitative methods in the study of news' in K. Bruhn Jensen and N.W. Jankowski (eds) *A Handbook of Qualitative Methodologies for Mass Communication Research*. London: Routledge.

van Zoonen, L. (1998) 'One of the girls? The changing gender of journalism' in C. Carter, G. Branston and S. Allen (eds) *News, Gender and Power*. London: Routledge.

———————————————— **Going further** ————————————————

Davis, L. (2000) 'Public relations, news production and changing patterns of source access in the British national media', *Media, Culture and Society* 22: 39–59. Davis examines the increasingly significant role of PR practitioners in the making of news.

Grossberg, L., E. Wartella, D.C. Whitney and J. Macgregor Wise (2006) *Mediamaking: Mass Media in a Popular Culture*. 2nd edn. Thousand Oaks, CA: Sage. An excellent introduction to the forces shaping mass media content. See Chapter 3, 'Media people and organizations' and Chapter 8, 'Producing identities'.

Howley, K. (2005) *Community Media: People, Places and Communications Technologies*. Cambridge: Cambridge University Press. Howley investiages the emergence of grassroots media focusing on street newspapers, radio and cable television.

Kitty, A. (2005) *Don't Believe It! How Lies Become News*. New York: The Disinformation Company. This highly entertaining book takes you behind the scenes of everyday journalism. It firmly debunks the myths of journalistic neutrality and objectivity.

5

MEDIA IDEOLOGY

Summary

This chapter introduces you to the following:

- The concepts of ideology, dominant ideology, hegemony and discourse.
- How these concepts have been applied towards furthering our under-standing of the ideological role of the mass media in contemporary societies.
- The debate between those who favour and those who oppose the contin-ued use of the concepts of ideology and dominant ideology within mass media analysis.
- A tripartite methodological approach to ideological analysis of the mass media that gives equal recognition to the production, content and recep-tion of media texts.
- An approach to ideological analysis that sees the concepts of ideology and discourse working together in a complementary way, thus furthering our understanding of the mass media's role in perpetuating unequal power relationships.

Key concepts

- Ideology
- Ideological state apparatus
- Relative autonomy
- Hegemony
- Dominant ideology
- Asymmetrical or unequal relations of power
- Counter-hegemonic ideologies
- Content analysis
- Discourse
- Discursive formation
- Hermeneutic approach
- 'Reading against the grain'
- Audience resistance

'Ideology, broadly speaking, is meaning in the service of power' (Thompson, 1990: 6).

Modern and postmodern societies continue to be characterized by the persistence of unequal relations of power, especially in terms of class, ethnicity and gender. Inequalities between men and women, between the social classes and between different ethnic groups – either singly or more usually in one or other combination – are just a few of the many kinds of inequalities that currently exist. Added to these are numerous material inequalities that exist on a global scale between the so-called 'developing' and 'developed' worlds, which result in absolute poverty, hunger, suffering and death. The question as to what role the mass media play in either sustaining or challenging these and other unequal relations of power through the reproduction of ideology has had a long and troubled history within social theory generally and within media studies in particular.

In this chapter we introduce you to the sometimes contentious concept of ideology and assess its continued usefulness in doing critical media analysis. In recent years the concept has come under increasing pressure from poststructuralism and postmodernism as well as from an ongoing critique within media studies itself, most notably from those following a reception analysis model of research (see Devereux, 1998: 17–23; 2006).

See Chapter 7 for a detailed account of audiences and reception analysis.

In accordance with Thompson (1990), we argue for the continued use of a revised definition of ideology within media analysis based upon a tripartite methodological approach that pays sufficient attention to the hermeneutic aspect of media texts. By this we mean that analysis of dominant and other ideologies within the mass media needs to pay sufficient attention not only to media organizations or institutions, the content or structure of the text(s), but also – and crucially – to the meanings that the text(s) have for audience members. This approach has the capacity to make up for the shortcomings of the two research traditions that have, until recently, predominated within ideological analysis of the mass media, namely the *political economy* and *content analysis* approaches. The political economy approach has been criticized for being overly deterministic in explaining why the media reproduce an ideological slant that is favourable to the ruling class and other dominant groups. The content analysis approach has been criticized for being too narrow in terms of the kinds of media genres it has chosen to analyse and in many instances for making simplistic assumptions about the ideological effect on audiences based on analysis of content alone.

See Chapters 3 and 6 for a discussion of both approaches.

We start by briefly outlining the history of the concept of ideology, sketching its key 'moments' within the Marxist heritage. Beginning with Marx and then considering how the Frankfurt School, Althusser and Gramsci developed the concept of ideology, we see a gradual move from an initial 'closed/materialist' conceptualization of ideology towards a more 'open/relaxed' understanding of the term. We then consider Thompson's (1990) attempts to rescue the concept of ideology from its many opponents. The chapter concludes by examining the more recent (and welcome) emphasis on the concept of discourse within ideological media analysis. The twin concepts of *discourse* and *discursive formation* underpin the recent attempts by media and communications scholars to understand the workings of ideology more fully.

> See Chapters 2 and 3 for an elaboration of this theme.

It is our belief that ideology continues to be an important, useful and necessary concept within both social theory and media analysis. In its reformulated state, it represents one of the most challenging areas of mass media analysis and debate. This is particularly so in an age of media globalization and at a time when the ownership of an increasing number of media organizations rests in the hands of a decreasing number of multimedia conglomerates.

It is somewhat ironic that many postmodernist scholars have called for the abandonment of the concept of ideology altogether, given that in the post-9/11 world we have seen an even greater focus on competing ideologies. As we have already noted in Chapter 2, one key outcome of the globalization process – which is itself founded upon the ideology of neo-liberalism – is the intensification of local and ethnic identities. Globalization and the reflexivity that it inculcates has, if anything, placed a greater emphasis on ideology. In addition to the many residual ideological differences between left and right (as evidenced in the ongoing tensions between Cuba and the USA, for example) the early twenty-first century has witnessed a variety of ideological clashes between Islamic and Western viewpoints, as well as the reappearance of fundamentalism of both the Christian and Islamic varieties. Ethnic conflicts such as that between Palestine and Israel or between Christians and Muslims in Darfur, has meant a continued war of attrition between competing worldviews. The shift to the right in many countries as well as the re-emergence of anti-immigrant ideologies are further evidence of the ongoing ideological battles that are occurring.

Perhaps the most obvious recent example of the need to continue with a critical media studies lies in the so-called 'war on terror' campaigns in both Afghanistan and Iraq. Media organizations on both sides of these conflicts have played a pivotal role in disseminating disinformation and propaganda about the United States, the West and the Islamic world. Ideologically loaded terms such as 'the civilized world', 'the democratic world', 'the free world', 'global terrorism', 'America at war', 'fighting back' and 'weapons of mass destruction' have been used by many media professionals in an unreflective way. The emergence of the 'embedded journalist' is a stark reminder of just how illusory the notion of journalistic objectivity actually is (see Kumar, 2006; Tumber and Palmer, 2004). These conflicts have presented media professionals in the Western world, and in the United States in particular, with a new set of challenges on how the practices of journalistic 'neutrality' and 'objectivity' might otherwise be observed. The coverage of the 'war on terror' and the images and language used to define 'the enemy' are obvious examples of where the ideological role played by the media comes into sharp focus (see Box 5.1(b)).

More often than not, however, the bulk of ideological activity that takes place in the context of media discourse happens unwittingly. Our main challenge is to consider how ordinary, everyday media content performs an ideological role in telling stories about power relationships. In this regard ideological power is exercised in five key ways through what Thompson (1990: 60) refers to as legitimation, dissimulation, unification, fragmentation and reification (see Box 5.1(a)). In terms of dissimulation, for example, relations of dominance can be concealed, denied or obscured. In *Devils and Angels*, Devereux (1998: 15, 139) demonstrates how dissimulation is achieved in television news and telethon programmes. Many television news reports on charitable acts by elite figures resort to using a discourse that stresses the 'human interest' angle in the relationship between the well-off and the poor. The poverty and exclusion experienced by the poor are framed in terms of their individual case histories. Structural context referring to the causes of poverty and inequality is, more often than not, ignored. Fundraising or telethon television is a good example of where this process takes place. The fact that telethons are needed at all is indicative of need and inequality in society. Telethons, however, typically concentrate on how the activities of (usually well-off) celebrities and the heroic deeds of 'ordinary people' help to alleviate poverty. The ideological work takes place in individualizing and personalizing poverty stories.

BOX 5.1(A)   HOW IS IDEOLOGICAL DOMINATION ACHIEVED? (THOMPSON, 1990)

Ideology functions through	How?	Examples
1 Legitimation	Unequal power relationships are created and maintained by being represented as legitimate and as being in 'everybody's' interest.	A key way in which legitimation works is through the process of universalization – i.e. creating the sense in society that in spite of the existence of material differences between different social groups, the present economic or political system benefits all or has the *potential* to benefit all members of society. At election time, for example, political parties of all hues argue that sometime soon everybody will benefit from one or other policy.

BOX 5.1 (A)

Ideology functions through	How?	Examples
2 Dissimulation	This occurs where relations of domination (such as gender inequality) are denied, hidden or obscured.	Dissimulation can occur for example, when unequal relationships of power are ignored altogether, glossed over or taken for granted.
		Dissimulation is regularly in evidence in the tabloid print media in the (mis) representation of women.
		Dissimulation also occurs through the practice of omission, whereby alternative accounts of events are not included in a news report for example.
3 Unification	Hegemonic or dominant ideology unifies members of a society into a collective entity usually in opposition to a real or imagined 'enemy'.	Uniting (all) members of society against the 'threat of terrorism' or the assumed threat that immigration brings.
	This serves to further deflect attention away from the unequal power relationships between the rulers and the ruled.	In this context, particular use is often made in political or state discourse, for example, of unifying terms such as 'community'; 'family'; 'society' and 'we'. The use of othering discourses sets up clear distinctions between 'us' and 'them'.
		(Continued)

BOX 5.1(A)

Ideology functions through	How?	Examples
4 Fragmentation	Hegemony is achieved and maintained through dividing or fragmenting the potential opposition and thus reducing or removing the perceived 'threat' they might otherwise pose. In short, the powerful adopt a 'divide and rule' approach.	A colonial power, for example, might foster divisions and enmity between different ethnic or class groups. A political party might encourage divisiveness between the underclass and immigrants around questions concerning work, social welfare or housing.
5 Reification	Unequal social structures are represented as being 'natural' and 'inevitable'. Relations of domination are represented as if they were divorced from history and were without specific economic and political contexts.	The belief, for example, that gender inequalities are based on 'natural' or biological differences between women and men. Third World poverty or underdevelopment being discussed without reference to the exploitative contexts of colonialism or more recent global capitalism.

BOX 5.1(B)   THE MOST DECISIVE IDEOLOGICAL STRUGGLE OF THE TWENTY-FIRST CENTURY

On 11 September 2006 the accompanying text formed part of a major speech by US President George W. Bush. His address, delivered from the Oval Office in the White House, was widely reported and commented upon in both the mainstream and independent media. Media reports referred to its key components as well as to how

Bush's political opponents had critiqued his speech – noting specifically concerns about how he had used a commemoration of 9/11 to justify prolonging the war in Iraq. Media reportage of Bush's speech contained both hegemonic and counter-hegemonic ideologies. Some media organizations such as SKY and CNN carried Bush's address live, whilst in a print media setting journalists reported on the content of Bush's address and made reference to the views of his critics.

> Since the horror of 9/11, we've learned a great deal about the enemy. We have learned that they are evil and kill without mercy – but not without purpose. We have learned that they form a global network of extremists who are driven by a perverted vision of Islam – a totalitarian ideology that hates freedom, rejects tolerance, and despises all dissent. And we have learned that their goal is to build a radical Islamic empire where women are prisoners in their homes, men are beaten for missing prayer meetings, and terrorists have a safe haven to plan and launch attacks on America and other civilized nations. The war against this enemy is more than a military conflict. It is the decisive ideological struggle of the twenty-first century, and the calling of our generation. . . .

> In the first days after the 9/11 attacks I promised to use every element of national power to fight the terrorists, wherever we find them. One of the strongest weapons in our arsenal is the power of freedom. The terrorists fear freedom as much as they do our firepower. They are thrown into panic at the sight of an old man pulling the election lever, girls enrolling in schools, or families worshiping God in their own traditions. They know that given a choice, people will choose freedom over their extremist ideology. So their answer is to deny people this choice by raging against the forces of freedom and moderation. This struggle has been called a clash of civilizations. In truth, it is a struggle for civilization. We are fighting to maintain the way of life enjoyed by free nations. And we're fighting for the possibility that good and decent people across the Middle East can raise up societies based on freedom and tolerance and personal dignity. . . .

> We are now in the early hours of this struggle between tyranny and freedom. Amid the violence, some question whether the people of the Middle East want their freedom, and whether the forces of moderation can prevail. For 60 years, these doubts guided our policies in the Middle East. And then, on a bright September morning, it became clear that the calm we saw in the Middle East was only a mirage. Years of pursuing stability to promote peace had left us with neither. So we changed our policies, and committed America's influence in the world to advancing freedom and democracy as the great alternatives to repression and radicalism. . . .

(Continued)

Across the broader Middle East, the extremists are fighting to prevent such a future. Yet America has confronted evil before, and we have defeated it – sometimes at the cost of thousands of good men in a single battle. When Franklin Roosevelt vowed to defeat two enemies across two oceans, he could not have foreseen D-Day and Iwo Jima – but he would not have been surprised at the outcome. When Harry Truman promised American support for free peoples resisting Soviet aggression, he could not have foreseen the rise of the Berlin Wall – but he would not have been surprised to see it brought down. Throughout our history, America has seen liberty challenged, and every time, we have seen liberty triumph with sacrifice and determination.

At the start of this young century, America looks to the day when the people of the Middle East leave the desert of despotism for the fertile gardens of liberty, and resume their rightful place in a world of peace and prosperity. We look to the day when the nations of that region recognize their greatest resource is not the oil in the ground, but the talent and creativity of their people. We look to the day when moms and dads throughout the Middle East see a future of hope and opportunity for their children. And when that good day comes, the clouds of war will part, the appeal of radicalism will decline, and we will leave our children with a better and safer world.

On this solemn anniversary, we rededicate ourselves to this cause. Our nation has endured trials, and we face a difficult road ahead. Winning this war will require the determined efforts of a unified country, and we must put aside our differences and work together to meet the test that history has given us. We will defeat our enemies. We will protect our people. And we will lead the twenty-first century into a shining age of human liberty.

Commentary

As an example of a text containing dominant or hegemonic ideology, note how Bush (and/or his speechwriter(s)) makes use of the following discursive strategies:

1   The ideas of the US's opponents are explicitly referred to as being ideological. In using the term *ideological* here, Bush is using it in its negative or pejorative sense. The ideas and political values (democracy, freedom and liberty) which Bush is purported to stand for are not in themselves seen as ideological, although he does make reference to a 'decisive ideological struggle' in which the US and its enemies are engaged.
2   Key historical facts – such as the US's previous support of Saddam Hussein – are omitted. There is no reference to the many thousands of innocent civilians killed

by the US in Iraq or Afghanistan. The presence of oil in the Middle East is alluded to but quickly glossed over.

3   Descriptors such as 'perverted', 'totalitarian', 'extremists', 'radicalism', 'radical Islamic empires', 'evil', 'repression', and 'despotism' are used in reference to the 'enemy'.

4   An attempt at unification is present through the use of terms such as 'we', 'us', 'our nation', 'a unified country', 'our people', 'our generation', 'the people of the Middle East' and 'good and decent people across the Middle East' (meaning presumably those who are supportive of the US). References to shared historical narratives try to draw parallels between the Bush administration's activities in the Middle East and the experiences of previous US presidents such as Truman and Roosevelt. Note how the President refers to the loss of life in previous battles as a means of countering those who are critical of the US's current intervention in the Middle East.

5   The deployment of affective or emotional language as evidenced in 'our children', 'their children', and 'moms and dads'.

6   The use of images associated with the desert are quite striking – thus Bush refers to 'Mirage'; 'Desert of Despotism' and the 'Fertile Gardens of Liberty.'

7   Contrasts are cleverly drawn between 'them' and 'us'. 'We' stand for 'freedom', 'liberty', 'moderation', 'tolerance' and 'personal dignity'. 'They' stand for 'extremism', 'repression' and 'radicalism'. (see Stabile and Kumar, 2005).

CRITICAL QUESTIONS 5.1   UNEQUAL POWER RELATIONSHIPS AND THE MASS MEDIA

1   Think of three recent examples of media coverage concerning unequal power relationships between men and women, the social classes or different ethnic groups.

2   What sorts of discourses, in your opinion, do these examples contain?

3   Can these discourses be considered to be ideological?

4   Is there more than one kind of ideological position/perspective evident within the media content?

Ideology: our approach

From the outset, it is useful to pin some colours to the mast. In using the term 'ideology' in this textbook, we mean the ideas that legitimize the power of a dominant social group or class (see Creeber, 2006; Devereux, 1998: 19–23; and van Dijk,

1998a, for a more detailed overview). Our interpretation of the term and our particular emphasis on ideology as dominant ideology is in broad alignment with the neo-Marxist tradition, but it is not solely confined to explaining class relations. Ideological analysis of the twenty-first century mass media might very well be concerned with discourses about class relations, but it might also be applied to, among other things, analyses of heterosexism, homophobia, disability, patriarchy, racism or 'terrorism'. We are not restricted to analysing hegemonic ideology. We should also examine the workings of counter-hegemonic ideologies circulating, for example, among oppressed groups such as ethnic minorities, sexual minority groups or the colonized.

We are interested in examining the interrelations of meaning and power and, more specifically, how meaning serves to maintain relations of domination. Furthermore, we favour using a 'relaxed' rather than a 'closed' definition of the term. In practice, when we engage in ideological analysis of the mass media, we are often confronted with competing ideologies rather than a single monolithic 'thing' called ideology. The challenge facing us as students of the mass media is to examine the workings of, and sometimes the tensions between, dominant and counter-hegemonic ideologies that audiences are exposed to in an increasingly complex media setting.

The mass media play an immensely powerful part in the production and circulation of ideologies. In *The Whole World is Watching*, Gitlin explains this complex process as follows: '[E]veryday, directly or indirectly, by statement and omission, in pictures and in words, in entertainment and news and advertising, the mass media produce fields of definition and association, symbol and rhetoric, through which ideology becomes manifest and concrete' (1980: 2). It is worthwhile acknowledging, however, that while counter-hegemonic ideologies are in circulation in, among other places, the alternative press, in underground dance music, on home-produced Web sites or in independent cinema/film, we are particularly interested in the ideological struggles between dominant and counter-hegemonic ideologies that take place in the mainstream media (see Boxes 5.2 and 5.3). While it may be tempting to identify – usually through one or other kind of content analysis – certain media texts as having dominant and other ideologies, analysis based on content alone is not sufficient in undertaking ideological analysis.

Content analysis, as we will see in greater detail in Chapter 6, is typically used to identify the intentions and other characteristics of communicators, detect the existence of latent propaganda or ideology, reflect cultural patterns of groups, reveal the foci of organizations, and describe trends in communication content. However, content analysis should be seen as only one important part in our overall attempts at examining the operation of dominant and other ideologies in a media setting. If the media have an ideological role, then their job is to help perpetuate or sustain unequal relationships of power among real people in the real world. Ultimately what is at stake is whether existing (dominant) ideas and discourses surrounding power relationships between men and women, between the social classes or between ethnic groups, for example, are reinforced or challenged and whether audiences accept, reject or appropriate these ideas or discourses. *Ideological and discursive analysis* of mass media content asks us to concentrate on the relationship between media language (in its broadest sense) and audience beliefs about the social world.

Communication with audiences could not exist without ideology and discourse. Mass media organizations engage in ideological work all of the time, so much so that the use of many ideas and assumptions about the social world are simply taken for granted by media professionals and others. However, when conflicts arise in society (involving, for example, challenges to patriarchy or institutional racism by the state or the police), then the mass media's ideological role becomes more apparent and the possibility of the hegemony or dominant ideology being challenged can arise for some audience members.

BOX 5.2 'FUCK EMI'

In certain media settings, counter-hegemonic ideology may be found side by side with dominant or hegemonic ideology. Many media conglomerates are happy enough to incorporate and sell media products (e.g. hard-core punk rock, rap etc.), which contain ideas that run counter to the status quo. Virgin Records (now owned by EMI) sell thousands of copies of the Sex Pistols' recordings singing about anarchy. In 1986, Morrissey (then distributed by a record company controlled by Time Warner) sang of his dream of 'Margaret On The Guillotine' – in reference to the then UK Prime Minister Margaret Thatcher. The anarchist group Chumbawawa contributed to a compilation record entitled 'Fuck EMI' in 1989. In response to Live Aid, they released a record entitled 'Pictures of Starving Children Sell Records' (1986). Yet major record label EMI signed them in 1997 and the band had a chart hit with the song 'Tubthumping One'. Their music is now for sale on Apple's iTunes store. A tiny minority of music groups have managed to remain independent of the mass media conglomerates and engage in self-distribution. Perhaps most famously, the Anarchist artists group, The K Foundation – who achieved significant levels of chart success in the early 1990s as the KLF – burnt one million pounds sterling and when retiring from the music industry they deleted their entire back catalogue of recordings.

A	Anarchism; Ageism; Anti-globalization
B	Bolshevism
C	Capitalism; Communism; Consumerism; Communitarianism; Colonialism
D	Dominionism
E	Ecological; Euro-communism; Egalitarianism
F	Feminism; Facism
G	Green; Globalism
H	Heterosexism; Humanism
I	Islamism
J	–
K	–
L	Liberalism/Neo-Liberalism
M	Marxism; Monarchism
N	Nationalism; Neo-Nazism
O	–
P	Patriarchalism; Pacifism; Post-Colonialism
Q	Queer
R	Racism; Republicanism; Religion
S	Sexism; Secularism; Socialism; Social Democracy
T	Terrorism; Totalitarianism; Trotskyism
U	Utopianism
V	Vegetarianism; Veganism
W	White-centrism
X	Xenophobism
Y	–
Z	Zionism

Figure 5.1 An A–Z of hegemonic and counter-hegemonic ideologies (but by no means an exhaustive list)

BOX 5.3   COUNTERING HEGEMONIC IDEOLOGY: THE FILMS OF MICHAEL MOORE

Michael Moore's films provide visual evidence of counter-hegemonic ideologies at work within a mainstream media setting. Commercially successful, Moore's film work manages to engage in a strong critique of many of the dominant ideas and beliefs within the USA. Typically adopting a documentary style, Moore's films have critiqued global capitalism as well as calling into question many of the orthodoxies of American politics. *Roger and Me* (1989) sought reasons for General Motor's decision to 'downsize' in Moore's hometown of Flint, Michigan. *The Big One* (1992) focused on the cheap labour strategies used by global firms such as Nike in order to maximize profits. The preponderance of gun culture within the USA was the theme of '*Bowling for Columbine*' (2002). That film placed the rising levels of gun ownership and deaths from legally held weapons in the larger context of the growth in the armaments industry. His most controversial film to date *Farenheit 9/11* (2004) explored the supposed links between the Bush and Bin Laden families as well as examining the dissemination of fear within a post-9/11 USA.

Moore's films, television programmes and books are sold and distributed by many of the mass media conglomerates he is directly critical of. It is worth noting that while his work is of significant commercial importance to the conglomerates who sell and distribute his work, he has fallen foul of some sections of the media industry. In 2004 for example, the Disney Corporation decided to disallow its subsidiary Miramax to distribute *Farenheit 9/11* in the USA. The impasse was resolved only when Disney allowed the joint chairmen of Miramax (Harvey and Bob Weinstein) to buy back the film for US$6 million and to arrange an alternative means of distribution.

Moore had previously encountered difficulties with the original publisher of his book *Stupid White Men* (2001). 50,000 copies of the book were printed and ready for release by ReganBooks (owned by HarperCollins, part of the News Corporation conglomerate) on 10 September 2001. In a subsequent edition of the book (published by Penguin, UK in 2002), Moore recounts the difficulties he had with his initial publisher. They asked that 50 per cent of the book be rewritten in the context of the changed political climate in which the USA found itself. Moore refused and there was a stand-off between him and his publishers, with the latter threatening to pulp the book altogether. The pressure brought to bear by senior librarians and ordinary readers ensured that this did not happen. Senior librarians told HarperCollins that they would stop buying their books. Ordinary readers purchased *Stupid White Men* through on-line bookstores such as Amazon.com and it became a bestseller as a result of a combination of audience agency and economic pressure.

(Continued)

Michael Moore's work as a filmmaker, television presenter and author has been the focus of much debate. His films, for example, have been criticized for telling stories about the powerful in a selective way. Whatever their merits and demerits, Moore's films are examples of where hegemonic ideologies are highlighted and questioned by reference to a liberal discourse. His films are also an example of where widely distributed media texts contain counter-hegemonic ideologies which are the source of significant amounts of profit for the multimedia conglomerates.

You should now read EXTRACTED READING 5.1, *A Propaganda Model* (McChesney and Chomsky, 1994) and consider the following issues:

1 Think of at least three examples where the mass media may be shown to disseminate propaganda.

2 What are the key arguments that you might make *against* McChesney and Chomsky's propaganda model?

BOX 5.4   POWERFUL TEXTS AND GUERRILLA READERS . . .

The debate about the contemporary mass media and their ideological effect (or not) may be caricatured as one in which there are, on the one hand, powerful media texts replete with dominant and other ideologies capable of shaping the thinking of audience members and, on the other hand, audience members who are 'guerrilla readers', capable of either recognizing dominant and other ideologies for what they are or subverting the intended ideological meaning altogether. The challenge for the media student is to recognize exactly how and in what circumstances either the former or the latter takes place and to what extent. Media content shapes audience perceptions about the social world but the interpretative repertoires of audience members – their agency – allow audiences in certain circumstances to 'read against the grain' of the preferred reading of the text. In what circumstances do you think a critical reading of a media text is more likely to occur?

What is ideology?

Defining ideology

Closed/materialist definitions of ideology.   Early attempts at defining what is meant by ideology are usually characterized as being restricted or closed. Karl Marx and more latterly the Frankfurt School developed a negative and largely deterministic understanding of ideology.

In Marx's work the ruling classes in capitalist society control not only the means of material production but also the production of ideas. Ideas perform an ideological function when they either mask the exploitative nature of capitalism or present these kinds of exploitative economic relationships as being natural and inevitable. In this understanding of the term, ideology can serve to create false consciousness among the exploited and only when it is recognized as such will there be a revolution and a new social order.

The Frankfurt School's attempts to apply Marx's understanding of ideology to the emerging twentieth-century mass media are a further example of a closed definition of ideology. In writing about the persistence of capitalism, and the destruction brought about by two world wars, the Frankfurt School were critical of and pessimistic about the mass media. As an economic system, capitalism had gone from strength to strength in the postwar era because capitalists controlled the mass media. Writing about this theme in his famous study *One Dimensional Man,* Marcuse argued that the media create products that 'indoctrinate and manipulate; they promote a false consciousness which is immune against its falsehood' (1964: 12).

> ◯◯◯
>
> *See Chapter 7 for an analysis of audience reception.*

Both Marx and the Frankfurt School emphasized the relationship, as they saw it, between the economic base and dominant ideas of capitalist society. Their understanding of the term is negative in that both imply passivity on the part of those who receive the ideas via the media or other ideological agencies. Active audience theorists, as you will see in Chapter 7, would firmly reject such blanket assertions of audience passivity.

Open/relaxed definitions of ideology. Louis Althusser and Antonio Gramsci are justifiably credited with broadening out the parameters of how we should understand ideology. In their work we can see the beginnings of a more open or relaxed definition of the term.

The French theorist Louis Althusser was concerned with explaining how the mass media created ideological meaning for audiences. In writing about ideology, Althusser developed the concept of the ideological state apparatus. By this he meant that institutions such as the media or the educational system reproduced ideology in such a way as to 'represent capitalism as being natural, inevitable and indeed desirable' (Devereux, 1998: 10).

Althusser's understanding of the term 'ideology' carried with it the concept of relative autonomy. To allow the continuation of class domination in capitalist society, the media must be perceived by their audience as being relatively autonomous from the direct control of the ruling class. Althusser's notion of relative autonomy allowed for dissenting voices to be heard within the mass media but the ideas that legitimized and facilitated the continuation of capitalism remained dominant.

BOX 5.5   OPEN AND CLOSED DEFINITIONS OF IDEOLOGY

Theorist(s)	Definition of ideology	Mass media's ideological role	Conceptualization of media audience
Karl Marx (1818–83)	Closed/materialist. Negative.	Only indirectly concerned with this issue. Nineteenth-century newspapers supportive of capitalism. Marx in his role as a journalist and commentator critiqued the capitalist system within the print media.	The working class or proletariat have 'false-consciousness'.
The Frankfurt School. Various members, including Theodore Adorno (1903–69) and Herbert Marcuse (1898–1979)	Closed/materialist. Various negative.	Mass media are a powerful source of propaganda. Specifically concerned with propaganda within radio and film in Nazi Germany.	Audiences are duped by emerging mass media.
Louis Althusser (1918–90).	Increasingly open.	Mass media's role as an ideological state apparatus is to legitimize the capitalist system.	The mass media have the appearance of being relatively autonomous from the powerful capitalist class. The mass media manage to give greater legitimacy to certain kinds of ideas over others.
Antonio Gramsci (1891–1937)	Increasingly open.	Mass media play a central role in the creation of hegemony in the interests of the capitalist class.	Applications of Gramsci's ideas see a continuous struggle within media texts in order to achieve hegemony.

(Continued)

BOX 5.5

Theorist(s)	Definition of ideology	Mass media's ideological role	Conceptualization of media audience
John B. Thompson	Open/relaxed. Emphasis on dominant and other counter-hegemonic ideologies.	A tripartite ideological analysis of the mass media is required to take account of the production context, the content of the text and the agency of audience members.	Audiences are active and capable of considerable agency. The effect or not of dominant ideology is based upon taking a depth hermeneutic approach.

Ideology and hegemony

The Italian Marxist Antonio Gramsci also added much to our understanding of ideology through his development of the concept of hegemony. Gramsci wanted to know more about how the capitalist class achieved and maintained a position of dominance in modern society. Hegemony or domination may be achieved through the use or threat of force or more typically through the creation of consensus. Domination of the latter kind in capitalist society comes about by means of the powerful being able to fashion a consensus between those with power and those with little or no power. From Gramsci's perspective the mass media create a 'commonsense' view of the world that portrays capitalism as being natural and inevitable. In accepting this viewpoint, the powerless allow themselves to be dominated by the ruling class through consent.

BOX 5.6   KEY THINKERS: MARX, GRAMSCI AND ALTHUSSER

Three European radical thinkers have influenced the ways in which we think about ideology and unequal power relationships. Born in Germany, Karl Marx (1818–83) was one of the founding fathers of contemporary sociology. His voluminous work focused on explaining the workings (and contradictions) of capitalist society. Drawing from his analyses of economics, politics, philosophy and history, Marx outlined his vision for a socialist society. He combined his work as a social theorist with an intermittent career in journalism, as well as an involvement in communist politics. Owing to his revolutionary activities, Marx and his family lived in a variety of locations in Continental Europe and the UK (see Wheen, 1999).

(Continued)

Like Marx, the Italian theorist Antonio Gramsci (1891–1937) was a committed political activist and journalist. Imprisoned in 1926 for his political activism, Gramsci spent much of the following ten years writing what have become known as the *Prison Notebooks*. The Italian theorist grappled with the failure of the socialist project and in doing so he began to write about how consent is achieved in a society in which inequalities are in evidence. It was in this context that Gramsci developed his thinking about the concept of *hegemony*. He theorized as to how domination was achieved by the capitalist class who used, he argued, either consent, force or the threat of force in order to dominate the social order. The work of both Gramsci and Louis Althusser (1918–90) represent attempts to develop further the ideas first circulated by Marx in the nineteenth century.

Althusser was a French theorist who, like his predecessors, was a committed political activist. He attempted to combine Marxist thinking with the ideas being developed within structuralism, in an effort to understand more about the deep structures that were said to underlie all texts. In contributing to the Marxist analysis of modern society, Althusser developed the concept of the ideological state apparatus. Of the three theorists, Althusser had perhaps the most tragic life. He was incarcerated in a psychiatric hospital in 1980 for the murder of his wife.

Plate 5.1   Gramsci's writings on the concept of hegemony added significantly to how we understand the workings of ideology in society and in a media setting in particular. Photo of Antonio Gramsci reproduced courtesy of the International Gramsci Society.

BOX 5.7   A CONCEPT UNDER ATTACK?

In the last two decades of the twentieth century the continued use of the concept of ideology was called into question (see Corner, 2001, for a very good summary). The attack happened on two key fronts. Within the field of social theory – and particularly in the context of the collapse of communism – it was argued by many that ideology was an ambiguous, outdated concept full of Marxist baggage that no longer had any use or relevance. Within cultural studies, and in media and communications studies in particular, the emergence of postmodernism as a dominant theoretical framework and the broad shift away from analyses of media effects and analyses of media content gave rise to a new emphasis on audience reception. Audiences were now conceptualized as being much more sophisticated in how they interpreted and engaged with media texts and thus the certainties of earlier ideological analysis were now in serious doubt (see, for example, Eagleton, 1991; Fiske, 1987; Frazer, 1992; van Dijk, 1998a; Hawkes, 2003 for further insights into the debate between those who favour and those who oppose the continued use of the concept.)

See Chapter 5 for an account of Hall's Encoding/Decoding model as an example.

Gramsci argued that the media managed to appear relatively autonomous from the capitalist class and yet they were engaged in the production and reproduction of ideology that helped in maintaining capitalism. (In reality, of course, the mass media can never ever be considered to be ideologically neutral.) The production and reproduction of ideology was not a static business, however. In Gramsci's estimation the capitalist class could not be certain of their hegemonic position and therefore in order for hegemony to be achieved, it had to be constantly negotiated and renegotiated. Gramsci saw the mass media as being a key source of hegemonic ideology. Gramsci's work has informed many of the attempts at undertaking mass media analysis from an ideological perspective. It has presented the production of ideology as an ongoing struggle between the dominant/hegemonic and the alternative/counter-hegemonic. His work has underpinned the approaches taken by feminist and Marxist media analysts in recent times.

You should now read EXTRACTED READING 5.2, *A Social Theory of Mass Communication* (Thompson, 1990) and consider the following issues:

1   What does Thompson mean by the term 'fallacy of internalism'?

2   Taking a media text of your choice, outline how you would apply Thompson's tripartite model of analysis.

Ideology as dominant ideology

John B. Thompson's *Ideology and Modern Culture* (1990) has made a very significant contribution towards how we now understand ideology and the mass media's role in the production and reproduction of ideology. Prior to describing his suggested model of media analysis, we briefly outline his attempts at rescuing the concept from a growing army of critics.

The importance of Thompson's work

Conceding that the concept has proved itself to be problematic in the past, Thompson argues that the concept 'should be used in its negative or critical sense' (Devereux, 1998: 13). Significantly, he asserts that our thinking about ideology: 'should be refocused on the interrelations of meaning and power and more specifically on how meaning serves to maintain relations of domination' (Devereux, 1998: 13). In Thompson's words, the concept of ideology:

> can be used to refer to the ways in which meaning serves, in particular circumstances, to establish and sustain relations of power which are systematically asymmetrical – what I shall call 'relations of domination'. Ideology, broadly speaking, is meaning in the service of power. Hence the study of ideology requires us to investigate the ways in which meaning is constructed and conveyed by symbolic forms of various kinds, from everyday linguistic utterances to complex images and texts; it requires us to investigate the social contexts within which symbolic forms are employed and deployed; it calls upon us to ask whether, and if so how, the meaning constructed and conveyed by symbolic forms serves, in specific contexts, to establish and sustain relations of domination. (1990: 6–7)

Thompson's (1990) emphasis on ideology as *dominant* ideology, used to perpetuate unequal power relations, carries with it a number of important implications (Devereux, 1998: 12–14). His approach underscores the fact that alternative or counter-hegemonic ideologies exist and that they may also circulate in a mass media setting. Not all media texts are ideological. They can be termed ideological only if they can be shown to help perpetuate unequal power relations. He also argues that it is not a prerequisite that ideology should be a form of false consciousness.

Thompson's work reasserts the importance of doing ideological analysis within media and communications studies. In repositioning the spotlight on ideology as dominant ideology, he concedes that ideologies other than dominant ideologies exist and circulate within media texts. In his reformulation, media texts that are ideological do not necessarily have to be false, erroneous or illusory, although they may be. By emphasizing the hermeneutic dimension, he privileges the role of the media audience in examining if and how an ideological effect takes place. Thompson's emphasis on the media audience mirrors the concentration on reception that had taken place in any event within media studies. The real value of his methodological framework is that he argues convincingly that we need to concentrate on all three key dimensions of the communication process – production, content and reception. We now outline his model of ideological media analysis.

Ideological analysis: a tripartite approach

Thompson's (1990) tripartite model takes what he terms a 'depth hermeneutics approach' in examining the media's ideological role. If we wish to understand more fully how media messages or texts help sustain or perpetuate relations of domination, then we need to place a firmer emphasis on the issues of meaning and interpretation.

A vast proportion of the media's activity is in the production of symbolic forms. Our attempts at understanding the ideological effect – if any – of the mass media need to recognize the crucial importance of the interpretative work that takes place around and with media messages or texts. It is only through a detailed consideration of what Thompson (1990: 274) calls 'the everyday appropriation' of media messages or texts that we can truly address questions surrounding their ideological effect.

Although individual analyses of production, content and reception may go some distance towards informing us about particular aspects of the ideological character of mass communication, a methodological framework using a combination of all three, and with particular emphasis on the reception and appropriation of media messages or texts, is potentially far more illuminating. According to Thompson:

> Rather than assuming that the ideological character of media messages can be read off the messages themselves (an assumption I have called the fallacy of internalism), we can draw upon the analysis of all three aspects of communication – production/transmission, construction, reception/appropriation – in order to interpret the ideological character of media messages. (1990: 306)

By engaging in what is admittedly a far more ambitious and demanding approach, we can begin to address many of the weaknesses traditionally associated with ideological media analysis.

Thompson (1990) asserts that his tripartite model is well suited to ideological media analysis for a number of reasons. It is worthwhile quoting him at length to understand his position:

> The analysis of production and transmission is essential to the interpretation of the ideological character of media messages because it sheds light on the institutions and social relations within which these messages are produced and diffused, as well as the aims and assumptions of the producers. The study of the construction of the media messages is essential because it examines the structural features by virtue of which they are complex symbolic phenomena, capable of mobilizing meaning. Finally, the study of the reception and appropriation of media messages is essential because it considers both the social-historical conditions within which messages are received by individuals and the ways in which these

individuals make sense of the messages and incorporate them into their lives. In drawing upon the analysis of these three aspects of mass communication, the process of interpretation may seek to explicate the connections between particular media messages, which are produced in certain circumstances and constructed in certain ways, and the social relations within which these messages are received and understood by individuals in the course of their everyday lives. In this way the process of interpretation can begin to explicate the ideological character of media messages, that is, the ways in which the meaning mobilized by particular messages may serve, in certain circumstances, to establish and sustain relations of domination. (1990: 306–7)

An investigation into:

1 The production and transmission or diffusion of symbolic forms.	2 The construction of the media message – especially its discursive dimension.	3 The reception and appropriation of media messages.

FIGURE 5.2   Three stages in ideological media analysis (Thompson, 1990)

This tripartite model is strongly interpretative in orientation and draws upon a range of research methodologies to achieve the desired end. The production and transmission of media messages or texts may be best understood through the uses of socio-historical analysis and ethnography. The structure of the media message is analysed through formal or discursive analysis. Audience reception and appropriation are explored through again using a combination of socio-historical analysis and ethnography.

We need therefore to combine these three aspects of media analysis in order to explore questions surrounding ideology. We need to understand the organizational circumstances in which specific media texts were produced; we need to closely examine the structure and content of these texts; and we need to examine what happens with media texts when they are put into circulation.

You should now read EXTRACTED READING 5.3, *Popular Culture and Ideology* (Abercrombie, Hill and Turner, 1990) and consider the following issue:

1   What are the main theoretical and methodological problems that researchers must overcome if they wish to undertake an ideological analysis of a media text?

The second part of Thompson's tripartite model makes explicit reference to formal or discursive analysis of media texts. In this final section we examine the importance of the discursive dimension of ideological analysis. Within media and communications studies the concept of discourse can go a long way in better informing analyses of ideology (see, for example, van Dijk, 1998a). A growing amount of research work has recently emerged using this conceptual framework and, to date, it has mainly examined media representations of unequal power relationships concerning race and class, for example, in a print media setting (see Bell, 1998; Fairclough, 2001; Fowler, 1991; van Dijk, 1991, 1998b).

BOX 5. 8   IDEOLOGICAL ANALYSIS IN PRACTICE

Dahlgren and discourse

Dahlgren's study 'Viewers' plural sense-making of TV news' (1992), while supportive of the concept of ideology, argues that previous ideological analysis suffers from an overly simplistic interpretation in terms of how texts function ideologically. Dahlgren argues that the crux of this problem is one of reconciling the polysemic 'openness' of a media text with the narrow parameters that a preferred (dominant ideological) reading requires. Dahlgren (1992) argues that the very openness of the text can actually assist in the reproduction of ideology through dissimulation. His analysis of viewer discourses on television news suggests that the openness of the text, irrespective of whether it contains contradictions or not, helps in the obfuscation and the circulation of ideology. Television news, he argues, presents a range of possible meanings, none of which assists the viewer in locating herself politically or socially. In masking the social structure through the use of open texts, dominant ideologies are produced and reproduced.

Radway and romance

<table>
<tr><td>

○○○

See Chapter 7 on
reception analysis

</td><td>

Janice Radway's *Reading the Romance: Women, Patriarchy and Popular Literature* (1987) is a good example of ideological analysis that opts to combine an examination of the production, content and reception of media texts. The study

</td></tr>
</table>

focuses on the role of romantic novels in the lives of forty-two women in a Midwestern US city. It is deservedly heralded as a milestone in the field of media and communications studies. Radway brings together interesting insights into the world of publishing, analysis of the narrative structure of romantic novels as well as a detailed account of the importance of these texts in the everyday lives of these female readers.

(Continued)

Racial stereotyping

Paek and Shah's (2003) examination of how US magazine advertising represents Asian Americans demonstrates how racial ideologies are employed within the media industry. Using a combination of quantitative content analysis and textual analysis, the researchers examine how advertising contained within three main-stream publications (*Time*, *Newsweek* and *US News and World Report*) resort to using stereotypes of Asian Americans. In a white-centric society, mass media discourse typically constructs ethnic groups through the use of negative media constructions. Historically, Asian Americans have been represented negatively. Paek and Shah's (2003) content and textual analysis shows however that their represen-tation has now changed and the discourses used within advertising suggest that Asian Americans are a 'model minority' group. In the context of racist media representations of non-white groups, this might seem like a positive development. It is however problematic for a number of reasons. The homogenizing of Asian Americans ignores differences within the Asian American diaspora and it also implies the existence of a hierarchy in terms of the various ethnicities which make up US society and specifically in terms of those groups who are more like 'us' – i.e. being enterprising, high-achievers and successful.

Hegemonic and counter-hegemonic accounts of racism

Fraley and Lester-Roushanzamir (2004) demonstrate how the print media engage in the dissemination of dominant ideology. By focusing on how race and class are por-trayed, they compare media coverage of the shooting dead of Fred Hampton, the Chicago-based Black Panther leader in December 1969. Fraley and Lester-Roushanzamir show how the mainstream print media operated not as a public sphere but rather as a state ideological apparatus reproducing an ideology sup-portive of the (white) ruling class.

The concepts of *dominant ideology* and *moral panic* are applied in order to reach a critical understanding of how the mainstream and Black press covered the killing of Fred Hampton and his colleague Mark Clark. The authors' textual analysis suggests that the *Chicago Tribune* clearly reproduced a dominant or hegemonic ideological position, whilst the *Chicago Daily Defender* countered this by offering an alternative account of the same set of events with particular reference to racism and unequal power relations. The hegemonic version relied heavily on police sources. This is an important example, they argue, of a 'discursive battle' (2004: 163) between main-stream/hegemonic and counter-hegemonic accounts of a single event. Fraley and Lester-Roushanzamir conclude that the mainstream print media fulfil an important ide-ological function for the powerful and that in the context of increased conglomeration, it is becoming more difficult to identify a set of alternative discourses.

Like ideology, the concept of discourse is notoriously problematic. It suffers greatly from the often ambiguous ways in which it is used. There are tensions in the field between those who use both concepts in a complementary way and those who have abandoned the concept of ideology altogether in favour of discourse.

Postmodern and more traditional approaches to media analysis are sharply divided over whether ideologies can be shown to actually exist at all outside of media texts or representations. The postmodern focus on the connections between language and social structure draws heavily on the late French theorist Michel Foucault's writings on discourse. Foucault was interested in examining how specific discourses or forms of knowledge exercise power over members of society. As Bilton et al. state:

> Foucault's perspective on social life is . . . fundamentally concerned with power. Prevailing forms of knowledge or discourse exercise power over us because they provide us with the language we use to think about the world, and thereby 'know' about it. These discourses constitute us (make us what we are and what we think) because we have to use their vocabularies to make sense of events and phenomena. (2002: 235)

In Foucault's work a discourse or discursive formation 'is at once singularly authoritative and deployed in the interests of existing structures of authority and power' (Deacon et al., 1999: 147). In attempting to understand the media, many postmodernists argue that the only 'reality' – ideological or otherwise – that exists resides within the multitude of discursive formations which individual audience members encounter in the course of their media consumption, i.e. within media texts.

The postmodern perspective ignores the numerous attempts by elite groups to shape certain media agendas such as news programming in favour of their chosen ideological position. It also ignores the increasingly concentrated nature of media ownership by elite groups and the fact that the mainstream media in actuality reflect the interests of these elite groups within much of their media content. A more traditional approach would hold that dominant ideologies such as racism or homophobia or capitalism, for that matter, do not merely reside within media texts. There are clear linkages between media representations of the social world and the existence and persistence of social inequalities.

Marrying ideology and discourse

It is our belief that the concepts of ideology and discourse play complementary roles in furthering our understanding of the media's role in the reproduction of unequal power relationships in society. A critical discourse analysis has the potential to deepen our understanding of the media's ideological role. It can be used to examine how media texts are structured and how they may ultimately function at an ideological level. It can also be used to analyse the discourses employed by both media professionals and media audiences in the production and reception of media texts.

Discourse analysis is sometimes referred to as the analysis of text and talk (for an overview see van Dijk, 1998a). Deacon et al. (1999) argue that, as a core part of a critical linguistics, discourse analysis has two main concerns. First, it is interested in examining the use of language in social life and, second, it is interested in investigating the relationships between language use and social structure. Deacon et al. argue that discourse analysis:

enables us to focus not only on the actual uses of language as a form of social interaction, in particular situations and contexts, but also on *forms of representation* in which different social categories, different social practices and relations are constructed from and in the interests of a particular point of view, a particular conception of social reality. (1999: 146; emphasis added)

It is this second strand of discourse analysis, with its emphasis on discourse within forms of representation and its focus on social structure/power relationships, that is of particular relevance to us, given our interest in the mass media's ideological role.

Empirical research work using a discourse analysis approach has an interest in the ways in which text and talk represent asymmetrical relationships of power. Discourse analysis, with its detailed emphasis on the workings of language in respect of power relationships, has much to offer the media student. It can help us unpack the possible readings that may reside in a media text. For Deacon et al. (1999), the 'critical scope and potential of discourse analysis resides most of all in its examination of how relations and structures of power are embedded in everyday language use, and thus how language contributes to the legitimisation of existing social relations and hierarchies of authority and control' (1999: 150). Furthermore, they argue that discourse analysis is well suited to doing detailed investigative work into the ideological dimensions of talk and texts:

Discourse analysis can show these processes at work in the realm of natural language by pointing to attempts to close meaning down, to fix it in relation to a given position, to make certain conventions self-evidently correct, to do creative repair work when something becomes problematic, and to make the subject positions of discourse transparently obvious without any visible alternatives. (1999: 154)

An understanding of the discursive dimension of media texts is a crucial aspect of doing ideological analysis. Discourses that are supportive of dominant ideology do so through legitimizing unequal relationships of power. Such relationships are reified and presented as natural and inevitable. By examining media texts at this micro-level in a detailed and systematic way, we can begin to appreciate how texts are structured as discourses and ask whether or not these discourses support or challenge dominant ideologies. A critical understanding of media discourses is necessary if we want to ask about the production and reception of media texts that we consider to be ideological in orientation.

BOX 5. 9 IDEOLOGY AND DISCOURSE

Van Dijk's study *Ideology: A Multidisciplinary Approach* (1998a) is an important account of how we should approach the analysis of dominant and other forms of ideology. Because of its very complexity, we need, he argues, to take a multifaceted approach in order to understand more about how ideologies work. Van Dijk proposes that we concentrate on the conceptual and disciplinary triangle of cognition, society and discourse. If we want to move away from abstract and ambiguous notions of ideology towards an undersanding of what ideologies 'actually look like' (1998a: 5), then we have to make use of the theoretical and methodological tools of analysis available to us from psychology, sociology and linguistics. In van Dijk's account, discourse plays a central (though not exclusive) role in the dissemination of ideology. He argues that:

> Discourse has a special function in the implementation and especially the reproduction of ideologies, since it is only through language use, discourse or communication (or other semiotic practices) that they can be explicitly formulated. This is essential in contexts of acquisition, argumentation, ideological conflict, persuasion and other processes in the formation and change of ideologies. (1998a: 316–17)

We need to examine, in detail, the discursive formations that occur in text, talk and other contexts if we wish to understand how ideologies are constructed, circulated and how they may change.

Chapter 6 will discuss an example from van Dijk's analysis of media.

Van Dijk proposes a rigorous and detailed model of analysis in examining the discursive dimensions of ideology. As well as taking account of the type of communicative genre and participants/participant roles involved, when we come to analyse communicative events in terms of their ideological aspect, our focus should not be restricted to their semantic properties. We should also consider, for example, their 'phonological, graphical, syntactic, lexical, stylistic, rhetorical, schematic (e.g. argumentative, narrative) pragmatic and conversational structures' (1998a: 317). The lexical dimension has received the bulk of attention from those interested in analysing the relationship between ideology and discourse. Here 'a negative concept of a group is represented in a model, and depending on context, the most "appropriate" word is selected, in such a way that an outgroup is referred to and at the same time an opinion about them' (1998a: 270). Thus we can read and hear about, for example, 'fundamentalists', 'welfare scroungers', 'bogus asylum seekers', 'the flood of refugees', 'foreign nationals', 'refugee rapist on the rampage', 'the devil's poor', 'militant and terrorist groups' and 'striking workers'. When we come to undertake ideological analysis of this kind, we are interested in examining how the lexical and the other aforementioned devices help to define 'us' and 'them'. How do they work to shape one group's thinking about another?

BOX 5.10   DISCOURSE ANALYSIS IN PRACTICE

Walker's (2005) examination of the liberal Mexican newspaper *La Jornada* uses a critical discourse analysis approach in order to understand how unequal power relationships in terms of both gender and race/ethnicity are narrowly constructed within media discourse. Her research reminds us that borders are not merely geographical, political or economic constructs; they also operate at a symbolic level. As symbolic entities they are 'sexed' and 'raced'. In examining the discourses within three selected newspaper articles, Walker (2005) demonstrates that hegemonic rather than counter-hegemonic discourses are in evidence – despite *La Jornada*'s liberal reputation. Using a qualitative content analysis approach and a close critical reading of the newspaper articles, Walker shows how 'discursive violence, "narratives of eviction" and silences are implicated in the construction of women as weak, sexualized objects, and Mexicans as raced, backward "others"' (2005: 95).

By focusing on the discourses employed within media content, Walker (2005) interrogates many of the assumptions contained within media discourse. A basic assumption is that underdeveloped Mexico can and should move along the same path of economic development as its neighbour the United States. The exploitation of women (in a variety of ways) is assumed to be a mere symptom of the globalization process. Walker (2005: 95–6) identifies four discursive moments in terms of the representation of women. These are discourses which construct women as (1) anonymous replaceable bodies; (2) victims of the border city; (3) dependent appendages; (4) 'Guada-Narco-Lupe' (combining images of virginity and criminality, especially in relation to drug-trafficking). Mexicans, as a whole, are constituted as a racialized 'other' to the inhabitants of the USA. She notes that within media discourses about Mexicans, the words 'poverty', 'lack', 'marginalization' and 'empty communities' appear repeatedly (2005: 106).

Walker situates the examination of discourse within a media setting in a much larger ideological context. Her critical reading of these three newspaper articles is grounded in the wider ideological context of US – Mexican political and economic relationships. The 'scripting' of women and Mexicans by hegemonic media discourse has to be read in terms of dominant patriarchal and racist ideologies in existence outside of the media texts examined.

CRITICAL QUESTIONS 5.2   CINEMA AND 'QUEER' DISCOURSES

Select a film of your choice that deals with being gay, lesbian, or bisexual. Try to identify the dominant and other discourses that reside within your chosen text. What are the key devices used by the filmmaker in constructing a particular discourse about being gay, lesbian or bisexual? How do these discourses relate to dominant hegemonic heterosexist ideologies? Is being gay pathologized or normalized? We recommend the following films: *Brokeback Mountain* (directed by Ang Lee, 2005); *The Adventures of Priscilla, Queen of the Desert* (directed by Stephan Elliot, 1993); *My Beautiful Laundrette* (directed by Stephen Frears, 1986).

∞∞∞

See Chapter 6 for further discussion on gender and sexuality.

In examining queer discourses in a cinematic context, compare any one of these films with the representation of gay men and women in mainstream television series such as *Queer as Folk*, *The L Word*, *Six Feet Under*, *Sex and the City*, *Queer Eye for the Straight Guy*, *Will and Grace* and *Ellen*.

For a discussion of 'Queer' discourses see P. Burston and C. Richardson (1995) (eds) A *Queer Romance: Lesbians, Gay Men and Popular Culture*. London: Routledge.

Conclusion

The postmodern world is often characterized as being fragmented. It is clearly a divided and unequal world. The collapse of communism and the decline in structuralist sociology in the 1990s had significant implications for the concept of ideology. At the beginning of this chapter we noted that at a time when the right is in resurgence, when the social world is being increasingly privatized, when citizenship is being downplayed in the context of the new-found emphasis on the market and consumption, and when fundamentalism – both Christian and Islamic – is re-emergent, the death knell of the concept of ideology is being prematurely heralded by many. This chapter has attempted to restate the significance of ideology as a concept within social theory and has warned against a metaphorical 'throwing out the baby with the bath water'. Ideological analysis of the mass media is clearly a contentious zone within media studies. Such analysis of the mass media – if undertaken properly – should be retained as a critical component in terms of how we understand the media. We need, however, to proceed with some caution.

One way of overcoming the kinds of pitfalls traditionally associated with doing ideological analysis is to combine analyses of production, content and reception. By emphasizing the hermeneutic dimension, we can begin to examine how certain kinds of media content reinforce or challenge existing public discourses by reference to what audiences ultimately believe.

The concentration in this chapter on ideology as *dominant* ideology means that, by definition, a wider range of ideologies potentially exist within media content.

A sophisticated ideological analysis of the media should pay particular attention to the potential range of ideological positions among the media professionals involved, the kinds of discourses (dominant and otherwise) used in the text, and the range of possible readings that audiences may place upon the text. The ideological import of media content, however, is not in itself obviated by alternative audience readings of a text. Moreover, we need to realize that certain kinds of media genres – such as television news, tabloid newspapers and magazines – are more amenable than others to the reproduction of ideologies that sustain unequal relations of power. A balance needs to be struck between the capacity of audience members to reject or reconstruct dominant ideology and the fact that media organizations and media content have been shown to possess significant power in constructing and shaping the ideological effect in the short, medium and long term.

Extracted readings

5.1 A propaganda model

E.S. Herman and N. Chomsky, *Manufacturing Consent: The Political Economy of the Mass Media*. London: Vintage, 1994, pp. 1–2

The mass media serve as a system for communicating messages and symbols to the general populace. It is their function to amuse, entertain, and inform and to inculcate individuals with the values, beliefs, and codes of behaviour that will integrate them into the institutional structures of the larger society. In a world of concentrated wealth and major conflicts of class interest, to fulfil this role requires systematic propaganda.

In countries where the levers of power are in the hands of a state bureaucracy, the monopolistic control over the media, often supplemented by official censorship, makes it clear that the media serve the ends of a dominant elite. It is much more difficult to see a propaganda system at work where the media are private and formal censorship is absent. This is especially true where the media actively compete, periodically attack and expose corporate and governmental malfeasance, and aggressively portray themselves as spokesmen for free speech and the general community interest. What is not evident (and remains undiscussed in the media) is the limited nature of such critiques, as well as the huge inequality in command of resources, and its effect both on access to a private media system and on its behaviour and performance.

A propaganda model focuses on this inequality of wealth and power and its multi-level effects on mass-media interests and choices. It traces the routes for which money and power are able to filter out the news fit to print, marginalize dissent, and allow the government and dominant private interests to get their message across to the public. The essential ingredients of our propaganda model, or set of news 'filters', fall under the following headings: (1) the size, concentrated ownership, owner wealth, and profit orientation of the dominant mass media firms; (2) advertising as the primary income source of the mass media; (3) the reliance of the media on information supplied by government, business and 'experts' funded and approved by these primary sources and agents of power; (4) 'flak' as a means of disciplining the media; and (5) 'anti-communism' as a national religion and control mechanism. . . .

The elite domination of the media and marginalisation of dissidents that results from the operation of these filters occurs so naturally that media news people, frequently operating with complete integrity and goodwill, are able to convince themselves that they interpret and choose the news 'objectively' and on the basis of professional news values. Within the limits of the filter constraints they often are objective; the constraints are so powerful, and are built into the system in such a fundamental way, that alternative bases of news choices are hardly imaginable.

5.2   A social theory of mass communication

John B. Thompson, 'A social theory of mass communication' in J.B. Thompson, *Ideology and Modern Culture*. Cambridge: Polity Press, 1990, pp. 267–8

This is a shortcoming because it cannot be assumed that the messages diffused by media institutions will have, by virtue of the organization of these institutions or the characteristics of the messages themselves, a given effect when the messages are received and appropriated by individuals in the course of their everyday lives. It cannot be assumed that the individuals who receive media messages will, by the very fact of receiving them, be impelled to act in an imitative and conforming way and thereby be bound to the social order which their actions, and the messages which allegedly impel them, serve to reproduce. The fact that the continuous and reverent portrayal of Ceauçescu and his entourage on Romanian state television did little to win them a secure place in the hearts and minds of the Romanian people is vivid testimony to the weakness of this assumption. Based on . . . the fallacy of internalism, this whole approach to the ideological character of mass communication takes too much for granted and must be replaced by an approach which considers more carefully the specific contexts and processes in which the messages produced and diffused by media institutions are appropriated by the individuals who receive them.

We can begin to make this reorientation by situating the analysis of the ideological character of mass communication within the framework of . . . technically mediated quasi-interaction. The structure and content of media messages must be analysed in relation to their production within the primary interactive framework and their reception within the primary reception region, as well as in relation to the quasi-interaction sustained between communicators and recipients and the subsequent social interactions in which the content of media messages is incorporated and elaborated. Moreover, these interlocking frameworks of interaction are always embedded in broader sets of social relations and institutions which are structured in certain ways. It is only by analysing the structure and content of media messages in relation to these frameworks of interaction and encompassing sets of social relations that we can examine the ideological character of media products. For these products, like all symbolic forms, are not ideological in themselves; rather, they are ideological only in so far as, in particular sets of social-historical circumstances, they serve to establish and sustain relations of domination.

5.3   Popular culture and ideology

Nicholas Abercrombie, 'Popular culture and ideological effects' in Nicholas Abercrombie, Stephen Hill and Bryan S. Turner (eds) *Dominant Ideologies*. London: Unwin Hyman, 1990, pp. 202–4

What would be meant by saying that popular culture has ideological force? Provisionally the following four features are relevant:

1   Popular culture encapsulates a particular (hegemonic) view of the world, even if it has to accommodate other views.
2   This particular view of the world is widely available in society, perhaps the most widely available.
3   Popular culture conceals, misrepresents and secures an order of domination.
4   This concealment is in the interests of a particular (ruling) group, social formation or form of society.

What are the conditions for these propositions to be true? To illuminate this question it is useful, following Hall (1980) to distinguish three moments – production, text and appropriation – when carrying out a sociological analysis of any cultural form. Generally speaking, any analysis of this kind is notoriously difficult and controversial. That reading, whether it is a television programme, film, book, or advertisement, establishes the dominant themes, codes, or discourses in the text. In so coding, a sociological problem is established, since the sociologist wants to know, on the one hand, why the text carries a particular discourse and, on the other hand, what an audience will do with the text. Therefore, a complete account has to start from the text but it has to move on from there to consider the means of production and appropriation. As Hall (1980) points out, it is not simply a matter of looking at the three moments independently; it is actually the way that they fit together that is of chief interest in considering the relationship between cultural form and ideology.

. . . Before looking at the three moments of ideology in detail, a methodological problem needs to be mentioned. Can one say that there is ideology in a text independently of any audience reaction? Are [they] separable or can one reduce ideology to ideological effect?

The proposal that ideology is really a particular effect of a discourse is seductive. If we are able to say that a discourse is ideological, to the extent that it affects an audience so that the existing relations of domination are secured, we would at least avoid traditional hermeneutic problems. Instead of arguing over rival interpretations of a text, we would only have to find out how audiences appropriate the text.

--------------------------- Exercise 5.1 ---------------------------

Ideology and dominant ideology in newspapers

This exercise requires you to combine some basic qualitative content analysis with an investigation into audience response to a small sample of newspaper articles on a selected theme.

Depending upon your individual circumstances, you may do this exercise on your own or as part of a collaborative effort with some of your fellow students.

The exercise

In the light of what you have read about ideology and ideological analysis in this chapter, write a critical commentary of no more than 1,000 words on the ideological content of a newspaper of your choice. Identify who owns the publication and, where possible, note its reputed ideological position. Select a maximum of ten articles on a specific theme from the publication in question and explain how, in your opinion, these articles function at an ideological level. It is essential that you give equal weighting in your report to the content analysis and the responses from your sample of audience members.

Content analysis

In doing the content analysis please highlight the following:

1   The author(s) of the selected articles.
2   The word length of the selected articles.
3   The kind of article (e.g. news story/feature/editorial/op. ed., i.e. opinion pieces that appear opposite the editorial).
4   The location of the article within the newspaper.
5   The stylistic devices employed in presenting the article.
6   If photographic images or other kinds of illustrations are used, how do these relate to the ideological dimension(s) of the specific article?
7   The use of sources and spokespersons if cited.
8   The kinds of ideological perspectives in evidence within the coverage.
9   The use of omission – of alternative perspectives or understandings of the phenomena in question – in so far as you can see such.

Audience response

In the second phase of the exercise, select at least three samples of audience groups. The structuring of the audience groups should be based upon age, gender and educational attainment. Each group member is asked to do a close reading of the selected texts and then, using informal or unstructured interviewing, you investigate the kinds of readings that your selected members place upon each of these texts.

The commentary

In beginning the commentary itself, please state clearly what you understand by the terms 'ideology', 'dominant ideology' and 'discourse'. The main body of the report should highlight the following:

(Continued)

1 What you consider to be the ideological nature of your selected articles and why?
2 What kinds of ideologies and discourses are reproduced within the coverage?
3 How do these ideologies relate to existing public discourses about your chosen research theme?
4 Does the coverage reproduce the dominant ideology, counter-ideologies or both?
5 What sorts of audience response(s) did you get from the various sample groups? To what extent did their readings of the articles vary from your initial content analysis?
6 If there was a variety of readings or interpretations of the selected articles by your audience groups, how do you explain this?

Questions for consideration and discussion

1 What arguments may be made for or against the proposition that 'In the twenty-first century ideology is a redundant concept'?
2 Outline and explain what you understand by 'open' and 'closed' definitions of ideology. How might these concepts be applied in a mass media setting?
3 Does media globalization mean more or less dominant ideology within mainstream media content?
4 If dominant ideology exists within media content what does this say about media professionals?

References

Abercrombie, N., S. Hill and B.S. Turner (eds) (1990) *Dominant Ideologies*. London: Unwin Hyman.

Bell, A. (1998) 'The discourse structure of news stories' in A. Bell and P. Garrett (eds) *Approaches to Media Discourse*. Oxford: Blackwell.

Bilton, T., K. Bonnett, P. Jones, T. Lawson, D. Skinner, M. Stanworth and A. Webster (2002) *Introductory Sociology*. London: Palgrave Macmillan.

Burston, P. and C. Richardson (eds) (1995) *A Queer Romance: Lesbians, Gay Men and Popular Culture*. London: Routledge.

Corcoran, F. (1984) 'Television as ideological apparatus: the power and the pleasure', *Critical Studies in Mass Communication* 1: 131–45.

Corner, J. (2001) 'Ideology: a note on conceptual salvage', *Media, Culture and Society* 23(4): 525–33.

Creeber, G. (2006) 'Television, ideology and discourse' in G. Creeber (ed.) *Tele-Visions*. London: BFI.

Dahlgren, P. (1992) 'Viewers' plural sense-making of TV news' in P. Scannell, P. Schlesinger and C. Sparks (eds) *Culture and Power*. London: Sage.

Deacon, D., M. Pickering, P. Golding and G. Murdock (1999) *Researching Communications*. London: Arnold.

Devereux, E. (1998) *Devils and Angels: Television, Ideology and the Coverage of Poverty*. Luton: University of Luton Press/John Libbey Media.

Devereux, E. (2006) 'Media and mass media' in A. Harrington, B. Marshall and H.P. Muller (eds.) *The Routledge Encyclopaedia of Social Theory*. London: Routledge.

van Dijk, T.A. (1991) *Racism and the Press*. London: Routledge.

van Dijk, T.A. (1998a) *Ideology: A Multidisciplinary Approach*. London: Sage.

van Dijk, T.A. (1998b) 'Opinions and ideologies in the press' in A. Bell and P. Garrett (eds) *Approaches to Media Discourse*. Oxford: Blackwell.

Dutton, B. (1986) *Sociology in Focus: The Media*. London: Longman.

Eagleton, T. (1991) *Ideology: An Introduction*. London: Verso.

Fairclough, N. (2001) *Language and Power*, 2nd edn. Harlow: Longman.

Ferguson, R. (1998) *Representing 'Race': Ideology, Identity and the Media*. London: Arnold.

Fiske, J. (1987) *Television Culture*. London: Methuen.

Fowler, R. (1991) *Language in the News*. London and New York: Routledge.

Fraley, T. and E. Lester-Roushanzamir (2004) 'Revolutionary leader or deviant thug? A comparative analysis of the *Chicago Tribune* and *Chicago Daily Defender's* reporting of the killing of Fred Hampton', *The Howard Journal of Communication* 15: 147–67.

Frazer, E. (1992) 'Teenage girls reading *Jackie*' in P. Scannell, P. Schlesinger and C. Sparks (eds) *Culture and Power*. London: Sage.

Gitlin, T. (1980) *The Whole World is Watching*. Berkeley and Los Angeles: University of California Press.

Gunter, B. (2000) *Media Research Methods*. London: Sage.

Hall, S. (1980) 'Encoding/decoding' in S. Hall et al. (eds) *Culture, Media and Language*. London: Hutchinson.

Hawkes, D. (2003) *Ideology*, 2nd edn. London: Routledge.

Kumar, D. (2006) 'Media, war and propaganda: strategies of information management during the 2003 Iraq war', *Communication and Critical/Cultural Studies* 3(1): 48–69.

Marcuse, H. (1964) *One Dimensional Man*. Boston: Beacon Press.

Moore, M. (2002) *Stupid White Men*, 2nd edn. London: Penguin.

Paek, H.J. and H. Shah (2003) 'Racial ideology, model minorities, and the "not-so-silent partner:" stereotyping of Asian Americans in U.S. magazine advertising', *Howard Journal of Communication* 14: 225–43.

Radway, J. (1987) *Reading the Romance: Women, Patriarchy and Popular Literature*. London: Verso.

Stabile, C.A. and D. Kumar (2005) 'Unveiling imperialism: media, gender and the war on Afghanistan', *Media, Culture and Society* 27(5): 765–82.

Thompson, J.B. (1990) *Ideology and Modern Culture*. Cambridge: Polity Press.

Tumber, H. and J. Palmer (2004) *The Media at War*. London: Sage.

Walker, M.A. (2005) 'Guada-narco-lupe, maquilarañas and the discursive construction of gender and difference on the US–Mexico border in Mexican media re-presentations', *Gender, Place and Culture* 12(1): 95–111.

Wheen, F. (1999) *Karl Marx*. London: Fourth Estate.

Teun van Dijk's homepage is an invaluable resource for students interested in learning more about ideology and discourse. See www.discourses.org. See also Noam Chomsky's homepage for a critical interpretation of current global events at www.chomsky.info. Norman Fairclough's website also contains downloadable articles on discourse analysis; see www.ling.lancs.ac.uk/staff/norman/norman.htm.

Bell, A. and P. Garrett (eds) (1998) *Approaches to Media Discourse*. Oxford: Blackwell. Nine essays by some of the world's key thinkers on discourse including van Dijk, Bell and Fairclough.

Blommaert, J. (2005) *Discourse: A Critical Introduction*. Cambridge: Cambridge University Press. This book focuses on the methods and theories involved in undertaking critical discourse analysis.

Gitlin, T. (2003) *The Whole World Is Watching*. California: University of California Press. This new edition of Gitlin's (1980) text contains an updated preface by the author. The text is an essential read for media students.

Hawkes, D. (2003) *Ideology*, 2nd edn. London: Routledge. The second edition of Hawkes' book examines the continued importance of ideology in a post-9/11 world. See his chapter 4 on Marxism in particular.

O'Keefe, A. (2006) *Investigating Media Discourse*. London: Routledge. O'Keefe's book is focused on how we analyse the spoken word in a mass media setting. Her text includes analysis of interviews with George Bush and Tony Blair.

6

ANALYSING MEDIA CONTENT: MEDIA 'RE-PRESENTATIONS' IN A DIVIDED WORLD

Summary

This chapter introduces you to the following:

- The main issues surrounding the analysis of media content.
- Quantitative and qualitative content analysis.
- Media representations of poverty in the developed world and the Third World.
- Media representations of class, ethnicity, gender and sexuality.

Key concepts

- Media content
- Representation and 're-presentation'
- Quantitative content analysis
- Qualitative content analysis

- Semiotic, discourse, frame and narrative analysis
- Social structure
- Class, ethnicity, gender and sexuality
- The 'deserving' and the 'undeserving' poor

Content is at the centre of the relationship between the media industries and media audiences. In this chapter we discuss the main issues involved in approaching the analysis of media content. In doing so, and in furthering our discussion of ideology and discourse from the previous chapter, we consciously place an emphasis upon how mass media content represents *unequal* relationships of power in the social world. Media content, as we noted in Chapters 4 and 5, is socially constructed. Content is not fixed but rather changes over time. It is socially and culturally determined. It contains many clues as to the make-up of the social structure that determines so much about all of our lives.

Media content matters because it is within media content that the shaping and framing of our understanding and perceptions of the social world takes place. Media content provides us with the many 'scripts' necessary for us to negotiate and make sense of the social contexts in which we find ourselves in our everyday lives. Media content informs us about the personal and the political. Understanding media content is crucial in terms of reaching a more informed understanding of how we form views, opinions and attitudes about groups who are considered 'other'. The 'other' may comprise a range of 'out' groups in any society. They may be the poor, the homeless, the colonized, the underclass, ex-prisoners, the mentally ill and immigrants, for example (see Triandafyllidou, 1998). Those who are othered are regularly constructed as a threat to the moral and social order (see Harding, 2006; Haynes et al., 2006).

Using the popular BBC (UK) situation comedy *The Royle Family* as an example, the chapter begins by highlighting some of the ways in which we can approach the analysis of media content. Content analysis of both quantitative and qualitative persuasions is then outlined. Generally speaking, two competing approaches to analysing media content exist. The first is enumerative, usually involving the analysis of specific aspects of a large volume of media texts. Quantitative content analysis has been extensively used in the analysis of the traditional print and broadcast media. The second form of content analysis is strongly interpretative in orientation. Selected media texts are analysed in terms of both their manifest (obvious) and latent (hidden) meanings. Qualitative content analysis has been employed to examine a wider range of media than its quantitative counterpart. It has been successfully used in conjunction with analyses of audience reception and ethnographic accounts of media production (Devereux, 1998).

Given the overt emphasis in this textbook on unequal power relations and the particular focus in this chapter on the 'divided world', we discuss a number of examples of how qualitative content analysis has been applied towards furthering our understanding of media representations of poverty, inequality and exclusion in the developed world and the Third World. The chapter proceeds to examine media representations of class, ethnicity, gender and sexuality. These aspects of social structure are discussed by drawing upon a range of qualitative methodological approaches applied to a mixture of media. The chapter contains three extracted readings. These examine the construction of a short media text from the perspective of a film director working on a fundraising or telethon television programme; the dominant themes in British print media coverage of so-called 'scrounging' or social welfare fraud; and media representations of gay men and women. In all of its guises, content analysis represents a crucial aspect of our overall endeavours in trying to understand the media. It is best used as part of a research approach that also examines production and reception.

Representation/re-presentation and 'reality'

An appreciation of how and why we should analyse media content is important for a number of key reasons. First, media content is a powerful source of meaning about the social world (see, for example, Breen, 2000; Dahlgren, 1981; Iyengar and Kinder, 1987). Take, for example, how ethnic minorities are represented in a media setting. That media coverage tends to problematize minorities is confirmed by a large number of studies. Gomes and Williams (1991), for example, examine how the media construct a connection between race and crime. Soubiran-Paillet (1987) investigates the representation of minorities in crime reports in the French and Swiss press (see also Winkel, 1990). Importantly, this kind of media coverage has been found to be of significance in the shaping of public attitudes towards minority groups such as refugees or asylum seekers (see, for example, Haynes et al., 2005, 2006; Schaffert, 1992, and our discussion of van Dijk, 1991, later in this chapter).

Second, while media content does not equate with social reality, it is essential that we examine how media content represents, or more accurately 're-presents', the realities involved in social, economic and political relationships. Given the apparent shrinkage of media content of a more critical nature – owing in no small part to growing concentration and conglomeration – this issue is particularly germane. Whose version of 'reality' do we mainly see or hear about in a media setting? Does the predominance of a hegemonic discourse about class, ethnicity, gender or sexuality have a bearing on what audiences believe about the social world?

In this regard it is essential that a critical media studies continues to ask questions such as:

1   What does media content tell us about unequal relationships of power?
2   Whose interests are served by misrepresentation (or under-representation) within media content?
3   What discourses and/or ideologies are employed in order to tell stories about the social world?
4   What aspects do they highlight?
5   What aspects do they ignore?
6   How do particular forms of media content shape public opinion and public policy?
7   How and why do particular forms of media representation about class, ethnicity, gender or sexuality change over time?

ANALYSING MEDIA CONTENT

```
○○○
See also
Extracted
Reading 7.1
```
Analysing media content, however, is a contentious business. If audiences are active agents in the construction of meaning, why should we bother to analyse content at all? A critical understanding of media content is an important part of understanding where power resides in creating meaning for audiences. In a strong defence of why we should continue to have an interest in the effects of media content, Kitzinger argues convincingly that: 'We cannot afford to dismiss inquiry into media influence as "old-fashioned" or doomed to failure as it confronts the complexity of text–audience relations. Cultural representations and media power matter' (1999: 15). They matter because they shape public beliefs and behaviour, a fact that is not lost on the economically or politically powerful. A balance needs to be struck therefore between the power of media audiences to deconstruct and resist media content and the power of media content to shape public perceptions about the world.

Many postmodernists would contest the very idea that we examine the relationship between media content and 'social reality'. (See for example Box 1.1 on Baudrillard.) From their perspective, media content constitutes a 'hyper-reality' for media audiences. An analysis of the relationship between media content and social structure would in this version of media studies appear to be redundant. Much of the empirical research work that has stemmed from the postmodern perspective has tended, however, to overstate the phenomenon of audience resistance. In examining some of the difficulties inherent in the postmodern perspective, Fenton notes that:

To claim that the media are our reality is further criticized by those who wish to point to the oppression of women as real. In this retort, reality is recognized as disorderly and fragmented but as also showing patterns of inequality. If the media are our reality it is argued that we effectively deny the existence of material inequalities unless they occur in representation. (2000: 729)

Quoting Kitzinger and Kitzinger, Fenton underlines the difficulties that postmodernism presents for a critical media studies:

Feminists struggled for decades to name 'sexism' and 'anti-lesbianism'. We said that particular images of women – bound and gagged in pornography magazines, draped over cars in advertisements, caricatured as mothers-in-law or nagging wives in sitcoms – were oppressive and downgrading. The deconstructionist insistence that texts have no inherent meanings, leaves us unable to make such claims. This denial of oppressive meanings is, in effect, a refusal to engage with the conditions under which texts are produced, and the uses to which they are put in the dominant culture (Kitzinger and Kitzinger, 1993: 15). (2000: 729)

In this book we are not proposing a simplistic 'effects' interpretation of media power. Understanding the complexity of media content and the reception of media texts calls for a model of analysis that is sophisticated, reliable and thorough.

We now demonstrate *some* of the choices available to us when thinking about approaching the analysis of media content by examining the British situation comedy *The Royle Family*.

CASE STUDY

Somewhere in the north of England (presumably Manchester) it is teatime in *The Royle Family* household. Jim Royle gets up from his armchair and switches on the television set. Soon he is joined by the rest of the family – his wife Barbara, son Anthony and daughter Denise – to talk about and to the television set. Later they will be joined by Barbara's mother Norma and Denise's husband Dave. From previous viewings we know that Jim Royle is unemployed and that Barbara has recently returned to work outside the family home.

Over three series, the subject matter of this BBC (UK) situation comedy has largely centred on the conversations that the Royles have in their sitting room about each other, about television, about their immediate neighbours (Mary, Joe and Cheryl) and, occasionally, about the wider social world outside of their home. Television is a constant presence in their everyday lives. The programme's production values are kept fairly simple, and, at times, as a viewer or spectator, one is looking at the Royles through their television set. The action rarely stirs from this one location. *The Royle Family*, arguably, may be read as a nostalgic and humorous look at (white) working-class life in post-industrial Britain, a theme that was also in evidence in other forms of British popular culture in the early years of the twenty-first century such as the 'Britpop' phenomenon, when uncertainties about British identity resulted in a media focus on the 'authentic' Northern English (white) working class. It could also be said, however, that it exemplifies how even representations of working-class life have been commodified in the post-industrial or postmodern era.

Although they only make occasional reference to the outside world, the social positioning of the Royles as working class may be decoded from the things that they say about other social class groups above and below their social position. There are further clues as to their diasporic Irish roots in the occasional presence of Irish relatives at family events such as Baby David's christening. Their acquaintances in the underclass are referred to by their nicknames such as 'flat-nosed Alan', 'Twiggy' and 'Leggings Lorraine'. Their leisure time outside the sitting room centres on their local pub – the Feathers. As well as commenting (usually in the form of lampooning or criticizing) upon 'real' television personalities, the programme's characters hold forth on a wide range of family and other issues. Much of their conversation is concerned with domestic politics, with money and with who is responsible for which domestic task. Invariably, Barbara or Anthony ends up with the job in question.

(Continued)

We could approach an analysis of *The Royle Family*'s content in a number of ways. We could examine how it compares to other situation comedies or dramas in terms of how it represents working-class life (see Box 6.4 on *Shameless* for example). We could investigate how as a situation comedy it compares with other genres (such as the 'social problem' film, soap opera or the realist television documentary) in representing family life, class, gender or sexual politics, (see Hill, 1985). What are the limitations and possibilities of situation comedy in terms of what a text can say about these and other issues?

Plate 6.1   Jim Royle of *The Royle Family*. The text may be read as a nostalgic and humorous look at white working class life in post-industrial Britain. Photograph courtesy of BBC Photo Library (London) and Ricky Tomlinson © BBC.

We could examine the narrative structure of the programme by viewing all the episodes in the three series produced. Does the programme conform to a particular narrative structure? What sorts of narrative conventions does the programme employ?

We could examine the production values used in the series by focusing on the styles of camera work or incidental music employed by the programme's director. What sort of visual and aural language does the programme utilize?

We could examine one or more episodes of *The Royle Family* to see how the text works at a semiotic or symbolic level. What sorts of signifiers do the programme makers use in order to convey to audience members that this programme is about a working-class Manchester family? What sorts of signifiers are to be found in the Royle household?

We could investigate the Royles' use of (bad) language and accent. More particularly, we could examine how the programme's characters discourse about themselves, each other, television and the wider world. Such a focus might consider how men and women talk among themselves and to each other.

What do these fictional characters say about gender roles or sexual orientation, for example? What does the text say about masculinity and femininity in post-industrial Britain? What do they say about the state or the government? What does the programme as a whole have to say about gender politics in the post-industrial world? What do the Royles say about the underclass or the middle class in their midst? Skeggs, for example, suggests that the series 'presents a sustained attack on middle-class pretensions. Yet the middle-class are likely to misrecognize the nature of the class hatred it contains; they must, since the show has won so many art-culture system awards.' (2005: 975). How do the representations of working-class life in the Royles compare to other forms of media representation on so-called 'Chav' or underclass culture?

In considering *The Royle Family* as a whole, we could speculate as to whom the text is aimed at in audience terms. How does it position its male and female viewers? Whose version of working-class life do we see? Given that *The Royle Family* has been distributed and consumed in the global television market, we could usefully ask how it has been interpreted in diverse geographical and varying cultural contexts? How is the text read and understood by audiences?

We have briefly outlined some of the ways in which we could examine the contents of *The Royle Family*. None of these individual approaches is without its pitfalls, however.

In my reading of the text I have decoded *The Royle Family* as being representative of the working class. How did I decide upon this? Could the text be read differently by audience members from different cultural contexts or by researchers with different research interests? I have referred to the semiotic dimension of the text. How can I be certain that others would not interpret or read specific symbols in a contrary way?

What matters most however is the decision to select a specific theoretical and methodological approach in order to attempt to make sense of a selected media text – an issue to which we now devote some attention to below.

ANALYSING MEDIA CONTENT

Content analysis

Content analysis is typically used to identify the intentions and other characteristics of communicators, detect the existence of latent propaganda or ideology, reflect cultural patterns of groups, reveal the foci of organizations, and describe trends in communication content. It is often used as a way of comparing media content with the 'realities' of the social world. Researchers compare media representations about gender, ethnicity or class, for example, with social reality, as they interpret it.

Two types of content analysis – quantitative and qualitative – are used within the field of media research. Both have proved themselves to be popular if sometimes contentious research methods. Quantitative content analysis has its roots in the positivist social science tradition, while the qualitative content analysis approach has been influenced by developments within both structuralism and postmodernism. Qualitative content analysis is in fact a broad amalgamation of approaches, with different camps stressing the importance of examining, for example, the semiotic, framing, discursive or narrative dimensions of media texts. Many researchers use these approaches either singly or in combination and, given the positivist associations of the original term, many would not describe their work as being a form of content analysis at all.

> ∞∞∞
>
> *See our discussion of Thompson's (1990) tripartite model of undertaking ideological analysis in Chapter 5.*

Content analysis (whether quantitative or qualitative) is best employed as a research method in conjunction with other methodologies that focus on media producers who create the content in the first place and/or on media audiences who receive the media texts in question. A small number of researchers have combined quantitative and qualitative content analysis approaches to good effect (see Box 6.1 on the early work of the Glasgow University Media Group). The obvious danger in relying solely on content analysis is that meaning cannot simply be 'read off' a selected text, either through atomizing individual parts of a media text (such as a newspaper headline or the cover photograph of a magazine) within the quantitative paradigm or as in a 'close reading' of a media text within the qualitative model.

BOX 6.1   CONTENT ANALYSIS RESEARCH IN PRACTICE

In *Bad News* (1976) the Glasgow University Media Group adopt what McQuail (1983) refers to as a 'hybrid' methodological approach in undertaking a content analysis of British television news. They combine traditional quantitative content analysis with a structuralist approach in an attempt to unpack the coding of television news about industrial relations issues. Their focus is not only on the various elements

---

that make up news content about industrial relations issues, but also on the cultural codes that predominate within the media organizations that produce the media texts in question. The Glasgow University Media Group's research is located between quantitative and qualitative poles. In undertaking this path-breaking research, their task was not simply a counting of industrial relations news items, but rather, it was an attempt to interpret the meaning of those messages by searching beneath the manifest text to reveal the latent assumptions about social class. It is worth noting that, in more recent times, the research group have developed the News Game exercise in order to examine how audiences interpret media texts. This exercise has been used in combination with content analysis of media texts. The News game is discussed in more detail in Chapter 7.

See Chapter 7 for a discussion of the News Game.

Quantitative content analysis

The technique of traditional quantitative content analysis developed primarily by Berelson (1952) is based on the counting of phenomena. Following Berger, we take this form of content analysis to be a:

> research technique based upon measuring (counting) the amount of something (violence, percentages of Blacks, women, professional types or whatever) in a sampling of some form of communication (such as comics, sitcoms, soap operas, news shows). The basic assumption implicit in content analysis is that an investigation of messages and communication gives insights into the people who receive these messages. (1982: 107)

Quantitative content analysis, if designed properly, can be a useful research tool. It allows us to compare selected aspects of large amounts of media content over time or between media organizations, for example. One obvious problem with traditional content analysis is its assumption that specific forms of media content will have an effect (usually a negative one) on audiences. Traditional content analysis does not deal with questions of either effects or the multiple meanings that media texts may have for audiences.

CRITICAL QUESTION 6.1

What types of media genre would you think best suit a quantitative form of content analysis?

ANALYSING MEDIA CONTENT

Qualitative content analysis

Despite the continued use of quantitative content analysis by some researchers (see, for example, Baxter et al., 1985; Evans et al., 1991), the quantitative approach came in for a great deal of criticism in the last quarter of the twentieth century and was eventually supplemented by a form of qualitative content analysis that emphasized the notion of discourse (Woollacott, 1982). The move within media analysis from quantitative to qualitative content analysis is best summarized as a shift from empiricism to discourse. Van der Berg and van der Veer trace the move away from enumerative content analysis to an approach of a more qualitative kind. Because of its tendency to isolate specific elements of a media text, quantitative content analysis, they argue, 'is not capable of analysing communications as discourses' (1989: 161).

The newfound emphasis on media texts as a whole rather than just specific parts (for example, instances of particular kinds of representation, such as the age or shape of women in television advertising) of media messages meant that traditional quantitative content analysis came to be displaced. The emerging, and ultimately more sophisticated, qualitative content analysis approach within media research was influenced, in turn, by developments within semiotic, discourse, frame and narrative analysis. Readings of media texts as a whole, examining the latent as well as the manifest elements of content, relating specific media discourses to other discourses, became more of the norm within media research. Qualitative content analysis focusing on the symbolic, discursive, framing or narrative dimensions of media texts has worked in tandem with the reception analysis model of audience-based research.

CRITICAL QUESTION 6.2

What types of media genre would you think best suit a qualitative form of content analysis?

BOX 6.2   CONTENT ANALYSIS: WHERE TO START?

The following books contain accounts of content analysis that are accessible and easy to understand. For qualitative content analysis techniques consult: K. Bruhn Jensen and N.W. Jankowski (eds) *A Handbook of Qualitative Methodologies for Mass Communication Research*, London: Routledge (1991) and D.L. Altheide

---

Qualitative Media Analysis, London: Sage (1996). For quantitative content analysis consult the following texts: A.A. Berger (1998), *Media Research Techniques*, 2nd edn, London: Sage; A. Hansen, S. Cottle, R. Negrine and C. Newbold (1998), *Mass Communication Research Methods*, London: Macmillan; K. Krippendorf (2003) *Content Analysis: An Introduction to its Methodology*, 2nd edn., Thousand Oaks, CA: Sage.

Exercise 6.1

Comic books, gender roles and content analysis

Taking two stories from a comic book of your choice, carry out both a quantitative and a qualitative content analysis of the representation of gender roles. In the case of the quantitative content analysis, itemize the variables that you intend to count. In doing the qualitative analysis, clearly identify the themes that you propose to analyse. Having undertaken this research exercise, what do you think are the implications of choosing either a quantitative or a qualitative research approach in the analysis of content?

Media representations in a divided world: four approaches outlined

We now briefly examine four examples of qualitative content analysis. All share an interest in examining how mainstream media content represents poverty and inequality. The approaches of the individual authors vary in terms of their use of semiotic, discourse, frame or narrative analysis.

Sebeok defines semiotics as: 'the study of the exchange of any messages whatever and of the systems of signs which underlie them, the key concept of semiotics remaining always the sign' (1974: 108). *Discourse analysis*, as we saw in Chapter 5, refers to the analysis of text and talk in terms of how unequal power relationships are reproduced. *Frame analysis* is concerned with the interpretative frameworks used by media professionals in telling stories to media audiences (see Caragee and Roefs, 2004; Kitzinger, 2000; Breen et al., 2006). The focus of narrative analysis is on the narrative structure of individual media texts. Many researchers use these approaches in one or other combination, with discourse analysis being the most popular choice in recent times.

Semiotic analysis

Taking a semiotic approach, Benthall's work *Disasters, Relief and the Media* (1993) examines media images of disaster and disaster relief. Relief agencies and the media are critically examined in terms of how they use (and abuse) children as potent sources of imagery in the construction of media texts about the Third World.

Benthall divides his analysis of the semiotics of disaster relief into two periods, namely the pre- and post-1980s. He argues that in the pre-1980 period the imagery tends to be of a patronizing sort: 'Virtually all appeals for charity until the 1980s tended to picture helpless passive victims and heroic saviours' (1993: 177). These campaigns involve using both realistic photographic styles and the flagrant abuse of starving children. In the post-1980s period, Benthall states, his semiotic reading of the dominant imagery reveals that, in the West, 'we' portray colonized peoples in the same way as men portray women. This portrayal, he argues, exhibits anxiety about our expendability and the fear of forces that are beyond our control. Thus the West views Third World poverty as a threat because of the perceived implications it may have for Western society in terms of mass migration. Benthall's semiotic analysis also suggests that in the West we both exaggerate and misunderstand Third World poverty. He argues that essential questions in the overall equation such as colonialism and global capitalism are absent in terms of how we explain the Third World at a visual and a symbolic level.

Benthall's fascinating study draws upon the work of the Russian formalist Vladimir Propp (1928). In doing so he suggests that we should examine media images of the Third World as a form of folk narrative. Just as the folk tale follows a set of narrative conventions (having villains and heroes, etc.), so do images and stories about the Third World. They have heroes (from the West, usually white and middle-class, often well known in another role as actress, politician or pop star); villains (often portrayed as greedy dictators or tyrannical Marxists); donors (who are given magical powers) and false heroes (such as fundraisers who make off with the proceeds of a collection for the poor and starving).

Discourse analysis

In *Mass Media Discourse on Famine in the Horn of Africa*, Sorenson (1991) uses a discourse analysis approach in order to examine the activities of media organizations and the stories that they produce about the Third World. The media content that Sorenson analyses draws upon a number of discourses. These discourses emphasize famine as crisis – Ethiopian rather than African famine – and that famine is as a result of either natural causes or native culpability. These media discourses, he concludes, may be read as ideological texts. They are ideological because they do not challenge or question the existing power relationships between Africa and the West.

Sorenson's (1991) work confirms the general invisibility of Third World issues in a media setting (see, for example, Nohrstedt, 1986). He notes that, despite the availability of film footage and information about African famine in the early 1980s, the mass media in the West were reluctant to cover the story. He cites an unnamed journalist as saying: 'the Third World isn't news and starving Africans in particular are not news' (Sorenson, 1991: 224). Sorenson argues that during the 1980s the African famine story was largely absent from the Western media's agenda because it had, in media terms, 'a low entertainment value'. Coverage only occurred when a crisis point was reached in the famine.

A key feature, Sorenson stresses, 'in the discursive construction of famine in the Horn [of Africa] is that of aestheticisation, the packaging of famine as a shocking and dramatic crisis' (1991: 225). Thus famine, itself a common feature of many African countries, is not in itself deemed to be 'newsworthy' and is only given coverage through a discourse of impending or actual crisis. A further key element in the 1980s media discourse on African famine is the emphasis on Ethiopia as opposed to other stricken areas (presumably because of the presence of the Western media – albeit belatedly – in Ethiopia in 1984; for a critical account see Philo, 1993). The 'naturalization' dimension of the coverage is also stressed – coverage tends to emphasize the notion that famine occurs as a result of natural causes (such as climate or crop failure) as opposed to man-made ones.

Sorenson's main assertion is that media coverage of famine represents an ideological parable:

> Analysis reveals imposition of a narrative structure through the use of standard rhetorical techniques to construct famine as an ideological parable. This parable demonstrates the abuse of Western charity by treacherous Third World regimes allied with the Soviet Union. Media reports are related to other discursive constructions of Africa which offer a similar narrative structure. (1991: 223)

Sorenson uses an analysis of *Newsweek* magazine (26 November 1984) to illustrate this argument. He concludes that the discourse of this edition 'reveals a mythologizing of famine and the imposition of a narrative structure which serves to emphasize the culpability of Africans' (1991: 227). Africans are represented as being either incompetent or greedy while the West is represented as a kind and generous benefactor.

Drawing on the approach taken by French theorist Roland Barthes in his book *Mythologies* (1973), Sorenson concludes that this type of media activity is in fact a form of inoculation. In engaging in this kind of practice, the media admit to the occurrence of 'accidental evil' (poverty and famine) and yet function to conceal the wider structural inequalities that cause Third World poverty and famine. Within this media discourse the locus of blame rests with Africans, especially the peasant farmers, who are portrayed as being backward and incompetent. Media coverage of this kind is loaded with assumptions about the 'primitivism' of our African opposites or cultural others (see also Dahlgren and Chakrapani, 1982).

Frame analysis

In a media setting it is commonplace to narrate stories about poverty in individual/biographical rather than structural terms (Devereux, 1998). One of the net results of individualizing stories about the poor is that it reduces the likelihood of threatening the status quo. This aspect of media coverage of poverty is not restricted to Third World poverty. In recognizing this, Iyengar's study *Is Anyone Responsible? How Television Frames Political Issues* (1991) subjects US media coverage of poverty to a frame analysis (see also Gamson, 1989; Gamson and Modligani, 1987). The study examines how network television frames issues about poverty, unemployment and racial inequality. Iyengar's results demonstrate how framing takes place in terms of attributions of responsibility for poverty and inequality.

Network news is analyzed in order to see whether it frames poverty, unemployment or racial inequality in terms of either 'thematic' or 'episodic' frames. Iyengar defines episodic news frames as those that 'take the form of a case-study or event-oriented report and depict public issues in terms of concrete instances (for example, the plight of a homeless person or a teenage drug user, the bombing of an airliner or an attempted murder' (1991: 14). Thematic news frames, on the other hand:

place public issues in some more general or abstract context and take the form of a 'take-out' or 'backgrounder', report directed at general outcomes or conditions. Examples of thematic coverage include reports on changes in government welfare expenditures, congressional debates over the funding of employment training programs, the social or political grievance of groups undertaking terrorist activity, and the backlog in the criminal justice process. (1991: 14)

Iyengar concludes that, in general, US network news is not overly concerned about poverty or racial inequality as news stories. In the coverage that did take place, 66 per cent of stories were found to be episodic. Iyengar suggests that audiences are twice as likely to encounter a story that was episodic as they were to encounter one that was thematic. Unemployment coverage, by contrast, was mainly thematic. This is explained by the fact that while unemployment is recorded on a monthly basis and is regularly the subject of government announcements, poverty receives much less attention because governments measure and report on it less frequently.

As part of the research project, Iyengar (1991) carried out a number of experiments using five news reports that were classified as having either thematic or episodic frames. After viewing the news reports in question, his study groups were asked to discuss whether poverty or racial inequality resulted from societal or individual inaction. His analysis suggests that news stories from network television were significant in shaping people's beliefs about the responsibility for poverty or racial inequality. Framing that was deemed to be episodic was found to increase the chances of audiences placing responsibility in the hands of the individual, while framing that was deemed to be thematic was found to increase the likelihood of audiences viewing the responsibility for the problem in structural or societal terms.

Narrative analysis

Campbell and Reeves's study *Covering the Homeless: The Joyce Brown Story* (1989) also makes reference to how media coverage of poverty relies upon individual rather than structural explanations. Their work analyses the narratives of news reporting on Joyce Brown, a New York 'bag lady' (who was allegedly schizophrenic). She refused the attentions and offers of help from social workers. They argue that network television framed and narrated the question of homelessness through four distinct stages of the routine news package. They suggest that: 'the major socio-economic problem of homelessness which requires collective participation for resolution often plays out in the news as an isolated personal problem demanding individual attention' (1989: 23).

CRITICAL QUESTION 6.3

How do the analyses by Benthall and Sorenson of media representations of the Third World compare with the findings of the case study on Third World news discussed in Chapter 2?

Media representations of social class

Media representations of social class have received less attention from mass media researchers. This may be, in part, due to the fact that many issues that are in fact class based are not framed, as such, within media content. Media content, can, as we have already noted in Chapter 5, obfuscate the very existence of structural inequalities whether they are based upon class, ethnicity or gender (or a combination of all three). Of the limited research work that exists, two important trends are worth commenting upon. There has been a particular focus on media representation of the working class and those who are dependent on state welfare. Two competing discourses emerge from this analysis. The working class are, in many instances, portrayed as the 'happy' or 'deserving' poor while those who are on welfare are regularly represented within media content in a negative light. Specific subgroups within the working and underclass are the targets of media-driven moral panics. Female lone parents, 'Chavs' in the UK and 'Trailer Trash' in North America – have been the subject of significant levels of negative media representation (see Boxes 6.3 and 6.4).

BOX 6.3 SHAMELESS AND SOCIAL EXCLUSION

In stark contrast to *The Royle Family*, Channel 4's (UK) BAFTA award-winning series *Shameless* portrays the lives of the underclass on Manchester's fictional Chatsworth 'sink' estate. Devised by Paul Abbott, the series examines the many trials and tribulations of the Gallagher family. Combining humour and social realism, the programme brings us into the lives of people who have been described (and dismissed) in other sections of the media as being 'Chavs' (see Box 6.4). Above all else, *Shameless* is a story of survival. Surrounded by dysfunction, the Gallaghers have been abandoned by their mother (who has run off with her lesbian lover) and their father Frank is unemployed, an occasional soft drug user and chronic alcoholic. Frank Gallagher lives elsewhere with his partner Sheila who suffers from chronic agoraphobia. Unlike the dominant view of the under-class as being lazy and unresourceful, *Shameless* demonstrates how the underclass manages to survive. Family and community ties are shown to be strongest in the face of adversity. The programme's main female characters (Fiona, Debbie and Veronica) are especially resilient. When 'establishment' or 'official' Britain – in the shape of the police, social welfare officials or social workers – intervenes into the lives of the Gallaghers, the family always wins the day by drawing upon their own resources or the help of their immediate neighbours.

The 'excesses' associated with the underclass are very much in evidence in the series, with soft-drug use, drunkenness and violence being common. *Shameless* has not been afraid of examining a range of social and personal issues such as 'coming out', inter-racial sexual relationships, welfare fraud, the black or informal economy and petty crime. It is somewhat ironic that Frank Gallagher's mother was once an (old) Labour Party representative. Although Frank makes reference to the rights of the 'working man' he has always been unemployed. *Shameless* represents a metaphorical 'two-fingers' to the Britain of New Labour with its newfound emphasis on 'social inclusion'.

Media coverage of the underclass: stories about welfare

Dedinsky (1977) stresses how media coverage of welfare and poverty in the United States tends to be sensationalist, short-lived and with very little in-depth analysis of the many complex issues at stake. She argues that the media have successfully convinced the public that the welfare system is a 'mess', but have not adequately explained why this might be. Barkin and Gurevitch's (1987) study 'Out of work and on the air: television news of unemployment' examines news coverage of unemployment in the United Kingdom in the 1980s. The authors focus on the thematic structure of news and the explanations given for unemployment. As such, few explanations for unemployment are offered by television news, and they argue that the very diversity of thematic structures reveals the societal frameworks within which television journalists construct stories about this issue.

Plate 6.2 *Shameless.* A powerful representation on the lives of the underclass in Blair's Britain. Reproduced by kind permission © Phil Fisk/Channel 4 2006.

Deacon (1978) examines the 'facts' behind scrounging or welfare fraud in the media. He investigates the reality of welfare abuse – which is in fact quite low – and the amount of undue attention given at times to this issue in the print and broadcast media. Golding and Middleton, similarly, in their studies 'Making claims: news media and the welfare state' (1979) and *Images of Welfare* (1982) examine media-generated moral panics about alleged welfare abuse. During their six-month, content analysis-based study, Golding and Middleton (1979) found that welfare issues, as such, did not make the news. Significantly, welfare was considered worthy of coverage only when it was connected with other issues such as crime, fraud or sex. A key theme uncovered in their analysis – and developed further in their 1982 study – was that the poor are constructed in a media context as either deserving or undeserving. Media demonization of certain sections of the underclass has contributed in no small way towards legitimizing both welfare cutbacks by the state and the furtherance of hegemonic ideologies about the poor and underclass.

> **You should now read EXTRACTED READING 6.1, *Luxurious Lifestyles* (Golding and Middleton, 1982) and consider the following issues:**
>
> 1 How, in your opinion, does media coverage of the crimes of the relatively powerless compare with coverage of the crimes of the powerful?
>
> 2 Reread this extract and highlight how lexicalization is used to define and express an opinion about those who engage in welfare fraud.

ANALYSING MEDIA CONTENT

The happy poor: representations in fictional media content

A number of critical studies have examined how the media represent social class within fictional genres. Thomas and Callanan's (1982) study 'Allocating happiness: TV families and social class' is critical of fictional television for disseminating the myth of the 'happy poor'. By analysing primetime television series on the US networks ABC, NBC and CBS, they conclude that fictional programmes such as *The Waltons* and *The Little House on the Prairie* all propagate a worldview that suggests that: 'money clearly does not buy happiness . . . in fact relative poverty does' (1982: 16). Thomas and Callanan argue that the poorer characters in these programmes were more likely to be portrayed as 'good' or 'straight' characters and they were more likely to see their problems resolved and to find happiness at the conclusion of a programme.

Gould et al. in 'Television's distorted vision of poverty' (1981) also explore how primetime US television portrays blue-collar or working-class life. They argue that in:

the depiction of poverty during prime-time broadcasts, television networks present a sentimentalised vision of economic deprivation that omits or minimises hardship while idealising the supposed benefits of a spartan way of life. Much happier than harried members of the middle and upper-income groups, poor and working people on television seldom strive against their economic fates or against the system. (1981: 309)

In *Upscaling Downtown: Stalled Gentrification in Washington DC* (1998), Williams explores the hermeneutics of television serials from a social-anthropological perspective. He explores the 'prime-time divide' whereby programmes that are aimed at specific social classes often portray members of one social class to another. The poor, he argues, watch television programmes about the wealthy, while the middle classes are drawn to programmes that feature the inner city and the down-and-out. In the middle-class Elm Valley viewers witness 'an uneasy and uncomfortable city, many crazed and violent people, but very few supportive creative people in charge of their own lives. Thus they may get from television an important sense of how poverty batters and victimizes people' (1988: 112). Programmes such as *Hill Street Blues* offer 'powerfully negative views of the poor in the city as exotic, often repellent "other", and these views are filtered through the eyes of the police' (1988: 113).

BOX 6.4   'CHAVS' AND MEDIA VISIBILITY OF THE UNDERCLASS

The reluctance of the mainstream media to frame social issues as being class-based ones has already been noted in this chapter. The world of the working or blue-collar class is disproportionately under-represented within media content. There have however been occasional moral panics engendered by the print and broadcast media

---

in Europe and the USA, for example, on the 'problem' of the underclass, with the 'problem' being defined mainly in terms of the cost of social welfare provision and that the underclass live – in labour market terms – unproductive lives. These moral panics have become increasingly gendered with a growing focus on female lone parents.

In the early years of the twenty-first century the British print and broadcast media began to focus more and more on the emergence, as they termed it, of 'Chav' culture. Skeggs notes the media's obsession '. . . with "chavs" (white working-class men and women depicted as tasteless, excessive, ungovernable and atavistic)' (2005: 966).

The term 'Chav' – based upon an old Romany/Gypsy word for a child – came to signify membership of the white (usually unemployed) underclass. Unlike older examples of the 'dishonest' or 'undeserving poor', Chavs were defined in terms of their excessive (but tasteless) consumption (Hayward and Yar, 2006). Clothing brands – such as Burberry – which were once seen as the preserve of the middle and upper classes, were appropriated to become a signifier of Chav identity. The conspicuous wearing of 'bling' jewellery such as gold chains or sovereign rings by both male and female Chavs was also criticized within media content. Within this media discourse Chavs lead excessive but feckless lives. An interesting twist within this media coverage was the focus on the 'celebrity Chavs' who were in evidence on reality television programmes and in tabloid newspapers and magazines (Hayward and Yar, 2006).

The pathologizing of the Chav represents an interesting example of how the mainstream media are directly involved in the forging and recasting of class identities. As an 'other', Chavs came to represent, in a very powerful way, a key component of the immoral poor. In spite of the dominant state discourse of social inclusion, which was a key aspect of New Labour ideology, Chavs exist outside of the pale. They are 'other' to the 'respectable' working class and expanding middle classes.

See http://www.chavscum.co.uk/

CRITICAL QUESTIONS 6.4

1   In addition to 'Chavs', what other social groups are demonized in a media setting?
2   If you live outside of the UK consider how the mass media represent members of the underclass in your country.
3   How do ethnicity and gender intersect with representations focused upon social class in a media setting?

You should now read EXTRACTED READING 6.2, *Film Producer B* (Devereux, 1998) and consider the following issues:

1 Why is it useful to take account of the media professional's perspective in undertaking an analysis of media content?

2 How does the film director in question view his potential audience?

Media representations of ethnicity: a discourse analysis approach

In Chapter 5 we referred to van Dijk's (1998a) work on ideology and discourse (see Box 5.9). Adopting a critical anti-racist perspective, van Dijk has undertaken detailed discourse analyses of the print media's role in reproducing racist ideologies in the Dutch and British press (van Dijk, 1988, 1991, 1998a, 1998b). In addition, in his text *Ideology: A Multidisciplinary Approach* (1998a) he subjects Dinesh D'Souza's (1995) book *The End of Racism: Principles for a Multiracial Society* to a detailed critical analysis in terms of how it understands race and ethnicity in the United States. Here, we will briefly examine his text *Racism and the Press* (1991) and focus, for reasons of space, on the semantic aspects of one selected example of media content about ethnic issues.

Van Dijk's (1991) study is a hugely detailed, multidisciplinary investigation into the British print media. In excess of 2,700 newspaper articles on ethnic issues were analysed for the period 1 August 1985 to 31 January 1986. In terms of an overall methodological approach, the researcher tells us that, in this study, when media discourses about ethnic issues are analysed:

> it is first established what is being said or written about ethnic minority groups or ethnic relations in general. This analysis yields an account of the contents of the discourse, namely in terms of global topics and local meanings. However, textual analysis pays special attention to how such contents are formulated, that is to style, rhetoric, argumentative or narrative structures or conversational strategies. (1991: 6)

Van Dijk's approach recognizes the importance of examining the connections between unequal power relations in society (in this instance in terms of ethnicity), media content and public or audience attitudes and beliefs. Thus the findings emanating from his discourse analysis of media texts are related to measured public attitudes and beliefs about ethnicity. The study seeks to explain how 'white ingroup members tend to express and communicate their ethnic attitudes to other members of the group and how such attitudes are spread and shared in society'

(1991: 6). Van Dijk's research is based upon detailed and systematic analysis of the print media's role in the reproduction and circulation of dominant ideological interpretations of race and ethnicity.

In the latter part of *Racism and the Press* van Dijk examines news discourse about ethnicity at the micro or local level. This is defined as: 'the meaning, style and rhetoric of its actual words and sentences' (1991: 176). In chapter 7, for example, he presents us with a powerful example of how we might examine the ideological aspect of media discourse. He reproduces an extract from an editorial on immigration published in the *Mail* newspaper on 28 November 1985. It states:

> That is why we have to be more brisk in saying no, and showing the door to those who are not British citizens and would abuse our hospitality and tolerance. To do that is not to give way to prejudice, but to lessen the provocation on which it feeds. (1991: 177)

This editorial conforms to a wider conservative or right-wing discourse about ethnic issues. Van Dijk identifies five meaning structures and strategies in this brief extract:

1 The editorial 'presupposes' that 'we [British] are hospitable and tolerant' (1991: 176).
2 It rejects the notion that 'showing the door to those who are not British' might be construed as being prejudiced (1991: 176).
3 The editorial represents immigrants 'in a negative way by the use of the verb "to abuse", which also presupposes that immigrants do indeed abuse British tolerance. At the same time, this use of "abuse" establishes a contrast between the negative properties of the abuser and the good ones of the "tolerant" British' (1991: 177).
4 The use of the phrase 'those who are not British citizens' (1991: 177) would, on the face of it, seem to suggest that the editorial is critical of those who do not hold British passports. Van Dijk contrasts this with the newspaper's more general coverage of immigration issues and concludes that it really means non-white immigrants.
5 The editorial employs a number of euphemisms when applied to how 'we' should deal with immigrants. We (or us) the tolerant and hospitable British must be 'brisk', 'in saying no', 'in showing the door' to them (immigrants).

Media representations of gender and sexuality

Within media content and across a variety of media genres we are presented with a range of representations about gender. Media content plays a hugely significant role in shaping our perceptions of what it is to be 'male' or 'female'. It also carries a set of hegemonic assumptions about human sexuality. Research on media representations of gender has focused on how women are objectified and exploited in a media context (especially in advertising and in pornography) and on the gap between social reality and media constructions of femininity and masculinity.

The feminist perspective has been to the fore in critiquing mainstream media content in terms of how it misrepresents and under-represents women (Rakow,

1990). Media representations pertaining to being 'a man' or being 'a woman' are not fixed entities and they, demonstrably, change over time. If you were to undertake even a brief comparative content analysis of the representations of roles ascribed to women and men on contemporary television advertising, for example, and compare it with representations in the 1960s or 1970s, you would undoubtedly see differences in the discourses employed. One obvious difference might be the shift from firmly locating women in the domestic sphere to one that now emphasizes an independent career in the world of paid employment – although even now some advertisers continue to stress both the domestic and the external world of work responsibilities for women!

Media content reflects changing dominant discourses about femininity and masculinity. That is not to say that media content is a mirror image of the realities of gender identities in the social world. The gulf between representations and reality has been much commented upon. Van Zoonen and Costera Meijer, for example, argue that:

It is indeed easy to see that real women are much more different and more diverse than their representations in the media would seem to suggest. If media images were indeed a reflection of reality, 'real' women would be relatively rare in most parts of the real world, and Black, older, disabled, lesbian, fat, poor, or Third World women would be virtually nonexistent. (1998: 298)

We could equally create a list of men who do not conform to the dominant discourses surrounding masculinity and who are largely invisible within mainstream media content. This is particularly true in terms of men who are gay or bisexual (see Extracted Reading 6.3).

In *Media, Gender and Identity* (2002) Gauntlett examines the invisibility of bisexuals, gay men and lesbians on television (see also Dow, 2001). He traces how mainstream television in both the United Kingdom and the United States is (slowly) beginning to examine the lives of bisexuals, gay men and lesbians in a fictional setting. Such coverage is not without its constraints, however. He notes that:

As recently as 1990, even the sight of two men sitting in bed together talking, with no physical contact – in the US drama series *Thirtysomething* – prompted half the advertisers to side with homophobic campaigners and withdraw their support, reportedly losing the ABC network over a million dollars . . . Even in 1997–1998, Ellen DeGeneres's coming out as a lesbian in her sitcom *Ellen* (as well as in real life) caused an even bigger controversy with advertisers fleeing, and ABC/Disney dropping the popular show after one 'lesbian' season. (2002: 82)

While changes are gradually occurring in terms of covering storylines concerning alternative sexualities, they are still novel.

Plate 6.3   Behind the picket fence: *Desperate Housewives* uncovers the anxieties of white middle-class America. Reproduced by kind permission of ABC Photography Archives ©.

You should now read EXTRACTED READING 6.3, *Villains or Victims: Media Representations of Gay Men and Lesbians* (Shugart, 2003) and consider the following issues:

1   Why do you think media representations of gay men and lesbians have become (relatively) more common within mainstream media texts?

2   Critically evaluate the way in which *Will and Grace* represents gay men. What are the main limitations evident within its portrayals?

ANALYSING MEDIA CONTENT

BOX 6.5 *DESPERATE HOUSEWIVES* AND THE POLITICS OF GENDER AND SEXUALITY

Desperate Housewives is an example of an immensely popular, globally distributed soap opera where the politics of gender and sexuality are explored. Created by Marc Cherry and produced by the ABC television network in the USA, *Desperate Housewives* (like HBO's *Sex and the City*) is aimed at a female audience (see McCabe and Akass, 2006). It manages to successfully combine elements of soap opera, melodrama and black comedy. The idyllic setting of the pastoral sounding 'Wisteria Lane' is also the place of many dark secrets such as suicide, drug addiction, murder and prostitution. Each episode of the series deals in turn with the desperation experienced by five housewives (see Coward, 2006).

An emerging body of scholarly work has examined *Desperate Housewives*. Chambers (2006), for example, has examined how the series has managed to subvert gender and sexual politics. Heterosexual norms are questioned and there are occasional references to queer sexuality. McCabe (2006) and Singleton (2006) examine hegemonic constructions of femininity (represented by the aptly named Bree Van de Kamp) and masculinity (represented by John the gardener). Kahn's (2006) reading of *Desperate Housewives'* representation of gay issues concludes that while the programme does have a few 'queer moments', it in fact manages to reinforce conservative hetero-normative interpretations of human sexuality. When it is fleetingly allowed to appear, gayness is a source of comedy, it is conflated with criminality, and it is suggested that it is something that can be 'cured'.

Conclusion

Formal analysis of media content remains important. This chapter has outlined the main models of content analysis available to students of the media. Your choice of opting for a quantitative, qualitative or mixed model of content analysis depends on your research question and the type of media genre you wish to study. Once again we stress the need to place the analysis of content within a research framework that might also consider the production and reception of the media texts in question. Media globalization has resulted in the wider circulation of many media texts. Concentration and conglomeration have altered the scope of media content. These structural changes add weight to the argument for a formal (and comparative) analysis of media content. A sophisticated content analysis of media texts drawing upon discourse, semiotic or framing analysis, for example, can assist us greatly in understanding more about the reception of media texts, a theme to which we now turn in Chapter 7. An appreciation of the intricacies of much media content can also deepen our understanding of how media content works to secure hegemonic definitions of social reality.

Extracted readings

6.1   Luxurious lifestyles

Peter Golding and Sue Middleton, *Images of Welfare: Press and Public Attitudes to Poverty*. Oxford: Blackwell, 1982, pp. 62–3

Every story made sure to mention cigars, suits and indolent comfort. For some time this was paramount. *The Daily Telegraph*, which had two separate stories the same day, headlined one '£10,000-a-year Lifestyle for Dole Fiddler', opening its coverage by noting Deevy's life of splendour. *The Sun* front-page headline '£36,000 Scrounger' was followed by an under-lined sub-headline, 'Six Years for Dole Cheat who Spent £25 a week on the Best Cigars'. *The Daily Express* coined the epithet King Con, and above their front-page headline 'Incredible Reign of King Con' was a strap '£200-a-week tycoon on social security'. The story gave great prominence to the Judge's remarks about people asking 'What's the good of working?' *The Daily Mail* front-page story 'Biggest Scrounger of the Lot' also drew attention to Deevy's Corona cigars and expensive suits. *The Daily Mirror* lead story 'King of the Dole Queue Scroungers' (a phrase clearly implying a host of like followers) began 'Nothing was too good for Derek Deevy. His weekly cigar bill came to £25 and he regularly bought expensive suits. The fact that he was out of work didn't spoil his life at the top.' . . . Deevy was immediately enthroned as King of a teeming population of scroungers and spongers. . . . The question 'How many others?' seemed always to be rhetorical, inviting the reader to nod knowingly in affirmation of the suspicion that prompted the question.

The Daily Express (14 July) carried a centre-page feature by Iain Sproat headed 'I believe we have seen only the tip of the iceberg,' which recounted the by now familiar tales from Mr Sproat's postbag to illustrate his point that the Deevy case exploded 'the myth that abuse of the welfare system is some minimal problem'. *The Daily Mirror* began to gather in the evidence in a story (15 July) headed 'Doing the Scrounge Rounds'. This featured four cases (three in Manchester) of people 'on the scrounge'. Given this massive evidence it was no surprise to learn in the first line of the story that 'Britain's army of dole-queue swindlers were on the run last night as a Government Minister warned he was going gunning for them'.

6.2   Film Producer B

Eoin Devereux, *Devils and Angels: Television, Ideology and the Coverage of Poverty*, Luton: University of Luton Press/John Libbey Media, 1998, pp. 34–5

This producer opted for a docudrama approach in making his appeal segments. His belief was that he should keep these ninety-second films documentary in style, but also incorporate elements of drama as well. True to his realism, he felt that there were certain things, which needed to be shown, and in the case of the Cork homeless boys piece, there was a necessity to act out certain otherwise unseen activities. In filming in Cork he spoke to the centre's founder about what he wanted to do. He maintained that the centre's founder realised that if he wanted to find young boys glue-sniffing or drinking spirits he could easily do so out on the streets, so instead he filmed some boys from the centre in a reconstruction of these activities. He maintained that it was essential for the audience to fully understand the implications for these young boys of allowing such a lifestyle to persist. He shot the piece of film in the backyard of the centre, using some of its clients – all of whom agreed to appear in the piece.

In describing the film segment he said:

I did it as a straight documentary, but dramatising one element. Why? Because I could talk about it . . . they sniff . . . and people would say we don't really believe that. So you show it. Then I had to make up my mind about creating it . . . If I had to go out and find it, it might take me a week . . . So I created it. I didn't put up a caption saying 'This is a reconstruction' because that again enters into the realm of disbelief on the part of the viewer.

In the context of . . . the unease . . . about this reconstruction, Producer B asserted his 'moral right' not to explain his filmmaking processes to the others in the production team, as he claimed the reconstruction was simply a creation in documentary form. His intention in making the piece of film was to create a connection between the message at the end of the film 'Our young people must not be allowed to die from drugs' and the images of solvent and alcohol abuse contained within the mini-dramatisation at the beginning. He maintained that what the audience was therefore being given was a certain degree of drama in two forms incorporating both the fictional and the factual documentary styles.

6.3 Villians or victims: *media representations of gay men and lesbians*

Helene A. Shugart (2003) 'Reinventing privilege: the new (gay) man in contemporary popular media', Critical Studies in Media Communication 20 (1): 67–91

Historically, representations of gay men and lesbians in the mainstream US media have been sparse and selective. . . . Although 'homoerotic images and behavior were used as comic devices' (Fejes and Petrich, 1993: 397) such as cross dressing and role reversals, 'as expressed onscreen, America was a dream that had no room for the existence of homosexuals... And when the fact of our existence became unavoidable, we were reflected, onscreen and off, as dirty secrets' (Russo, p. xii). When presented in mainstream film or television until quite recently, gay characters were almost exclusively portrayed negatively, as either villains or victims (Gross, 1994). In both capacities, they were rendered as problems to be solved and almost always reflected gendered stereotypes that characterize gay men as effeminate and lesbians as masculine.

Attendant to the emergent gay rights movement in the 1970s, although standard negative tropes did not disappear, mainstream film and television began to feature more positive portrayals of gay characters. . . . By the 1990s, the representation of gay men and lesbians in the popular mainstream media became *de rigueur* for film and even obligatory for television fare. Major box-office hits like *Philadelphia*, *The Birdcage*, *To Wong Foo, Thanks for Everything! Julie Newmar*, and *In & Out* featured sympathetic gay protagonists, and the secondary-but-permanent character became a staple of the majority of mainstream television dramas and situation comedies, including, for example, *NYPD Blue*, *Chicago Hope*, *ER*, *Mad About You*, *Roseanne*, *Spin City*, and *Friends*. This television trend ultimately culminated in prime-time shows that featured lead gay protagonists in dramas like *Melrose Place* and *Dawson's Creek* and, more prominently, in the situation comedies *Ellen* and *Will & Grace*.

As many critics have argued, however, the 'chic' visibility of gay men and lesbians in the mainstream media is not unproblematic. . . . Nearly all of these portrayals skirt the realities and implications of homosexuality by desexualizing the characters – i.e. by almost never depicting them in romantic or sexual situations. . . . Some of these representations, as in *Personal Best*, depict homosexuality 'as a temporary interruption in the flow of heterosexual life' (Gross, 2001: 74). More common themes are that, first, gay characters are presented as devoid of gay social and political contexts . . . thus capable of being grafted onto established heterosexual communities and contexts; and second, that their presence is used as a catalyst for heterosexual characters' growth and understanding.

--- **Exercise 6.2** ---

Analysing media content

1 Select three posters or print media advertisements about the Third World and carry out a semiotic analysis of their content. What symbols are used to create meaning for their readers? How do the three selected examples compare in terms of their semiotic dimensions?
2 Select a magazine primarily aimed at a male readership and carry out a thematic analysis of its contents. In what way(s) does the magazine construct masculinity?
3 Select a television news report about asylum seekers or refugees and write a detailed analysis of the discourses employed in the piece.

Questions for consideration and discussion

1 Why does media content matter?
2 In representational terms why is the complexity of social class particularly problematic?
3 What sorts of forces shape media content?

--- **References** ---

Barkin, S.M. and M. Gurevitch (1987) 'Out of work and on the air: television news of unemployment', *Critical Studies in Mass Communication* 4: 1–20.

Barthes, R. (1973) *Mythologies*. London: Paladin.

Baxter, R.L., C. de Riemer and A. Landini (1985) 'A content analysis of music videos', *Journal of Broadcasting and Electronic Media* 29 (3): 333–40.

Benthall, J. (1993) *Disasters, Relief and the Media*. London: Tauris.

Berelson, B. (1952) *Content Analysis in Communication Research*. Glencoe, IL: Free Press.

van den Berg, H. and C.G. van der Veer (1989) 'Ideologies in the news: on the measurement of ideological characteristics of news reports', *Gazette* 14: 159–94.

Berger, A.A. (1982) *Media Analysis Techniques*. London: Sage.

Breen, M.J. (2000) 'When size does matter: how Church size determines media coverage of religion' in J. Thierstein and Y.R. Kamalipour (eds) *Religion, Law and Freedom*. Westport, CT: Praeger.

Breen, M., A. Haynes and E. Devereux (2006) 'Citizens, 'Loopholes' and Maternity Tourists: Media Framing of the 2004 Citizenship Referendum' in M. Corcoran and M. Peillon (eds) *Uncertain Ireland*. Dublin: IPA.

Campbell, R. and J.L. Reeves (1989) 'Covering the homeless: the Joyce Brown story', *Critical Studies in Mass Communication* 6: 21–42.

Caragee K.M. and W. Roefs (2004) 'The neglect of power in recent framing research', *Journal of Communication*, June.

Chambers, S.A. (2006) 'Desperately straight: the subversive sexual politics of *Desperate Housewives*' in J. McCabe and K. Akass (eds) *Reading* Desperate Housewives*: Beyond the White Picket Fence*. London: I.B. Tauris.

Coward, R. (2006) 'Still desperate: popular television and the female Zeitgeist' in J. McCabe and K. Akass (eds) *Reading* Desperate Housewives: *Beyond the White Picket Fence*. London: I.B. Tauris.

Dahlgren, P. (1981) 'TV news and the suppression of reflexivity' in E. Katz and T. Szecsko (eds) *Mass Media and Social Change*. London: Sage.

Dahlgren, P. and S. Chakrapani (1982) 'The Third World in television news: Western ways of seeing the "other"' in W. Adams (ed.) *Television Coverage of International Affairs*. Washington, DC: George Washington University Press.

Deacon, A. (1978) 'The scrounging controversy: public attitudes towards the unemployed in contemporary Britain', *Social and Economic Administration* 12 (2): 120–35.

Dedinsky, M. (1977) 'The public image of welfare', *Public Welfare* 35 (4): 12–16.

Devereux, E. (1998*) Devils and Angels: Television, Ideology and the Coverage of Poverty*. Luton: University of Luton Press/John Libbey Media.

van Dijk, T.A. (1988) *News Analysis: Case Studies of International and National News in the Press*. Hillsdale, NJ: Erlbaum.

van Dijk, T.A. (1991) *Racism and the Press*. London: Routledge.

van Dijk, T.A. (1998a) *Ideology: A Multidisciplinary Approach*. London: Sage.

van Dijk, T.A. (1998b) 'Opinions and ideologies in the press' in A. Bell and P. Garrett (eds) *Approaches to Media Discourse*. Oxford: Blackwell.

Dow, B.J. (2001) '*Ellen*, television and the politics of gay and lesbian visibility', *Critical Studies in Media Communication* 18 (2): 123–40.

D'Souza, D. (1995) *The End of Racism*. New York: Free Press.

Evans, E.D., J. Rutberg, C. Sather and C. Turner (1991) 'Content analysis of contemporary teen magazines for adolescent females', *Youth and Society* 23 (1): 99–120.

Fenton, N. (2000) 'The problematics of postmodernism for feminist media studies', *Media, Culture and Society* 22 (6): 723–42.

Gamson, W.A. (1989) 'News as framing', *American Behavioral Scientist* 33: 157–61.

Gamson, W.A. and A. Modligiani (1987) 'The changing culture of affirmative action' in *Research in Political Sociology III*. Greenwich, CT: JAI Press, pp. 137–77.

Gauntlett, D. (2002) *Media, Gender and Identity*. London: Routledge.

Glasgow University Media Group (1976) *Bad News,* vol. I. London: Routledge.

Golding, P. and S. Middleton (1979) 'Making claims: news media and the welfare state', *Media, Culture and Society* 1: 5–21.

Golding, P. and S. Middleton (1982) *Images of Welfare: Press and Public Attitudes to Poverty*. Oxford: Blackwell.

Gomes, R.C. and L.F. Williams (1991). 'Race and crime: the role of the media in perpetuating racism and classism in America', *Urban League Review* 14 (1): 57–69.

Gould, C., D.C. Stern and T. Dow Adams (1981) 'Television's distorted vision of poverty', *Communication Quarterly* 29 (24): 309–14.

Harding, R. (2006) 'Historical representations of aboriginal people in the Canadian news media', *Discourse and Society* 17 (2) 205–35.

Haynes, A.,M.J. Breen and E. Devereux (2005) 'Smuggling zebras for lunch: media framing of asylum seekers in the Irish print media', *Etudes Irlandaises* 30 (1).

Haynes, A., E. Devereux and M.J. Breen (2006) 'Fear, framing and foreigners', *International Journal of Critical Psychology*, Spring.

Hayward, K. and M. Yar (2006) 'The "chav" phenomenon: consumption, media and the construction of a new underclass', *Crime, Media, Culture* 2 (1): 9–28.

Hill, J. (1985) 'The British "social problem film": *Violent Playground and Sapphire*', *Screen* 26 (1): 34–48.

Iyengar, S. (1991) *Is Anyone Responsible? How Television Frames Political Issues*. Chicago: University of Chicago Press.

Iyengar, S. and D.R. Kinder (1987) *News that Matters: Television and American Opinion*. Chicago: University of Chicago Press.

Kahn, K.T. (2006) 'Queer dilemmas: The "right" ideology and homosexual representation in *Desperate Housewives*' in J. McCabe and K. Akass (eds) *Reading* Desperate Housewives: *Beyond the White Picket Fence*. London: I.B. Tauris.

Kitzinger, J. (1999) 'A sociology of media power: key issues in audience reception research' in G. Philo (ed.) *Message Received*. Harlow: Addison Wesley Longman.

Kitzinger, J. (2000) 'Media templates: patterns of association and the (re)construction of meaning over time', *Media, Culture and Society* 22 (1): 61–84.

Kitzinger, J. and C. Kitzinger (1993) '"Doing it": representations of lesbian sex' in G. Griffin (ed.) *Outwrite: Lesbianism and Popular Culture*. London: Pluto Press.

McCabe, J. (2006) 'What is it with the hair? Bree Van de Kamp and policing contemporary feminity' in J. McCabe and K. Akass (eds) *Reading* Desperate Housewives: *Beyond the White Picket Fence*. London: I.B. Tauris.

McCabe, J. and K. Akass (2006) *Reading* Desperate Housewives: *Beyond the White Picket Fence*. London: I.B. Tauris.

McQuail, D. (1983) *Mass Communication Theory*. London: Sage.

Nohrstedt, S.A. (1986) 'Ideological news reporting from the Third World: a case study of international newspaper and magazine coverage of the civil war in Nigeria, 1967–70', *European Journal of Communication* 1: 421–46.

Philo, G. (1993) 'From Buerk to Band Aid: the media and the 1984 Ethiopian famine' in J. Eldridge (ed.) *Getting the Message*. London: Routledge.

Propp, V. (1928) *Morphology of the Folktale*, trans. L. Scott. Austin, TX: University of Texas Press.

Rakow, L. (1990) 'Feminist perspectives on popular culture' in J. Downing, A. Mohammadi and A. Sreberny-Mohammadi (eds) *Questioning the Media: A Critical Introduction*. Thousand Oaks, CA: Sage.

Schaffert, R.W. (1992) *Media Coverage and Political Terrorists: A Quantitative Analysis*. New York: Praeger.

Sebeok, T. (1974) 'Semiotics: a survey of the state of the art' in T. Sebeok (ed.) *Current Trends in Linguistics,* Vol. I. The Hague: Mouton.

Singleton, B. (2006) 'Hunters, heroes and the hegemonically masculine fantasies of *Desperate Housewives'*, in J. McCabe and K. Akass (eds) *Reading* Desperate Housewives: *Beyond the White Picket Fence*. London: I.B. Tauris.

Skeggs, B. (2005) 'The making of class and gender through visualizing moral subject formation', *Sociology* 39 (5): 965–82.

Sorenson, J. (1991) 'Mass media discourse on famine in the Horn of Africa', *Discourse and Society* 2 (2): 223–42.

Soubiran-Paillet, F. (1987) 'Presse et delinquance, ou, comment lire entre les lignes', *Criminologie* 20 (1): 59–77.

Thomas, S. and B.P. Callanan (1982) 'Allocating happiness: TV families and social class', *Journal of Communication* 32 (3): 184–90.

Triandafyllidou, A. (1998) 'National identity and the "other". *Ethnic and Racial Studies* 21 (8): 593–612.

Williams, B. (1988) *Upscaling Downtown: Stalled Gentrification in Washington DC*. Ithaca, NY: Cornell University Press.

Winkel, F.W. (1990). 'Crime reporting in newspapers: an exploratory study of the effects of ethnic references in crime news', *Social Behaviour* 5 (2): 87–101.

Woollacott, J. (1982) 'Messages and meanings' in M. Gurevitch, T. Bennett, J. Curran and J. Woollacott (eds) *Culture, Society and the Media*. London: Routledge.

Van Zoonen, L. and I. Costera Meijer (1998) 'From Pamela Anderson to Erasmus: women, men and representation' in A. Briggs and P. Cobley (eds) *The Media: An Introduction*. Harlow: Longman.

Going further

Breen, M., A. Haynes and E. Devereux (2006) 'Citizens, "Loopholes" and maternity tourists: media framing of the 2004 citizenship referendum' in M. Corcoran and M. Peillon (eds) *Uncertain Ireland*. Dublin: IPA. This essay is an example of how framing theory may be applied towards reaching a better understanding of media discourse about a contentious social issue.

Chandler, D. (2007) *Semiotics: The Basics,* (2nd edn.) London: Routledge. Along with the author's website, this text introduces you to the key aspects of semiotics and their application in a research setting. See also www.aber.ac.uk/media/Documents/S4B/semiotic.html.

Class Dismissed (2007) is available on video/DVD. Introduced by Pepi Leistyna and directed by Loretta Alper, *Class Dismissed* examines the invisibility and misrepresentation of the working or blue-collar class on mainstream American television. Using a wide range of historical and contemporary examples, the film shows how inequalities based upon ethnicity, gender, and sexuality all intersect with social class in the make-up of how television represents social class. The video/DVD is accompanied by a useful study guide for teachers and students. For further details see www.mediaed.org.

Kendall, D. (2005) *Framing Class: Media Representations of Wealth and Poverty in America*. Lanham: Rowman & Littlefield Publishers. Kendall uses a content analysis of newspaper and television to examine the underlying assumptions contained within US media content about social class.

Media coverage of asylum seekers and refugees

A range of studies using a variety of research methods have examined the 'othering' of asylum seekers and refugees. See for example L. d'Haenens and M. de Lange (2001) 'Framing of asylum seekers in Dutch regional newspapers' in *Media, Culture and Society* 23 (6) 847–60. Coole (2002) examines through a content analysis how the print media covered the murder of a Turkish asylum seeker in Scotland in 2001. See C. Coole, (2002) 'A warm welcome? Scottish and UK media reporting of an asylum-seeker murder', *Media, Culture and Society* 24 (6) 839–52. Van Gorp uses a framing theory approach towards understanding Belgian print media coverage of asylum and 'illegal' immigration. See B. Van Gorp (2005) 'Where is the frame? Victims and intruders in the Belgian press coverage of the asylum issue', *European Journal of Communication* 20 (4): 484–507. Lynn and Lea (2003) apply a discourse analysis approach to letters to the editor written by members of the British public concerning asylum issues. See N. Lynn and S. Lea (2003) 'A phantom menace and the new Apartheid: the social construction of asylum-seekers in the United Kingdom', *Discourse and Society* 14 (4): 425–52.

7

AUDIENCES AND RECEPTION

Summary

In this final chapter we aim to understand mass media audiences more clearly by highlighting the following:

- The continuing importance of reception analysis based upon a model that stresses the notion of discourse.
- The main quantitative and qualitative methodological approaches to mass-media audience analysis.
- The 'ethnographic turn' within audience research.
- The ongoing debate over the extent to which audiences have agency in the face of powerful media messages.
- The importance of marrying the understandings we may get from a reception-based model of media analysis with those obtained from a content or production-based approach.
- The need to apply a broadly defined model of reception analysis to both factual and fictional media content.
- The usefulness of understanding audiences as fans.
- The relationship between audiences and new forms of media technologies.

Key concepts

- Reception analysis
- Media discourse
- Active audiences
- Open and closed texts
- Audience resistance
- Resistive reading
- Public knowledge
- Popular culture
- Interpretative repertoires
- Fans and fandom

In this chapter we come to examine the third, and arguably the most intricate, part of the 'trinity' of production, content and reception. In discussing media audiences, and more particularly the processes involved in the reception of mass media texts, we recognize from the very outset the increasing level of complexity involved. Such complexity has been accentuated as a result of media globalization and technological changes producing a radically altered mediascape for media audiences. Indeed, some commentators have questioned whether we can usefully talk about a mass media audience any more. (See Stevenson, 2002, for a critical overview of these developments and changes and Livingstone, 2004, for an assessment of the implications of these developments and changes for audience studies in particular.)

This chapter does not rehearse, at any great length, the histories of the various traditional approaches to media audiences (effects; uses and gratifications; encoding and decoding models) that have come to typify many introductory textbooks (see Ruddock, 2000, for a comprehensive overview). Rather, it specifically examines the question of reception in some detail. Our particular focus here is on the *hermeneutic* dimension of the relationship between media texts and media audiences. We have already discussed this issue in the context of our examination of the workings of ideology, dominant ideology and discourse in Chapter 5 and in terms of audiences' media globalization and glocalization in Chapter 2.

While certain kinds of behaviourist-inspired quantitative research methodologies may tell us more about specific aspects of the audience (rates of listenership, viewership or readership, for example) – and are regularly used to this end by the media industries (see, for example, Krotz and Hasebrink, 1998, and Downing, 2003, for a critical view) – this chapter argues for an essentially qualitative approach to the media audience.

Our focus is on how meaning, in a media context, is generated in everyday life. We wish to restate the importance of the 'ethnographic turn' in reception research. The circumstances that allow more or less audience agency or reflexivity are our prime concern. While we recognize the capacity of audiences – in certain conditions – to be active in their reception of media texts, it must be stated that we are not dealing with what Fenton (1999) aptly terms an 'interpretative free-for-all' that has come to typify the postmodern perspective on media audiences. Mainstream media content, as we pointed out in Chapter 6, continues to play a significant role in the shaping of public attitudes and beliefs about the social world. Dominant discourses, many of which are ideological in orientation, are part and parcel of everyday mainstream media content. These media frames or discursive formations were shown to have a power in the social construction of reality for audience members.

In its own right, and in spite of some shortcomings, *reception analysis* has much to offer us in our attempts to comprehend the contemporary media. Some of the most exciting and insightful work within media analysis has come from this research tradition. When undertaken in conjunction with analyses of production and content, it offers us the opportunity to understand more fully how meaning is created.

The chapter begins with an overview of the three key paradigms that attempt to explain reception analysis, namely the encoding/decoding, ethnographic and constructionist models. Feminist and postmodern perspectives have now come to a position of prominence within reception analysis and have informed the growth and development of the ethnographic and constructionist approaches. We briefly outline the main quantitative and qualitative methodological approaches to media audiences and, given the particular emphasis in this chapter on the processes associated with the reception of media texts, we examine the ethnographic turn in greater detail. While much ethnographic research has been concerned with examining the meanings associated with popular culture or fictional genres, there is another strand of reception analysis that is concerned with broadcast and print media news. With this in mind, we outline the 'News Game' as devised by Greg Philo of the Glasgow University Media Group.

> ∞∞
> *See Box 6.1 for more on the Glasgow University Media Group.*

Starting with Morley's (1980) classic *Nationwide* study, we present three examples of reception analysis research. These are concerned with current affairs and news television, and women's magazines. As well as being concerned with different media genres, the selected studies utilize a range of methodological approaches in their attempts to understand audience reception.

The chapter concludes with a consideration of audiences in terms of participation within specific fan cultures and in the use of new media. In terms of fandom, our focus will be on the consumption of specific forms of media genres and the related media-based activities engaged in by fans. The fandom of the second-generation Irish singer Morrissey is explored in the form of a case study. As well as three extracted and contrasting readings on audiences and reception, the chapter contains three exercises that focus on media audience beliefs about the socially excluded, cinema fandom and the adoption of new media technologies in a domestic setting in terms of gender.

CRITICAL QUESTIONS 7.1   ON BEING AN AUDIENCE MEMBER

Before you read about how audiences, and reception in particular, have been understood by media theorists and empirical researchers, reflect for a while on your own experiences as an audience member. Compile a list of the variety of situations in any one day in which you may be a member of a media audience and consider the following issues in particular:

1   How many media audiences do you actually belong to?
2   What sorts of media genres are you predominantly interested in?
3   In what social situations are you mainly an audience member?

---

4   Do these social contexts have a bearing on how you interpret the multiplicity of media messages that you encounter?
5   How active or reflexive are you as an audience member?
6   Where might you see agency or reflexivity in your everyday media experience?

Understanding media audiences: changing paradigms in reception research

In a highly succinct essay, Alasuutari (1999) refers to the existence of three 'phases' or 'generations' of reception research. These are the encoding/decoding paradigm, the audience ethnography paradigm and the newly emerging constructionist or discursive paradigm. While these developments within reception research have been neither smooth nor linear, the last three decades have witnessed a series of significant theoretical and methodological ruptures in terms of how audiences are conceptualized and researched. These developments mark a radical break with the behaviourist/effects understanding of the media audience, because they stress the potential power of audiences to reshape and resist the contents of media texts. They also underscore significant changes in the kinds of media genres analysed, the methodologies used, and the nature of the questions raised within empirical audience research. Reception analysis has focused predominantly on television, although this has recently given way to a new set of concerns about the role of new media technologies in the home and the emergence of postmodern mediascapes.

Encoding/decoding

In Chapter 4 we discussed Hall's (1974) encoding/decoding model in some detail. The encoding/decoding paradigm was highly influential in the initial development of reception research. Heavily influenced by semiotics, Hall concentrates on two important 'moments' in the communicative exchange, namely the encoding undertaken by media professionals in the making of media messages and the decoding that takes place among audience members once the message has been received. Typically, audience members can make use of four codes in the process of interpreting a media message.

See Chapter 4 for an elaboration of the encoding/decoding model.

These are the dominant code, the professional code, the negotiated code and the oppositional code.

The encoding/decoding paradigm allows for audience agency in that individual audience members can reconstruct or resist the media message. Hall's (1974) model gave rise to a growing amount of empirical research on how audiences variously decode media messages. The most famous is Morley's (1980) *Nationwide* study, which we discuss later in this chapter. The period that followed Morley's application of Hall's encoding/decoding model saw the beginnings of a move towards analysing the content and reception of fictional television genres. Focus group interviews and in-depth interviews with individual audience members were used to explore the readings that were made of specific media texts. This shift in emphasis gave rise to a new phase of qualitative audience research that engaged with questions about the gendered realities of media use and consumption.

Audience ethnography

The second phase or generation of reception research usually describes itself as ethnographic. In describing its emergence, Alasuutari (1999) argues that three key features characterize the new audience ethnography. First, it is strongly influenced by the feminist perspective. Alasuutari states that:

> This can be seen . . . in the fact that a slackening of interest in the reception of public affairs programmes was balanced out by a growing interest in fictional programmes, particularly romantic serials. These studies concentrated on the politics of gender, on the discourses within which gender is dealt with in the programmes, and how women viewers interpret and make use of the offered readings against the background of everyday life and experiences. (1999: 5)

Second, the earlier concentration on the content and reception of media texts as evidenced in the encoding/decoding model gave way to a much broader interest in the functions of specific kinds of media in people's day-to-day lives. Researchers examined the uses of new media technologies in a domestic setting: the 'television talk' of everyday life as well as the ways in which gender discourses shape the uses of television in the home (see Lull, 1980; Morley, 1986; Silverstone et al., 1991). Third, the audience ethnography phase of reception research placed a new emphasis upon understanding reception in the context of people's daily lives.

Constructionist approach

The third and newly emerging phase of reception research is referred to as the constructionist or discursive approach. The certainties that once characterized the encoding/decoding and ethnographic approaches have been replaced with a new set of concerns (and doubts) within audience research. Under the influence of postmodern theory, the youngest of the three generations of reception research seeks to understand more about the mediascapes that define the postmodern experience. In explaining this approach, Alasuutari argues that:

> The third generation entails a broadened frame within which one conceives of the media and media use. One does not necessarily abandon ethnographic case studies of audiences or analyses

of individual programmes, but the main focus is not restricted to finding out about the reception or 'reading' of a programme by a particular audience. Rather, the objective is to get a grasp of our contemporary 'media culture', particularly as it can be seen in the role of the media in everyday life, both as a topic and as an activity structured by and structuring the discourses within which it is discussed. One is interested in the discourses within which we conceive of our roles as the public and the audience, and how notions of programmes-with-an-audience or messages-with-an-audience are inscribed as media messages and assessments about news events and about what is going on in the 'world'. The third generation resumes an interest in programmes and programming, but not as texts studied in isolation from their usage as an element of everyday life. Furthermore, it adds a neglected layer of reflexivity to the research on the 'reception' of media messages by addressing the audience's notions of themselves as the 'audience'. (1999: 6–7)

In the newly emerging constructionist understanding of media audiences, there is an emphasis on discourse and reflexivity that was previously absent in the encoding/decoding and audience ethnography paradigms. Alasuutari (1999) argues that there has been a shift from an emphasis on audience psychology to audience sociology. In this account the encoding/decoding model of audience reception is decidedly cognitive in its orientation. In the face of a media text with a preferred dominant ideological encoding on patriarchy, homophobia or 'terrorism', does an audience member accept, reconstruct or reject the encoding? In the constructionist version of audience reception, we are more concerned with the broader social and discursive context in which reception takes place. As Alasuutari notes:

From this perspective, the 'reception' of a programme or genre can be given a more sociological meaning. We are interested in it as a topic in a given society. What are the embedded problems and concerns that evoke it as a topic? What are the viewpoints and subject positions taken in the discourse? How, and by whom, is it discussed in public and how do people in everyday-life conversations refer to or comment on the public discussions about it? (1999: 16)

CRITICAL QUESTION 7.2   MEDIA DISCOURSE

List three examples of where and when you might talk about media content in your daily life. How, in your opinion, does talking about media discourse affect its influence on you and others?

You should now read EXTRACTED READING 7.1, *Reading and Reception* (Kitzinger, 1999) and consider the following issues:

1   Why in Kitzinger's view is the question of media effects still important?

2   What are, according to this extract, the potential problems with the terms 'audience reading' and 'audience resistance'?

Fractures and factions: competing methodologies in audience-based research

Quantitative and qualitative paradigms

The methodological fractures and factions evident within the larger project of media analysis – and within the social sciences more generally – come into clearer focus when we examine how empirical research is undertaken on media audiences. Two competing methodological paradigms – the quantitative and the qualitative – have traditionally been used within audience-based research. Despite the calls in recent times by some researchers for a more integrated methodological approach, the marked 'stand-off' between quantitative and qualitative camps remains (Schroder, 1999). Crucial epistemological, theoretical and methodological differences exist between these two contrasting approaches (see Figure 7.1). The degree to which audiences are conceptualized as either active or passive in their encounters with media texts and technologies is a key debating point. These two paradigms are divided over the relative amount of power attributed to either the media text or the media audience.

The quantitative approach makes use of experiments and surveys in order to measure both media power and audience behaviour. Those following an effects or uses and gratifications model of media analysis have typically examined large numbers of audience members in an attempt to examine the power of specific media texts. The media industry – and the advertising and marketing sectors in particular – continue to draw upon a quantitative approach in their analysis of audience behaviour and preferences. Ratings data on audience response to television programmes, for example, are used to sell air time to the advertising industry. Quantitative research can provide useful information to those in the commercial sector who wish to target a specific demographic group in society.

The qualitative approach uses interviews, focus group interviews and participant observation as the main methodological tools in examining media audiences. Here there is an emphasis on how meaning is created by media audiences. Media discourses are examined in the context of the workings of other – and sometimes more powerful – discourses that may prevail on questions of gender, ethnicity or class in the day-to-day lives of audience members. The qualitative paradigm examines the reception of media texts in a wider social context than its quantitative counterpart. While the reception and ethnographic approaches are generally accepted to be 'rich' in terms of the data yielded, many of these studies are based upon relatively small sample sizes, are genre-specific, raising questions as to the extent of their representativeness and the extent to which we can generalize about the wider process of media effects. Qualitative methodologies are also used by the media industries. It is common, for example, for the movie industry to pre-test audience response to a series of alternative endings for films that are intended for mainstream consumption and distribution.

Quantitative paradigm	Qualitative paradigm
Behaviourist/positivist	Interpretivist

Main methodologies:
    Experiments
    Surveys
    Questionnaires
	Main methodologies:
	    Interviews structured
	    Interviews unstructured
	    Participant observation
	    Observation
	    Focus group interviews
	    Journal/diary keeping

Effects Uses and gratifications	Encoding/decoding Ethnographic Constructivist

FIGURE 7.1   Methodological approaches to media audiences

Reception analysis and the 'ethnographic turn'

See Box 5.8 for
more on Radway
and romance.

Critical ethnography has dominated qualitative audience analysis in recent times. Championed by feminist and post-modern researchers alike, the so-called 'ethnographic turn' within audience research constructs audience members as active agents, capable of resisting and reconstructing media texts. Lull (1991), for example, used the ethnographic approach to examine how Chinese television viewers engaged in resistive practices. Radway (1987), similarly, explored female readers' resistance in her celebrated study of romantic fiction (see Chapter 5). In this research approach, audiences are celebrated as being active and resistant in their everyday encounters with media texts. Far from being the slaves of hegemonic ideology, audience members have, it is argued, the capacity to resist, to read against the grain of dominant and other ideologies. In the postmodern account, audiences are characterized as being more sophisticated in their encounters with media discourses. They possess the power to play with and subvert media texts. Some proponents of the ethnographic approach like to stress their empathy with those who have less power in society and this is reflected in many of the research themes that have been chosen for investigation (Gray, 1999; Ruddock, 2000).

The rise of the ethnographic approach marks a new emphasis on audience reception in its own right and not merely as one constituent part of the longer communicative chain of production, content and reception. From the ethnographic perspective, media discourses may be understood only in what Ruddock (2000) terms the 'total context of reception'. The rationale for the ethnographic turn within reception analysis is given by Moores as follows:

In attending to the meanings produced by social subjects and to the daily activities they perform, qualitative audience researchers have frequently sought to explain those significances and practices by locating them in relation to broader frameworks of interpretation and to structures of power and inequality. This is the mark of . . . a 'critical' ethnography. It is an approach which takes seriously the interpretations of the media constructed by consumers in their everyday routines. At the same time, it is not afraid to interrogate and situate their spoken accounts. (1993: 4–5)

Ethnographers use a range of interviewing styles (in-depth interviews; structured and semi-structured interviews; focus group interviews) as well as observation and participant observation in order to understand how audience members construct meaning. The reception of fictional genres such as romantic novels, women's magazines, serialized television dramas and soap operas has been a major focus of this research approach.

Unlike more traditional ethnographic research, where the researcher spends a long period of time observing and interviewing in the 'field', audience ethnographers typically have to rely upon far more restricted contact with their subjects. (For an exception to this rule see Miller and Slater's (2000) detailed ethnography of Internet culture and consumption in Trinidad.) The taped in-depth interviews are often no more than one hour in length. Prolonged access to informants or interviewees in their private domestic settings may also prove problematic. Observation of media consumption in the private sphere raises many ethical questions. For practical as well as budgetary reasons, sample sizes are usually small, leading some to question just how representative individual studies are. Nevertheless, as Gray points out:

We can learn a great deal more from these audience reception studies which are not necessarily very much to do with audiences themselves but rather the processes by which media forms and technologies take their place in everyday settings. Furthermore, critical and analytical empirical work can enter into a productive dialogue with our theorization of audiences and consumption practices. (1999: 32)

According to Moores (1993: 5), the ethnographic turn has made a worthwhile contribution that has deepened our understanding of media audiences. It has contributed much to the debate over the power (or not) of media texts to shape audience readings and interpretations. It has helped explain the variations in audience tastes for different media genres (see, for example, Lull, 1980). Audience ethnographies have focused on the politics of the private domestic sphere in order to understand more about the gendered realities of media consumption and interpretation (see, for example, Radway, 1987). A growing amount of ethnographic work is focused on the uses of new ICTs as well as older media technologies in the home (see, for example, Silverstone et al., 1991; Livingstone, 1998).

BOX 7.1   SEX DIFFERENCES IN VIDEO GAME PLAY

At the outset of this chapter we noted that mass media audiences are becoming disaggregated. A particular focus in recent years has been on the adoption and use of newer forms of media technology in the home, with a particular concentration on the gendered realities behind these developments. Lucas and Sherry (2004), for example, examined gender differences in video game playing. Drawing upon the results of a large-scale survey of 593 college students who were aged between 18 and 24 years, they found significant differences between female and male respondents. Females played video games less frequently and were not as motivated to play video games in social situations. Unlike their male counterparts, female respondents were less interested in games that were competitive in orientation.

See also Kerr (2006) for an excellent introduction to games and gaming.

You should now read EXTRACTED READING 7.2, *Living Room Wars* (Ang, 1996) and consider the following issue:

1   List ways in which you think your gender is of significance in understanding your television viewing patterns.

Alternative styles of reception analysis: the 'News Game'

As part of its ongoing research into media effects and audience beliefs, the Glasgow University Media Group make use of an innovative research technique known as the 'News Game' (see Philo, 1990, 1993, 1999; Kitzinger, 1990, 1993, 1999). The method has been used to examine media effects and audience beliefs about a wide range of 'public knowledge' issues, including media coverage of strikes, AIDS, mental health, the war in Northern Ireland and most recently the Israeli–Palestinian conflict (see Philo, 2002). The News Game has been a central part of the group's attempts at investigating the workings of dominant and other ideologies in a media setting.

The News Game was devised initially as a teaching aid. It was intended as a means of generating debate among students on how the media engage in the social construction of reality. In this research model audience groups are given a set of photographs from actual media coverage of a specific theme. The members of each audience group are then asked to pretend that they are journalists and are requested to write a story or a report to accompany the photographic images that they have selected. Greg Philo first used the News Game in audience-based research when he examined audience understandings of the 1984–5 miners' strike in the United Kingdom. In addition to the research group's dissatisfaction with the behaviourist model of effects research, a primary motivation behind using the News Game was to establish what attitudes and beliefs existed among audiences before the research exercise was undertaken. In Philo's words:

It seemed clear that much of the process of attitude and belief formation would have taken place before such an experiment could be conducted. In a sense we needed to establish what people already 'knew' and to show the processes by which they had arrived at their beliefs. We devised a new method which involved asking audience groups to write their own news programmes. This would show what they thought the content of news to be on a given issue. It would then be possible to compare this with what group members actually believed to be true and to examine why they either accepted or rejected the media account. . . . This approach has enabled us to look at long-term processes of belief, understanding and memory. (1993: 258)

In the miners' strike study (Philo, 1990), for example, sixteen 'naturally occurring' audience groups, with a total of 169 participants, were interviewed concerning their beliefs about and memories of the strike. Working in groups of three or four, they also took part in the News Game. Their 'journalistic' accounts of the strike were then compared with actual coverage on BBC and ITN. Philo (1990) found a remarkable similarity between the participants' and the television news versions of the strike. The third and final part of the study involved asking the participants about their beliefs about what had actually taken place. The research found that significant numbers of audience members believed the accounts given to them by television and the press. Dominant ideological constructions of the strike – such as the notion that the strike was a violent one – were not only reproduced in the News Game exercise but also surfaced in the interviews and discussions held with the study's audience groups.

Qualitative audience research: three examples

We turn now to examine three examples of qualitative research on media audiences. These studies focus on factional and fictional genres from the print and broadcast media. A variety of research methodologies are used (interviews; focus group interviews; observation as well as narrative analysis) in order to examine audiences. The studies vary in terms of whether they examine audience members in a 'natural setting', i.e. the home, or whether 'naturally occurring' groups (based on occupation, gender or ethnicity) were convened for the purposes of the study. In all three examples, audiences are constructed as being active and reflexive in their encounters with media texts.

> *See Chapter 4 for an elaboration of Hall's encoding/decoding model*

Morley's (1980) analysis of the popular BBC current affairs programme *Nationwide* is justifiably hailed as a classic within the field of empirical audience research. Reflecting a seismic shift in emphasis from textual to reception analysis, it sought to examine the complexity of audience response to current affairs television using Hall's encoding/decoding model of media analysis. Using a semiotic approach, Brunsdon and Morley (1978) had previously examined the *Nationwide* programme in terms of its mode of address and its ideological make-up. Following on from this, Morley's (1980) study set out to examine audience interpretations of *Nationwide* using Hall's dominant, negotiated and oppositional readings as his key. However, as Abercrombie and Longhurst point out, Morley 'assumed that there would be also differences within them [dominant, negotiated and oppositional readings] and his research design aimed to tap those internal differences in interpretation' (1998: 16). Morley was interested in investigating whether there was a demonstrable link between the readings produced by audience members and their socioeconomic status. He was also interested in investigating how media consumption practices were shaped by factors such as class, gender and race.

Twenty-nine audience groups made up of apprentices, managers, trade unionists or students were shown one of two selected recordings of *Nationwide*. These groups were already involved in education or training. They were convened for the purposes of the research project outside their usual domestic viewing contexts. Using the group interview method, their responses to the style and ideological orientation of specific episodes were tape-recorded and analysed in order to ascertain whether they engaged in dominant, negotiated or oppositional reading of the texts in question. The analysis of audience response was related to the ideological structure, mode of address and style employed in the selected texts.

In summarizing the main findings of the *Nationwide* study, Taylor and Willis (1999) argue that:

> the most important aspect of Morley's findings was the discovery that the socioeconomic background of the respondents did not necessarily determine their readings. In fact, respondents who shared similar backgrounds sometimes produced different responses. He also found that other cultural frameworks and institutions, for example, affiliation to institutions such as trade unions as well as the impact of informational sources such as the press, worked to shape audience responses to the text. For example, he found that the three reading positions simply could not accommodate the black students he interviewed. These students found very little in *Nationwide* to engage with; in fact, they declined to respond at all to the text and as a result their responses fell outside the three dominant positions. But it was not the only limitation Morley found in the reading positions laid out in the encoding/decoding model. He also found that while the managers broadly affirmed the ideological sentiments of

Nationwide, they were disparaging about the populist presentational style of the programme. The shop stewards he interviewed, however, were comfortable with the programme's populist production values, but voiced dissatisfaction with what they saw as its favourable treatment of management. As Shaun Moores argues, this type of difference between cultural ideas about taste could not be accounted for within the confines of Hall's model (1994: 21). Yet the findings do reveal important information about the relationship between audience decoding and class habitus. (1999: 173–4)

Morley's analysis then pointed to significant differences of interpretation between and among the four main audience groupings. His findings emphasized the complexities involved in audience interpretation of media texts and to the limitations of the encoding/decoding model. Morley's study found that one's class position did not necessarily determine the way in which one read or decoded a media text. Rather it pointed to a wider range of contexts that were influential in shaping the meanings derived from a media text. Proponents of reception-based research deservedly celebrate the *Nationwide* study. As Gray states, its significance rests upon the fact that it:

sought to combine textual construction and interpretation, it granted viewers interpretative status (but always within shaping structural determinations) and developed ways of conceiving of the audience as socially structured, suggesting that decoding is not homogeneous. Thus the text and audience are conceptualized within and as part of the social structure organized in and across power relations of dominant and subordinate groups, of which the media were seen to be occupying a crucial position and role. Although the viewer was considered to be interpreting specific programmes in different ways, these were not entirely and absolutely open to the viewer; she or he was limited, shaped by her or his own social positioning as well as the limitations and closures of the text itself. (1999: 27–8)

'Discursive texts, reflexive audiences: global trends in television news texts and audience reception' by Andy Kavoori

Using a combination of narrative and reception analysis, Kavoori (1999) examines news texts about 'political conflict' and their reception by audience members in an age of media globalization. This detailed qualitative study is based upon comparative research carried out in Britain, France, Germany and the United States. The research analyses the narrative structure and audience interpretation of news texts concerning political conflict broadcast by the BBC and ITN, A2N, ZDF and ABC television channels.

The stories in question reported on rioting by students in South Korea and a politically inspired slaughter of train passengers in South Africa. Kavoori's work is informed by two key research questions. In terms of news content he asks, 'How does television news portray foreign news events? (What is its narrative construction of the outside world?) Specific to stories on "political conflict", what vision of cultural "others" becomes narrative?' (1999: 387). With respect to audience interpretation he asks, 'How do audiences make sense of foreign news on television? What patterns of mediation of the narratives on political conflict emerge as constructed by television news?' (1999: 387).

The first stage of the study involved recording television news programmes in 1987 and 1990 in Britain, Germany, France and the United States. The content of individual news programmes was subjected to a narrative analysis and subsequently compared. The second stage of the study examined audience reception of the stories concerning the Korean unrest and the South African train violence. Six focus groups comprising between nine and twelve members per group were convened in each of the four countries. Kavoori's study did not segment the focus groups according to age, race or gender. Instead, there was an attempt to involve a wide range of socioeconomic groups. The audience groups were constructed on the basis of income and were recruited by academic institutions in each of the respective countries. Kavoori (1999) describes how the reception analysis was undertaken:

> Focus group transcripts were analysed for issues of variation across countries and power (the extent to which the audience reiterated the discursive features of the text). Each question by the moderator was followed by discussion. Transcripts were divided into discussion segments. Summary statements were written for each discussion segment. These statements were used as the basis for identifying modes of interpretation comprising audience mediation.
>
> Each focus group began with viewing of the news story aired in that country. The audience was asked to retell the story in their own words. This was followed by questions about media coverage and content, including the dominant themes identified by the researchers. (1999: 388)

Kavoori argues that, in terms of its narrative dimension, television news represents the 'other' world as 'a violent, unstable world' (1999: 395). He finds striking similarities across the four countries in how stories about 'violence' and 'democracy' are framed. He suggests that 'The effect of television news discourse . . . is discursive, i.e. the news the narrative constructs in each country draws upon frameworks common in each country. But the news also displays cross-cultural, global trends. Thes cross-cultural trends provide a narrow and negative construction of the "other"' (1999: 396). In its television news coverage, the global media industry continues to construct the world in terms of the West and the (uncivilized) rest.

Kavoori's (1999) reception analysis found a significant amount of reflexivity among audiences in their encounters with foreign news on television. The findings of his study suggest that audiences are increasingly critical in their engagement with news texts. Kavoori argues that '[p]art of political work that television news audiences perform is reflexive, re-articulating the terms of the news texts through a specific set of analytical practices' (1999: 396). His research suggests that we are now witnessing the arrival of a 'global culture of critical media consumption'

(1999: 396). Audiences are increasingly critical because of 'a familiarity with the narrative conventions of the genre; an awareness of the institutional imperatives of the media industries and, more generally, the cultural, political and ideological contexts of media coverage' (1999: 396).

Reading Women's Magazines by Joke Hermes

> ∞∞
>
> *See our earlier discussion in this chapter, 'Fractures and factions', on the potential problems with the ethnographic approach vis-à-vis sample size.*

Hermes (1995) used a postmodern feminist perspective to analyse the everyday use of women's magazines. Starting from a position of 'respect' rather than 'concern' for her research subjects, her work is an exemplary qualitative study. With the exception of Winship's (1987) celebrated work *Inside Women's Magazines*, Hermes expresses her disillusionment with the ways in which this popular media genre has been traditionally approached by researchers. Using analytical techniques associated with socio-linguistics and discourse analysis, she draws upon detailed interview data based upon eighty conversational interviews with fifteen men and sixty-five women. Unlike many other 'ethnographic' studies of popular media genres where sample sizes are notoriously small, Hermes's sample is sufficiently large for her to draw sound conclusions from the findings.

The study focuses on the everyday uses of Dutch and British magazines. Hermes's work is written in an accessible style and is strongly reflexive, particularly in terms of her chosen methodological approach. Her specific focus is on meaning and therefore she is steering a middle-ground position between audience research that has either combined textual and reception analysis with a clear focus on texts or genres (e.g. Ang, 1996; Radway, 1987) and audience research that has focused on the uses of media technology and form in the context of power relationships in everyday (domestic) life (e.g. Morley, 1986; Gray, 1999). Hermes's ambitious task was 'to find out how women's magazines become meaningful in everyday life and what "meaning" can be taken to be in everyday contexts' (1995: 11).

What sorts of 'interpretative repertoires' do ordinary readers bring to women's magazines? Hermes tells us that she:

wanted to know how women's magazines became meaningful for readers and readers told me that women's magazines have hardly any meaning at all. They are convenient, my informants said, easy to put down when other things need to be done, but of little cultural value and therefore not very meaningful. They would also point out that while women's magazines have little cultural value, they do have practical value: all those tips, recipes and dress patterns. What more meaning would a medium need than to be of such a practical use? Although reading women's magazines is a complex activity that certainly has more than one side to it, readers would mainly speak of its cultural insignificance. (1995: 143)

Hermes (1995) uses an interview-based ethnographic approach. With an average length of one and a half hours, the interviews were recorded and transcribed, giving the author a large volume of research data. She stresses that due to the 'inherently unequal positions of interviewer and interviewed, I cannot claim this text is a series of dialogues or a polylogue – a goal interpretative ethnography should aim for according to some of its practitioners' (1995: 11).

The text provides an insightful account of both the female and the male readers of women's magazines. We are given detailed portraits of two readers based upon interviews with the author's mother and one of her informants – Joan Becker. Both interviews provide us with important contextual information on the everyday use of women's magazines, and the author's interview with her mother is particularly moving. While even the most cursory glance at a magazine shelf in a newsagent's would suggest that the publishing industry segments its readership base according to age and interests (gossip, clothes, celebrity, lifestyles, domestic know-how, etc.), Hermes found that 'readers read unpredictable and changing combinations of magazines' (1995: 155).

Hermes concludes that:

> the most important aspect of women's magazines for readers was not that they are so full of practical information, even if that is a common justification for spending money and time on them, but that they blend easily with other obligations, other duties and activities. Women's magazines as a text are not highly significant, but as an everyday medium they are a means of filling a small break and of relaxing that does not interrupt one's schedule, because they are easy to put down. (1995: 144)

Furthermore she argues that:

> A second, less manifest aspect of reading them is that women's magazines offer material that may help you imagine a sense of control over your life by feeling prepared for tragedy, or a more perfect version of yourself by supposing that you would be able to answer any questions regarding the difficult choices in life someone else might ask. (1995: 144)

Audiences as fans

Although fans and fandom are often maligned within public and media-based discourse, analyses of fans and the phenomenon of fandom represent a further important trend within audience research (see Jenson, 1992). Typically focused on popular forms of mass media, this work attempts to understand more about the significance of media content and their related activities in people's everyday (media) lives. This recent development mirrors a more general concern within sociology and cultural studies which has tried to make sense of the complexities of identity formation and subcultural affiliation – particularly in terms of sport (soccer) and music (punk rock, Goth) for example (see Bennett, 2006; Hodkinson, 2002).

Conceptualized as fans, audience members are viewed as possessing considerable agency. They have the power to subvert intended meanings and to produce and circulate new media texts either replacing the original text altogether or creating new texts, which in turn may influence how the original text is understood. Researchers have used interviews, focus groups, observation/participant observation and discourse analysis in order to understand audience members as fans. As we will shortly see in our case study of the singer Morrissey, there is a strong emphasis on the question of identity formation within fan studies as well as its performative and affective or emotional dimensions.

In its popular usage, being a fan often implies an obsessive or unhealthy interest in a star, a football team or a particular media genre. Defining fandom in this pejorative or negative way is highly problematic in that nearly all of us who live in a media-saturated world are fans or followers of one or more kinds of media genre (De Kloet and van Zoonen, 2007). Fandom is not monolithic. It has to be understood as a continuum. One fan of David Bowie may buy all of his recordings and listen to his music regularly. Another fan may also buy the same set of recordings but also be an active member of the subscription-based service Bowie.net. She may trade bootleg recordings and other items of interest such as posters or badges with other collector fans. She may also contribute regularly to a range of fora discussing Bowie's latest touring or recording plans with people she has never met. Similiarly a fan of *Sex and the City* may watch the programme when she has the time, whereas another may watch all episodes when they are broadcast, purchase all of the series on DVD and discuss the programme's characters and storylines with other fans in either a real or virtual setting. The fans of David Bowie and *Sex and the City* may also be fans of other types of media genres. In this regard Abercrombie and Longhurst (1998) suggest that we need to differentiate between *fans*, *cultists* and *enthusiasts* in terms of reaching a more critical understanding of audiences as fandom.

Fan studies have been strongly influenced by postmodern theory, cultural studies and feminist approaches to media. It is hardly surprising then that fans have been examined in terms of their attachment to specific popular media genres (e.g. soap operas, romantic novels, women's magazines, 'reality' television shows and science-fiction series such as *Star Trek* (Jenkins, 1992; Jenkins and Tulloch, 1995) and Hollywood blockbusters) and/or attachment to particular 'stars' or 'celebrities' such as Britney Spears, Kylie or Beyoncé.

Fandom is now usually understood in terms of its affective dimension in that researchers have examined the role that being a fan plays in people's everyday emotional lives. They ask: What sorts of connections occur between the content of the chosen media text(s) and the everyday emotional experiences of fans? How are these connections cemented? Vroomen (2004), for example, has examined the listening practices of older fans of Kate Bush who consume her music in a private setting. Does being a fan of a particular media genre alter in any way the meanings and pleasures derived from the text? Does a committed fan of say *Queer As Folk* interpret an episode differently than a less-regular viewer?

Fandom is increasingly participatory. The merging of old and new media technologies allows for greater audience participation through voting, texting or email. Fans, as Jenkins (1992) has argued, may be textual poachers as well as cultural nomads. They are not necessarily restricted to one medium and migrate across media in search of texts concerning the object of their interest. Livingstone notes that

> Fandom is increasingly important as audiences fragment and diversify. And as media become interconnected, increasingly intertextual, it is content irrespective of medium that matters to people *qua* fans, for they follow it across media, weaving it seamlessly also into their face-to-face communications. (2004: 81)

As we pointed out at the start of this textbook, fandom can also be about audience members becoming producers – albeit in a basic sense. Fans produce publications such as fanzines and e-zines. The fans of *Buffy the Vampire Slayer* who were disappointed at the decision to axe the programme after its seventh series wrote their own follow-up series (see Box 0.1). Fans are active in the blogosphere, sharing ideas and thoughts with fellow fans about their mutual interest. Increasingly, being a fan is about being a member of an imagined community which exists only in cyberspace. Fans of *Arcade Fire* (www.arcadefire.net), for example, converse with one another about the Canadian band and share their thoughts and ideas. Membership of an imagined transnational community allows individual fans to take on assumed identities.

At its core, fandom is about identity formation. It is at once both public and private. It is about saying to the world (or at the very least to your family, friends, neighbours and work/study colleagues) that 'I am a fan of X, Y or Z'. It involves laying down all sorts of semiotic markers as to who you think you are. It is not just about media consumption *per se* but may involve shaping how you present yourself to the world in terms of your overall style/dress code or involvement in related leisure activities such as attending a concert or a fan event such as a *Star Trek* or Elvis convention. Being a fan is also a private act in that the relationships that fans have with media texts or genres can come about as a result of subjective or personal experiences. Such experiences are of course determined in turn by one's relative amount of power in terms of one's class/ethnicity/gender.

Political economists may argue that there has been too strong an emphasis on examining popular culture within everyday life to the detriment of a focus on more important economic and political questions. Furthermore, fandom – in its more extreme guises – can be seen as the manifestation of conspicuous consumption much favoured by the global capitalist class. Whatever the shortcomings, analyses of fandom have something to say about audience members in terms of consumption, meaning and identity formation.

Plate 7.1   An iconic figure, Morrissey attracts a fandom that is sometimes seen as fanatical. Photograph reproduced by kind permission of Sanctuary Music (London) © 2005.

CASE STUDY

From Manchester to 'Moz Angeles': Morrissey, identity and fandom

As leader of the seminal post-punk group The Smiths and as a solo recording artist since 1987, the singer Morrissey has attracted a fandom that is sometimes seen as fanatical. His fans have been described, somewhat unfairly, as being 'High-IQ misfits and fervent introverts' (Evans, 1993). His sell-out concerts are the site of quasi-religious fervour with (typically male) fans competing to touch his hand or hug this reluctant icon. Even a cursory scan of the many fan websites and fanzines dedicated to Morrissey indicate the centrality of the star in the very meaning that fans make of their own lives (see for example www.morrissey-solo.com). On a daily basis, fans dissect the latest piece of news about Morrissey and communicate with one another via bulletin boards about concerts, recordings or rumours. Fans have published on-line essays on the significance of Morrissey in their personal lives (see for example, Nylén, 2004; Taylor, 2006).

While Morrissey's fans are predominantly male and aged 35 or older, his fan base is quite heterogeneous. Viitämaki (1997: 40) suggests, for example, that Morrissey's American fans include 'androgenic teenagers, Latino gangsters, skinheads, well-dressed 30 year olds, gays and some older fans'. Morrissey's songs speak to an audience that may be gay, straight, bisexual, celibate or transgendered. Queer discourses are strongly in evidence in much of the iconography (record covers; posters; t-shirts etc.) associated with both The Smiths and Morrissey.

Morrissey occupies a contradictory space. Famously shy and reclusive, he is a narcissistic star. He is heralded as a gay icon but he appeals to 'straight' men. His previous band The Smiths are sometimes (somewhat problematically) seen as being the quintessentially 'English' band of the 1980s, yet all four members were the children of Irish immigrants. The songs of The Smiths and Morrissey are just one example of a larger shift within British popular culture, which has fetishized and commodified a particular version of (white) Northern English working-class life – a theme which is also very much in evidence in the later so-called 'Britpop' phenomenon of the early 1990s (see, for example, Stringer, 1992; Zuberi, 2001).

Morrissey's songs have crossed many geographical and cultural boundaries in terms of their meaning and their appeal. He has attracted a cult following in places like Bogotá, Columbia, as well as, most notably, amongst Latino immigrants in the United States. In Los Angeles, for example, a group of Mexican immigrants play in a Smiths/Morrissey tribute band called 'Sweet and Tender Hooligans.' As a tribute to their (anti) hero, Morrissey's Latino fans have re-named their adopted hometown as 'Moz Angeles'. This phenomenon of tribute bands is replicated elsewhere in the USA as well as in New Zealand, Italy, Finland, Ireland and the UK. Concerts by tribute bands allow fans to re-create their experiences of attending 'real' Morrissey/Smiths concerts. Participation in Karaoke style events takes this one step further in that fans can 'become' their hero for 4 minutes or longer. Using musicians from Bogotá, Columbia, the video artist Phil Collins has recorded a Karaoke soundtrack of a Smiths' compilation called *The Songs That Saved Your Life*. This has been used as the basis of a series of videos recorded to date in Ireland, Turkey and Greece involving fans (both male and female) who 'become' Morrissey during their performance.

Fandom is graduated however. Amongst Morrissey's fans are those who are effectively 'full-time' in their fandom – whom Morrissey himself has termed the 'regular irregulars'. Cheaper air travel has resulted in a core group of fans following entire concert tours. Information on tickets, travel and cheap places to stay is exchanged on fan websites. Full-time Morrissey fans have been known to drop out of school, college or paid employment in order to follow their idol's concerts. Some fans collect a wide range of artefacts associated with the singer. Ticket stubs, autographs, photographs and bootleg recordings are regularly traded on eBay.

At Morrissey concerts many fans mimic their idol in terms of their personal appearance. In an ethnographic account of one Morrissey concert, Devereux notes that:

> A specific hairstyle and style of dress mark out the (male) Morrissey fan. The dress code involves wearing either a Morrissey t-shirt usually emblazoned with Morrissey's face . . . Many of the t-shirts make use of gay iconography. Additional items of clothing include the wearing of a Harrington-style jacket and Dr. Martens shoes or boots. The James Dean/Elvis-style quiff is the most common hairstyle. Some fans have the nickname 'Moz' shaved into the back of their heads. Tattoos, of either Morrissey's image or selected quotes from his songs, are also used as signifiers of fandom. Other fans wear t-shirts quoting lyrics from his songs. (2006: 239–40)

(Continued)

Morrissey's appeal is often explained by reference to themes of his songs. His lyrics are abundant with sadness, humour and irony. Morrissey sings, typically in the first person, about depression, suicide, failed relationships and relationships that will never happen. He sings about the dispossessed, the long-term unemployed, the disabled and the lonely. The displacement experienced by immigrants has also been explored. There has been a recurring focus on themes associated with gay subculture. He has written about boxers, football hooligans and skinheads. Songs are written invariably from the point of view of the outsider. The realities of adolescent experience are a recurring theme. Reynolds (1995: 332) asserts that 'Morrissey exposed the hidden truths of adolescence: awkwardness, sexual incapacity, neurasthenia, emasculation'. Fans repeatedly refer to the personal connection they feel with Morrissey's lyrics and relate them to their own emotional experiences, thus agreeing with Wells's (1990) research into the affective aspects of fandom.

Identity politics are central to understanding Morrissey's fandom. In combining social realism and ambiguity about sexuality and gender (often in a wry and humorous fashion), Morrissey provokes strong feelings of empathy from his fans. His attraction may be explained by reference to his ability to write well-crafted songs which draw upon a bricolage of images associated with white, Northern English, working-class life, which manage to present a sense of authenticity and 'realness' to his fans. He taps into a nostalgia for a particular version of working-class life whose key elements are now disappearing or have gone altogether. At a more general level, he expresses feelings of loss, alienation and *anomie*, which may help explain his transnational appeal. As the perennial outsider, Morrissey's songs speak directly to the disenfranchised and the disenchanted.

Side by side with this, is a consistent gay and camp discourse. Hawkins notes that the ambiguity in evidence in his songs and associated imagery means that both gay and heterosexual fans are allowed to 'address the complexity of their own sexualities and desires'. (2002: 75). Morrissey manages to sing from a range of viewpoints that address both male and female subjects. Sometimes it is not altogether clear whom exactly he is addressing. In recognizing this ambiguity, Hubbs (1996) stresses the variety of ways in which Morrissey's audience can read his songs and points out that whilst gay fans have no difficulty in decoding the gay discourse inscribed in Morrissey's work, many heterosexual fans do not adopt a so-called 'queer' reading of his texts.

Morrissey once described his music as being for 'the fourth gender' (Hubbs, 1996). Apart from his obvious ability as a songwriter, Morrissey's appeal may be explained in terms of how he manages to combine both ambiguity and authenticity all at once.

His refusal to be classified in terms of one specific sexuality and his ability to sing from a range of gender perspectives (male to male; male to female; female to male; female to female) serves to create an ambiguity and fluidity in which a wide range of fans can see themselves. In doing so, Morrissey's creative output and his concerts deviate significantly from the usual patriarchal – or so-called 'cock rock' aspects of rock and roll culture. Morrissey's concerts are places where many male fans can express the complexities which have come to typify masculinity in the early twenty-first century.

> You should now read EXTRACTED READING 7.3, *Fans: Poachers and Cultural Nomads* (Gray, 2003) and apply Gray's ideas to the case-study of Morrissey's fans.
>
> 1   Do you think Morrissey's fans inhabit an imagined community?
>
> 2   How is it possible that a wide variety of fans (male/female; gay/straight) can identify with the same performer?

Conclusion

While quantitative audience research has its place within the broad church of media studies, a qualitative approach is potentially the most fruitful in assisting us in our efforts to better understand media audiences. As an antidote to the crude determinism evident in the behaviourist/effects model of audience research and as a bulwark to the often simplistic assumptions made about media effects within public (and media) discourse, the qualitative approach recognizes the dynamic and often complex nature of the relationship between media audiences and media texts.

While we accept that media texts have the power to shape and frame audience interpretations, we can never be fully sure how audiences will interpret media content. The research methodologies used by those following a reception or ethnographic research approach offer us the best chance of understanding more about these processes. Interpretative activity has to be examined in terms of where audience members are socially situated and in terms of the relative amount of power they possess. Ideally, analyses of reception should be undertaken not in isolation but rather as part of a research framework that gives adequate attention to questions concerning production and content. Reception analysis need not be confined to analysing fictional genres. It is applicable to both factual and fictional media genres. The ethnographic approach has produced valuable insights into the processes associated with media globalization and on the gendered dimensions of new media technologies. It has been particularly insightful in terms of understanding the world of the fan and fans, of popular cultural forms in particular.

Extracted readings

7.1   Reading and reception

Jenny Kitzinger, 'A sociology of media power: key issues in audience reception research' in Greg Philo (ed.) *Message Received*. Harlow: Addison Wesley Longman, 1999, pp. 15–18

. . . Cultural debate and intervention must include engaging with the production, content and reception of such messages. In this sense, mass communication is too important to leave to the mass communication experts . . . It would be a sad irony if communication studies researchers only communicated with each other, and if communication itself failed to lead to productive dialogue.

First . . . the ability to deconstruct media messages and develop a critical reading in a research setting is not necessarily the same as being able to reject the message conveyed via the media on a day-to-day level. It was sometimes only when invited to do so, within the research setting, that people challenged attitudes or facts conveyed by the media which they had previously accepted without question. Evidence of critical readings from organised research sessions should not be unproblematically extrapolated to routine media–audience encounters.

Second . . . the term 'reading' itself needs to be unpacked. . . . sometimes people do not just 'read' a report 'differently' but simply refuse to believe the facts conveyed, or blatantly disagree with the media's interpretation. An intertwined issue is that the polysemy of texts has been exaggerated

. . . Third, it is important to recognise that 'deviant readings' may be as much influenced by other media messages as by some kind of counter-cultural reservoir of alternative perspectives. Observing that people 'resist', or read against the grain of any individual media product, does not mean that the media lack power.. In any case, it is misleading to play off textual power against reader 'freedom' as if the reader came to the text with an independent view.

. . . This leads to the fourth point . . . the 'active' audience is not immune from influence. Indeed, the way in which people use the media (and incorporate soap opera plots, media stories or slogans from advertisements into their everyday lives) can strengthen, rather than weaken, media effects. The way people re-read individual texts or take unexpected pleasures can actually reinforce, rather than undermine, broad media influence over public understandings.

The fifth . . . point . . . is that 'resistance' becomes a problematic concept, once applied empirically to substantive topics. . . . Should 'audience resistance' be celebrated if people reject the primary message of a mass media campaign to encourage safer sex or violence against women? . . . Clearly audiences do not always accept the dominant message, but I would argue that the normative implications of a word such as 'resistance' should be questioned.

7.2   Living room wars

Ien Ang, 'Politics of empirical audience research' in *Living Room Wars: Rethinking Media Audiences for a Postmodern World*. London: Routledge, 1996, pp. 50–2

What clearly emerges here is the beginning of an interpretative framework in which differences in television-viewing practices are not just seen as expressions of different needs, uses or readings, but are connected with the way in which particular social subjects are structurally positioned in relation to each other. In the context of the nuclear family home, women's viewing patterns can only be understood in relation to men's patterns; the two are in a sense constitutive of each other. Thus, if watching television is a social and even a collective practice, it is not a harmonious practice. Because subjects are positioned in different ways towards the set, they engage in a continuing struggle over programme choice and programme interpretation, styles of viewing and textual pleasure.

. . . Television consumption . . . contributes to the everyday construction of male and female subjectivities through the relations of power, contradiction and struggle that men and women enter into in their daily engagements with the television sets in their homes. At this point, we can also see how [David] Morley's research enables us to begin to conceive of 'the ideological operations of television' in a much more radical way than has hitherto been done. The relation between television and audiences is not just a matter of discrete 'negotiations' between texts and viewers. In a much more profound sense the process of television consumption . . . has created new areas of constraints and possibilities for structuring social relationships, identities and desires. If television is an 'ideological apparatus', to use that old fashioned-sounding term, then it is not so much because its texts transmit certain 'messages', but because it is a cultural form through which those constraints are negotiated and those possibilities take shape.

. . . [D]o we need empirical research, or more specifically, ethnographic audience research, to arrive at such theoretical understandings? Why examine audiences empirically at all? After all, some critical scholars still dismiss the idea of doing empirical research altogether, because, so they argue, it would necessarily implicate the researcher with the strategies and aims of the capitalist culture industry.

. . . Ethnographic work, in the sense of drawing on what we can perceive and experience in everyday settings, acquires its critical edge when it functions as a reminder that reality is always more complicated and diversified than our theories can represent, and that there is no such thing as 'audience' whose characteristics can be set once and for all.

7.3   Fans: poachers and cultural nomads

A. Gray, *Research Practice for Cultural Studies.* London: Sage, 2003, pp. 47–8

. . . Jenkins has carried out some work to identify fan groups (for a particular programme, performer, musical style, film genre) who inhabit an imagined community which is likely to be dispersed and connected, not within locatable or bounded space or community, but through a variety and number of mediated practices: media text, fanzines and websites. Jenkins argues that in order to understand the 'fan' we must:

> focus on media fandom as a discursive logic that knits together interests across textual and generic boundaries. While some fans remain exclusively committed to a single show or star, many others use individual series as points of entry into a broader fan community, linking to an intertextual network composed of many programmes, films, books, comics and other popular materials. (1992: 40)

'To focus on any one media product – be it *Star Trek* or *"Material Girl"* is to miss the larger cultural context within which that material gets embedded as it is integrated back into the life of the individual fan' (ibid.: 41). Thus, the studies of investments which fans make in a popular culture takes us back to the importance of how these practices relate more broadly to the cultures of everyday life.

As Jenkins suggests, many of the traditionally assumed boundaries, such as that between the producer and consumer and between commercial and creative products are broken down. 'Fandom here becomes a participatory culture which transforms the experience of media consumption into the production of new texts, indeed of a new culture and a new community' (ibid.: 46). And we might add, the boundaries of researcher and researched as they share their pleasures in the consumption of popular texts.

Those scholars who have studied fans and fan cultures have looked at the appeal of specific genres or texts for individuals. To be a 'fan' is to have extraordinary recognitions and identifications with aspects of popular culture. The insights gained here, especially into the construction of subjectivities, are very interesting indeed and reveal the complex processes of such identifications. They take us into the realm of fantasy, desire and give us some understanding of the role of the popular in giving us a sense of who we are, or who we might be.

Exercise 7.1

Researching media audiences: audience beliefs and public discourses about the socially excluded

You have been invited by a public service broadcasting organization to tender for a research project on audience beliefs about the socially excluded. The terms of the research brief state that you must concentrate on the broadcast media and that you must use an 'active audience' theoretical perspective. It is further proposed that you carry out the research in the context of existing public discourses about poverty. You are required to submit a detailed research proposal showing how you would intend to undertake this proposed research project.

   Your research proposal should focus on the following:

1 Explain what you understand by the term 'active audience' and state why you think this theoretical perspective is applicable to the research project in hand.
2 Outline and discuss your understanding of the term 'the socially excluded'. What is your understanding of the causes, extent and nature of poverty and social exclusion in your society? Which groups in your society are most likely to fit into this categorization? State whether your research is going to concentrate on one or more categories of groups who are considered to be poor or are more likely to be poor or excluded, e.g. children, women, immigrants, the homeless, the disabled or the long-term unemployed.
3 Show how you will select audience groups from the general population. What factors (e.g. age, gender, socioeconomic status, ethnicity) will you consider in terms of defining and selecting audience groups?
4 What research methodologies will you use in order to examine audience beliefs about poverty?
5 In the context of existing public discourses about poverty and social exclusion, how will your findings on audience beliefs be analysed?
6 What media genres would you intend using and why?
7 Outline the benefits for the broadcasting organization that may result from this research.

―――――――――――――――― Exercise 7.2 ――――――――――――――――

Researching media audiences: going to the movies

Focusing on a film genre of your choice, carry out a short research project on cinema and fandom.

1   The audience group should consist of at least six fans of the genre in question.
2   As in the previous exercise, some consideration should be given to the make-up of your selected groups in terms of age, gender, socioeconomic status or ethnicity.
3   The group's members should attend the showing of a particular film at the cinema. Ask them to write a short journal – say no more than 500 words – on the overall experience.
4   Interview each of the group's members separately, using the semi-structured interview technique. Your questions should focus on the appeal of the genre in question and on the meanings derived from the chosen film.

―――――――――――――――― Exercise 7.3 ――――――――――――――――

Researching media audiences: gender and new media technologies

Carry out a short qualitative research project on the use of new media technologies in a domestic setting. Focusing on gender as a key variable, examine the acquisition, use and control of new media technologies in the private sphere.

Questions for consideration and discussion

1   What are the advantages and disadvantages of the ethnographic approach to media audiences?
2   Think of three ways in which:

  •   audience members exhibit agency.
  •   audience members do not have agency.

―――――――――――――――― References ――――――――――――――――

Abercrombie, N. and B. Longhurst (1998) *Audiences*. London: Sage.
Alasuutari, P. (1999) 'Introduction: three phases of reception studies' in P. Alasuutari (ed.) *Rethinking the Media Audience*. London: Sage.

―――――――――― 241 ――――――――――

Ang, I. (1996) *Living Room Wars: Rethinking Media Audiences for a Postmodern World*. London: Routledge.

Bennett, A. (2006) 'Punk's not dead: the continuing significance of punk rock for an older generation of fans', *Sociology* 40(2): 219–35.

Biltereyst, D. (1995) 'Qualitative audience research and transnational media effects', *European Journal of Communication* 10(2): 245–70.

Brunsdon, C. and D. Morley (1978) *Everyday Television: 'Nationwide'*. London: BFI.

Cobley, P. (1994) 'Throwing out the baby: populism and active audience theory', *Media, Culture and Society* 16: 677–87.

Corner, J. (2000) '"Influence": the contested core of media research' in J. Curran and M. Gurevitch (eds) *Mass Media and Society*, 3rd edn. London: Arnold.

Devereux, E. (2006) 'Being Wild(e) about Morrissey' in M. Corcoran and M. Peillion (eds) *Uncertain Ireland*. Dublin: IPA.

Downing, J.D.H. (2003) 'Audiences and readers of alternative media: the absent lure of the virtually unknown,' *Media, Culture and Society* 25(5): 625–45.

Evans, P. (1996) cited in N. Hubbs 'Music of the Fourth Gender: Morrisey and the Sexual Politics of the Melodic Contour' in T. Foster, C. Stiegal and E. E. Berry (eds) Bodies of Writing, Bodies in Performance. New York: New York University Press, 266–96.

Fenton, N. (1999) 'Mass media' in S. Taylor (ed.) *Sociology: Issues and Debates*. London: Macmillan.

Gray, A. (1987) 'Behind closed doors: video recorders in the home', in H. Baehr and G. Dyer (eds) *Boxed In: Women and Television*. London: Pandora.

Gray, A. (1999) 'Audience and reception research in retrospect: the trouble with audiences' in P. Alasuutari (ed.) *Rethinking the Media Audience*. London: Sage.

Hall, S. (1974) 'The television discourse: encoding and decoding', *Education and Culture* 25: 8–14.

Hawkins, S. (2002) *Settling the Pop Score*, Aldershot: Ashgate.

Hermes, J. (1995) *Reading Women's Magazines: An Analysis of Everyday Media Use*. Cambridge: Polity Press.

Hodkinson, P. (2002) *Goth: Identity, Style and Sub-Culture*. Berg: Oxford and New York.

Hubbs, N. (1996) 'Music of the "Fourth Gender": Morrissey and the sexual politics of melodic contour', in T. Foster, C. Stiegel and E.E. Berry (eds), *Bodies of Writing, Bodies in Performance*, New York: New York University Press, pp. 266–96.

Jenkins, H. (1992) *Textual Poachers: Television Fans and Participatory Culture*. London: Routledge.

Jensen, J. (1992) 'Fandom as pathology: the consequences of characterization' in L. Lewis (ed.), *The Adoring Audience: Fan Culture and Popular Media*. London: Routledge.

Kavoori, A. (1999) 'Discursive texts, reflexive audiences: global trends in television news texts and audience reception', *Journal of Broadcasting and Electronic Media* 43(3): 386–98.

Kerr, A. (2006) *The Business and Culture of Digital Games*. London: Sage.

Kitzinger, J. (1990) 'Audience understandings of AIDS media messages: a discussion of methods', *Sociology of Health and Illness* 12(3): 319–335.

Kitzinger, J. (1993) 'Understanding AIDS: researching audience perceptions of Acquired Immune Deficiency Syndrome' in J. Eldridge (ed.) *Getting the Message: News, Truth and Power*. London: Routledge.

Kitzinger, J. (1999) 'A sociology of media power: key issues in audience reception research' in G. Philo (ed.) *Message Received*. Harlow: Addison Wesley Longman.

De Kloet, J. and L. van Zoonen (2007) 'Fan cultures – performing difference', in E. Devereux (ed.) *Media Studies: Key Issues and Debates*. London: Sage.

Krotz, F. and U. Hasebrink (1998) 'The analysis of people-meter data: individual patterns of viewing behaviour and viewers' cultural backgrounds', *Communications* 23(2): 151–74.

Liebes, T. and S. Livingstone (1994) 'The structure of family and romantic ties in the soap opera', *Communication Research* 21(6): 717–41.

Livingstone, S. (1998) 'Mediated childhoods: a comparative approach to young people's changing media environment in Europe', *European Journal of Communication* 13(4): 435–56.

Livingstone, S. (2004) 'The challenge of changing audiences: or what is the audience researcher to do in the age of the Internet?', *European Journal of Communication* 19(1): 75–86.

Lucas, K. and J.L. Sherry (2004) 'Sex differences in video game play', *Communication Research* 31(5): 499–523.

Lull, J. (1980) 'The social uses of television', *Human Communication Research* 6(3): 197–209.

Lull, J. (1991) *China Turned On: Television, Reform and Resistance*. London: Routledge.

Miller, D. and D. Slater (2000) *The Internet: An Ethnographic Approach*. Oxford: Berg.

Moores, S. (1993) *Interpreting Audiences: The Ethnography of Media Consumption*. London: Sage.

Morley, D. (1980) *The 'Nationwide' Audience*. London: British Film Institute.

Morley, D. (1986) *Family Television, Cultural Power and Domestic Leisure*. London: Comedia.

Nylén, A. (2004) 'Morrissey and Me', www.eurozine.com.

Philo, G. (1990) *Seeing and Believing: the Influence of Television*. London: Routledge.

Philo, G. (1993) 'Getting the message: audience research in the Glasgow Media Group' in J. Eldridge (ed.) *Getting the Message: News, Truth and Power*. London: Routledge.

Philo, G. (1999) *Message Received*. London: Longmans.

Philo, G. (2002) 'Missing in action', *Guardian*, 16 April.

Radway, J. (1987) *Reading the Romance: Women, Patriarchy and Popular Literature*. London: Verso.

Reynolds, S. (1995) *The Sex Revolts: Gender, Rebellion and Rock 'n' Roll*. Cambridge, MA: Harvard University Press.

Ruddock, A. (2000) *Understanding Audiences: Theory and Method*. London: Sage.

Schroder, K.C. (1999) 'The best of both worlds? Media audience research between rival paradigms' in P. Alasuutari (ed.) *Rethinking the Media Audience*. London: Sage.

Seiter, E. (1999) *Television and New Media Audiences*. Oxford: Oxford University Press.

Silverstone, R., E. Hirsch and D. Morley (1991) 'Listening to a long conversation: an ethnographic approach to the study of information and communication technologies in the home', *Cultural Studies* 5(2): 204–27.

Staiger, J. (2000) *Perverse Spectators: The Practices of Film Reception*. New York and London: New York University Press.

Stevenson, N. (2002) *Understanding Media Cultures: Social Theory and Mass Communication*, 2nd edn. London: Sage.

Stringer, J. (1992) 'The Smiths: repressed (but remarkably dressed)', *Popular Music* 11: 15–26.

Taylor, L. and A. Willis (1999) *Media Studies: Texts, Institutions and Audiences*. Oxford: Blackwell.

Taylor, M. (2006) 'The songs that saved my life', *Guardian* 3 April.

Tulloch, J. and Jenkins, H. (1995) *Science Fiction Audiences Watching* Doctor Who *and* Star Trek. Toronto: Atticus Books.

Viitamäki, T. (1997) 'I'm not the man you think I am: Morrissey's fourth gender', *Musical Currents*, 3: 29–40.

Vroomen, L. (2004) 'Kate Bush: teen pop and older female fans' in A. Bennett and R.A. Peterson (eds) *Music Scenes: Local, Translocal and Virtual*. Nashville, TN: Vanderbilt University Press, pp. 238–53.

Wells, A. (1990) 'Popular music: emotional use and management', *Popular Culture* 24(1): 105–17.

Winship, J. (1987) *Inside Women's Magazines*. London: Pandora Press.

Zuberi, N. (2001) 'The last truly British people you will ever know: The Smiths, Morrissey and Britpop', *Sounds English: Transnational Popular Music*. Chicago: University of Illinois Press.

Going further

Abercrombie N. and B. Longhurst (1998) *Audiences*. London: Sage. This engaging text is a critique of the dominant paradigms within audience research. See in particular chapter 5, 'Fans and enthusiasts' for the authors' differentiation of fans, cultists and enthusiasts.

Bennett, A. (2006) 'Punk's not dead: the continuing significance of punk rock for an older generation of fans', *Sociology* 40 (2): 219–35. Bennett's fascinating essay on older British fans of punk rock uses an ethnographic approach in order to understand how fans have internalized the punk ethos.

Brooker, W. and D. Jermyn (2003) *The Audience Studies Reader*. London: Routledge. Contains essays by a wide range of well-known audience theorists including Ang, Gillespie, McRobbie, Schlesinger and Radway.

Gray, A. (2003) *Research Practice for Cultural Studies*. London: Sage. Gray's text is invaluable for students of media and cultural studies. She offers a critical account of ethnographic research as well as practical advice on how to undertake research of this kind.

Gillespie, M. (ed.) (2005) *Media Audiences*. Maidenhead: Oxford University Press. This is an excellent introduction to the study of media audiences. It has a strong focus on audiences in the contexts of technological change, debates and debates about citizenship. See in particular chapter 1 by Livingstone and chapter 4 by Gillespie.

Ross, K. and V. Nightingale (2003) *Media and Audiences*. Maidenhead: Open University Press. A well-written and highly accessible text. See in particular chapters 5, 6 and 7 which deal with audiences, in turn, as citizens, fans and as consumers of new media.

Schroder, K., K. Drotner, S. Kline and C. Murray (2003) *Researching Audiences*. London: Arnold. This practical text is a must for students intent on undertaking reception analysis. See in particular chapters 7, 8 and 9 on the realities of doing reception-based research.

GLOSSARY

Active Audience: The term refers to the agency or creativity of media audiences. Audiences are seen to be active interpreters of media texts.

Agency: By agency we mean the capacity that human beings have for creativity and critical self-reflection in the face of structures or constraints. (See also STRUCTURE.)

Asymmetrical Relations of Power: Unequal relationships of power in the social world with particular reference to how inequality manifests itself in terms of people's position in the social structure of modern capitalist societies based upon one's class, ethnicity or gender in one or other combination.

Blogs: A commonly used abbreviation for a web-log. Web-logs or Blogs are on-line journals and are used as a key tool in citizen-based journalism. Those who blog are usually referred to as 'bloggers' who communicate within the blogosphere. While mainstream media organizations make use of blogs, blogging by 'ordinary' people is an example of the emergence of public sphericules. (See also PUBLIC SPHERE.)

Blue Collar: See WORKING CLASS.

Class: The categorization of members of a society according to socio-economic status. Class is one of three key variables (the others being ethnicity and gender) used to understand inequality and social stratification in modern societies. While some theorists have dismissed class as a key determinant of our life-chances, it remains important and is best understood in terms of how it intersects with other forms of social stratification such as ethnicity and gender. (See also WORKING CLASS; ETHNICITY and GENDER)

Conglomerate: Large-scale corporations that operate at national and transnational levels. Conglomerates are made up of a range of corporations that have strong monopolistic tendencies and are either vertically or horizontally integrated in terms of their ownership structure. Media corporations may be part of larger media conglomerates or conglomerates of a more general nature who have economic interests outside of the media industry. (See also INTEGRATION, VERTICAL and HORIZONTAL.)

Constructionist: Researchers interested in media audiences use the term 'constructionist' to describe the discursive and reflexive activities of media audiences.

Content Analysis: Traditionally, content analysis referred to a research method used to count the occurrence of specific phenomena – e.g. particular kinds of representations – within media texts. More recently content analysis has come to refer to either quantitative or qualitative analysis of media texts. Qualitative content analysis can involve a close critical reading of a media text – focusing for example on its discursive dimensions – rather than an attempt to count the occurrence of specific phenomena within a text.

Convergence: As used in this textbook the term convergence means the coming together or merging of media technologies and media organizations. Media organizations, for example, concerned with 'old media' and 'new media' converge through the process of conglomeration. Recent developments with the mobile or cell phone allowing video-streaming or photography are an example of how a range of media technologies can converge.

Core, Peripheral and Semi-Peripheral Societies: World System Theory sees the world as being divided into core, peripheral and semi-peripheral societies. The labour forces and raw materials of peripheral and semi-peripheral societies are exploited in order to create goods and services for the core societies in the western capitalist world. (See also DEVELOPING and DEVELOPED WORLD and THIRD WORLD.)

Counterhegemonic: See HEGEMONY; IDEOLOGY and RESISTANCE.

Deserving Poor: The poor or socially excluded who are deemed to be worthy of assistance or help. The deserving poor are believed to be poor through no fault of their own and are deserving of state or other forms of support or assistance. The deserving poor are sometimes referred to as 'God's Poor'. (See also UNDESERVING POOR.)

Developing and Developed World: Both of these concepts are problematic, particularly the former. The term 'developing world' seems to imply that the poorer regions of the globe are (slowly) catching up with the more prosperous parts. The notion of the developed world is also troublesome in that it masks the existence of poverty and inequality in the northern hemisphere. (See also THIRD WORLD; CORE, PERIPHERAL and SEMI-PERIPHERAL SOCIETIES.)

Diaspora: Of Greek origin, this term means quite literally the 'scattering of seeds'. The diaspora is a collective term for immigrant communities e.g. the Irish in the USA or the Turkish guestworker in Germany. Within media analysis the focus is on how diasporic audiences make use of media technologies to stay in touch with their homelands or indeed to forge new hybrid identities.

Digital Divide: A concept used to highlight the gap between the information rich and information poor. While the digital divide is most apparent between northern and southern hemispheres, the concept may also be used to understand information inequalities in the 'developed world'. The concept of the digital divide warns us to be skeptical about the widely used concepts such as the global village, the 'wired world' and the information society.

Discourse: A form of knowledge.

Discourse Analysis: A method of research focused on the analysis of text and talk, discourse analysis is concerned with the use of language in a social context and the relationship between language use and (unequal) power relationships.

Dominant Ideology: See IDEOLOGY.

Effects: The effects model of media analysis stresses the power of media content over media audiences. The latter are usually constructed as being passive in the face of powerful media messages. The metaphor of the hypodermic syringe injecting its contents into the minds of audience members has long been used as a way of conceptualizing the media effects paradigm.

Empirical: That which is observable.

Epistemological: Epistemology is a branch of philosophy concerned with truth or knowledge.

Ethnicity: Within sociology the term ethnicity has come to replace the problematic concept of race. By ethnicity we mean the shared common cultural heritage of a group. Membership of an ethnic group (and not always a minority ethnic group) can have a strong bearing on one's life-chances and opportunities. Ethnicity is one of three key variables (along with class and gender) used to understand inequality in modern societies. There is an important body of content analysis-based media research on how ethnic groups are problematized in a media setting.

Ethnography, Ethnographic: A research method that has its roots in social anthropology, ethnography seeks to understand and describe social behaviour in its natural everyday setting. The ethnographic approach uses a wide range of qualitative research methodologies such as participant observation, observation and interviews as a source of data. Traditionally, doing ethnographic work meant engaging in fieldwork for long periods of time, but a marked feature of recent ethnographic work within media analysis is the truncated nature of the fieldwork. (See also PARTICIPANT OBSERVATION.)

E-zines: Internet-based magazines or newsletters. These are often aimed at specific interest groups.

Focus Groups: A research method using unstructured or semi-structured group interviews. The groups in question might be selected on the basis of gender, age or occupation. Focus groups may be used either as a sole or supplementary research method.

Feminist: The feminist perspective is concerned with gender inequalities in modern and post-modern societies. Inequalities are seen to stem from the patriarchal character of these social systems.

Frame Analysis: Influenced by the work of the sociologist Erving Goffman, frame analysis in a media setting examines the use of interpretative frames in constructing media content. Media professionals resort to using interpretative frames in telling stories about the social world. The agenda-setting perspective would suggest that the selective framing of news stories, for example, has an important bearing on public beliefs about matters of social, economic and political importance.

Genre: In a media studies context genre means distinct types or categories of media content such as punk rock or heavy metal music; television soap operas or news programming, action movies or romantic dramas. (See also INTERTEXTUAL.)

Gender: One's gender is not the same as one's biological sex. The categories male and female are social constructs. Through the process of socialization individuals are taught that particular sets of values, behaviours and roles are 'natural' to their biological sex. The mass media play a hugely significant role in this process.

Globalization: The term globalization is at once both multi-faceted and ambiguous. As a process globalization refers to a number of things – the restructuring of economic activities on global lines; the apparent 'shrinkage' of time and space as a result of new information and communications technologies; the increased awareness of the global in everyday life; cultural homogenization and the intensification of local identities. The media industries (and conglomerates especially) have globalized in terms of both their reach and their presence in a range of core, peripheral and semi-peripheral societies. Media globalization has resulted in the wider circulation of media texts and has given rise to new kinds of concerns and questions for audience researchers in particular. (See also GLOCALIZATION.)

Glocalization: Occurs when media audiences appropriate, localize and hybridize globally circulated media texts. In interpreting such texts audiences 'make their own' of them.

Hegemony: The dominance of one social group over another. Hegemony may be achieved through either force or consent. Hegemonic ideologies are those ideologies that facilitate or enable domination to take place. Counterhegemonic ideologies are ideas that run counter to those expressed within the dominant ideology.

Hermeneutic: Interpretative.

Homogenization: Refers to the sameness evident in the world as a result of economic and cultural globalization. McDonaldization is one of the more obvious examples of homogenization.

Hybrid: The term can have two key meanings. Hybrid media texts may be created when their producers or creators mix the ingredients from more than one media genre. Hybridization also occurs when globally circulated media texts are appropriated by audiences and are localized.

Hyperreality: According to Baudrillard, in the media saturated post-modern world it is no longer a question of us having to examine how the media represent 'reality'. Media 'reality' has become the (hyper) reality for most members of society.

ICT: An abbreviation for Information and Communications Technologies.

Ideology: At its most basic ideology means the 'Science of Ideas'. In media analysis the emphasis is on examining how the mass media construct and disseminate ideas that are of benefit to the dominant class or other social group. We usually differentiate between dominant or hegemonic ideologies about class, ethnic or gender relations and other counter-hegemonic ideologies evident in media content.

Information Rich, Information Poor: See DIGITAL DIVIDE.

Infotainment: The merging of information and entertainment usually in a news setting. It may also refer to the increasing tendency within more serious media content of entertainment masquerading as information.

Integration, Horizontal and Vertical: The terms 'vertical' and 'horizontal' integration refer to two contrasting styles of media ownership structure. With vertical integration a media company (usually a conglomerate) owns and controls all aspects of the production, marketing, distribution and selling of a media product. Media companies that are horizontally integrated own and control a range of media companies involved in different kinds of activities such as printing, broadcasting and ICT.

Intertextuality: The tendency for media texts to make reference to or make use of some of the component parts of other kinds of media texts or genres that audiences are likely to be familiar with. A television advert for soap powder making use of some of the ingredients of a James Bond movie would be an example.

Localization: The term 'localization' is used in two ways in this textbook. A key facet of the globalization process is the tendency for local identities to intensify. Globally circulated media texts may be appropriated by local audiences to fit local conditions. Global media conglomerates also engage in localization in that they will create media products to suit the characteristics of the local market in order to ensure greater market penetration and domination.

Marxist Perspective: The Marxist perspective is concerned with explaining the inequalities (and contradictions) inherent in capitalist society, in terms of media analysis, the focus is on media companies as examples par excellence of capitalist organizations and more particularly on how the mass media facilitate the continuation of capitalism (and globalization) by representing it as being inevitable and desirable.

Mass Media: Media industries and technologies capable of communicating with large numbers of people in diverse social situations.

Media Moguls: Powerful individuals who have a controlling interest in multimedia conglomerates. In addition to their economic power, media moguls are believed to wield considerable political influence in the shaping of state policy about media and other matters of economic and political importance.

Methodology/Methods: The means by which research is undertaken. Researchers may use quantitative or qualitative research methods. In recognition of the complexity of the social world, and the fact that no one research method is trouble free, a growing number of researchers make use of a combination of research methods in order to more fully understand their particular research question.

Modernity: Increasingly a contentious term modernity refers to the era in which societies became industrialized, secular and urban. The contention arises from whether or not modernity has given way to postmodernity. (See also POSTMODERN, POSTMODERNITY.)

Narrative Analysis: A research method concerned with the narrative structure of media texts. How do individual media texts such as reports broadcast on television news programmes tell or narrate stories about the social world? What conventions are employed in explaining 'Terrorism' for example?

Oligopolies: Powerful media conglomerates who dominate and control the global media industry.

Participant Observation: A research method most associated with the ethnographic approach. The individual researcher immerses herself in the society, community or organization under study, usually for a long period of time. Participant observation may be covert or overt. It may be used as the sole method of data collection or as a precursor to other forms of data collection such as interviews. (See also ETHNOGRAPHIC APPROACH.)

Patriarchy: The control and domination of women by men. Patriarchal ideologies are ones that legitimize the continuation of male dominance in positions of influence and power.

Political Economy Perspective: A theoretical perspective concerned with understanding how the capitalist class promote and ensure their dominant position in capitalist society.

Postmodern, Postmodernity: A lively debate has ensued in recent years as to whether the era of modernity has come to pass. Postmodernists argue that modernity has been replaced by a postmodern era characterized by cultural and economic globalization; homogenization; increased fragmentation of local identities and media saturation. Proponents of postmodern theory treat the certainties inherent in more traditional sociological approaches towards understanding the social world in general and the mass media in particular with some skepticism. The postmodern perspective celebrates what it sees as the fragmented nature of postmodernity. Media reality has become hyper reality or more real than reality itself. A key criticism of postmodernism is the lack of empirical evidence to support the many arguments which state that we have moved on from the era of modernity. (See also MODERN, MODERNITY.)

Power: The term 'power' is used in two key ways in this textbook. First, in terms of the power of media texts to shape audience understandings of the social world and second in terms of unequal power relationships based upon class, ethnicity, gender or geographical location.

Public Service Broadcasting: Traditionally dominant in Western Europe, Public Service Broadcasting refers to publicly owned media companies engaged in the production and broadcast of radio and television programmes. In the face of increased competition from privately owned (and increasingly transnational) media companies, Public Service Broadcasting organizations have re-iterated their public sphere function.

Public Sphere: A space allowing discourse and debate of political importance. The public sphere is seen as an essential element in the democratization of modern societies and ideally the mass media should facilitate such a space. The processes of privatization, homogenization, 'dumbing down'and the rise of infotainment all militate against the mass media providing a public sphere for media audiences. Some theorists warn against the notion that a single public sphere is ever truly possible and instead suggest that smaller public sphericules (such as on-line communities, blogs and alternative media) are in fact emerging.

Qualitative: Researchers who are interested in questions about meaning and inter-pretation tend to make use of non-quantitative or qualitative research methods. Key qualitative methods include interviewing, participant observation and semiotic analysis.

Quantitative: The term 'quantitative' refers to research methods such as content analysis or surveys that seek to count the occurrences of specific phenomena e.g. racist ideologies within media content such as newspaper editorials or the measurement of public attitudes and beliefs about welfare recipients.

Queer Theory: A theoretical perspective which is highly critical of the heteronormative assumptions of much public discourse. Queer theory has re-captured a once pejorative term for gay men and women and instead uses the term in a celebratory way. This perspective allows a queer reading to be made of mainstream (and other) media texts as well as pointing out the invisibility of queer issues within dominant discourse.

Reality Television: In many respects the term 'reality television' is a misnomer. It is a television genre which allows audiences to engage in surveillance of programme participants who are either 'ordinary' people or celebrities placed in a simulated situation such as in a house or on a remote island. Reality television attempts to create the illusion for audiences that programming of this kind is unscripted and unedited.

Reception/Reception Analysis: A model of media analysis concerned primarily with the interpretative work engaged in by audiences in their engagement with media texts.

Reflexivity: The concept of reflexivity refers to the capacity of social actors for reflection, criticism and self-awareness.

Representation: This form of media analysis is primarily concerned with how media texts represent the social world.

Resistance: The ways in which audience members may reject the preferred or intended readings or meanings in a media text. The term is often used to describe how audience members reject the dominant or hegemonic codes evident within a media text. Audience members are said to be 'reading against the grain' in rejecting or subverting dominant or hegemonic ideology.

Semiotic(s):   A method of analysis concerned with the functioning of signs and symbols within a text.

Socialization: Socialization theory examines how we learn to become members of society. Agents of socialization include the family, peer group, the education system and the mass media. We learn from each of these agencies about norms, beliefs, values, rules and ideologies.

Structure(s):   Constraints that determine or shape human behaviour. In doing media work, for example, media professionals may be constrained by rules imposed by an employer, by the laws governing broadcasting or print journalism and by audience expectations.

Third World: The poorer and dependent parts of the world especially in the southern hemisphere. (See also DEVELOPED & DEVELOPING WORLDS.)

Texts: The increased concentration within media analysis on the agency or creativity of audience members came hand in hand with an emphasis upon seeing media content as texts rather than messages. Implicit in the notion of audience members 'reading' media texts is the process of active, interpretative work in the creation of meaning.

Transnational: As used in this textbook the term 'transnational' refers to both media companies or organizations and media texts. Many media texts are increasingly transnational because they are circulated globally. Transnational media conglomerates are media companies that operate in several countries.

Undeserving Poor: The undeserving poor are those categories of poor or socially excluded who are demonized and who are personally blamed for their poverty and exclusion. They are sometimes termed the 'Devil's Poor.' Examples might be female lone parents, 'chavs' or 'trailer-trash' (See also DESERVING POOR.)

Working Class: The term working class is more and more difficult owing in small measure to the restructuring of work itself. Broadly speaking the term refers to those engaged in manual work. The working class may be further sub-divided into skilled manual workers; semi-skilled manual workers and unskilled manual workers. The term blue-collar is used in North America to refer to the working class.

INDEX

ideology cont.
  discourse relationship 173–5
  dominant 154–62
independent producers 139–41
Indymedia 139–41
inequalities
  power relations 150, 168, 173–4,
    176, 186
  social 13–15, 47, 103, 150
influence 24, 92, 95, 188
information and communication
    technologies (ICTs) 10, 13–14,
    48, 224, 233
information-rich/-poor 47, 55–6, 67
infotainment 103, 112, 124
integration, horizontal and vertical 94–6
Internet, public sphere 14–15, 31,
    49, 67, 108–9
Internet Service Providers (ISPs) 108
interviews
  ethnography 224
  production research 126–7, 133–4
  reception research 222,
    224, 230–2
Irish Times 75–7
ISPs see Internet Service Providers
Iyengar, S. 198–9

Jenkins, H. 233
Jones, P. 173
journalism, Indymedia 139–41
journalists see media professionals

Kavoori, Andy 228–30
key thinkers
  Louis Althusser 166
  Jean Baudrillard 22
  Antonio Gramsci 166
  Jürgen Habermas 106–8
  Stuart Hall 128–30
  Marshall McLuhan 47
  Karl Marx 165
Kim, Kyung-Hee 143
Kitzinger, C. 188
Kitzinger, Jenny 188, 237–8
Kraidy, Marwan M. 80–1
Kuhling, Carmen 79–80

La Jornada 176
language 50, 72, 174
Lawson, T. 173
legitimation 152–3
Lester-Roushanzamir, E. 172
liberal pluralism 126
lifestyle 52–3
literary criticism 21
Livingstone, S. 14–15, 233
localization 69–70
Longhurst, B. 227
Lull, J. 46, 223

McChesney, Robert W. 34–5, 113–14
McLuhan, Marshall 47
McQuail, D. 11, 101, 102, 103, 192
Marcuse, H. 163
Marx, Karl 162–3, 164, 165
mass media, definitions 11–13
Matheson, D. 32
media analysis 19–24
media professionals
  constraints 120–1
  contemporary challenges 151
  ideologies 124–5
  message encoding 129
  pressures 136
mediation 77
methodologies
  choice 20–1
  content analysis 192–4
  production research 126–30
  reception research 222–4
Middleton, Sue 209
migration 48, 70
mobile phones 54
moguls 103–4
Moore, Michael 161–2
Moores, S. 223–4
moral panic 172, 199
Morley, David 227–8
Morrissey 234–7
MP3 players 54, 59–60
Murdoch, Rupert 104
Murdock, G. 92, 174
music industry see recording industry;
    technological change

Nardi, B.A. 32
narrative analysis 195, 199
Nationwide 227–8
negotiated code 129, 219
neo-Marxism 124–5, 158
new media, examples 54, 72, 232
news
   air time 92
   globalization 68
   Indymedia 139–40
   production 120–1
   reception 227–30
   reporting 25–6, 51, 77–8, 137, 198–9
   Third World 51, 75–7
News Corporation 105
News Game 225–6
North–South divide 108–9
not-for-profit media 89–90

oppositional code 129–30, 219
O'Sullivan, T. 92
ownership 14, 55, 87–118
   forms 89–91
   political economy perspective 100–3
   up to date information 102

Paek, H.J. 172
Parker, Alan 137–9
participant observation 126–7, 133,
   222, 232
Patelis, Korinna 114–15
patriarchy 125, 221
peripheral societies 51–2
Peters, S. 46
Peters, T. 46
Philo, Greg 143–4, 225–6
Pickering, M. 174
Pilger, J. 46
Platon, S. 140
pluralism 69
podcasts 32
political economy
   globalization 68–9
   media concentration 100–3
   production research 124
   shortcomings 150
politics 11, 136, 228–30

popular culture 16–19, 26–31, 231–7
Postman, N. 91
postmodernism 13, 14, 46
   content analysis 188, 192
   ideology 150–1, 173
   reception research 220, 223, 230
poverty
   content analysis 196–9
   media portrayal 130, 133–4,
     152, 199–202
power
   ideological 152–4
   media moguls 103–4
   unequal relations 150, 168, 173–4,
     176, 186
print media 72, 75–7, 104, 137,
   176, 230–1
privately owned media 90–1
production
   new media 10
   research 120–39
   transnational 26–9
   tripartite media analysis 23–4, 169
professional code 129, 219
profit 52, 95, 102, 107
promotional products 95
propaganda 15, 151, 178–9, 192
psychology 22, 175, 221
public knowledge 225
public ownership 90–1
public service broadcasters 90–1
public sphere 106–9

qualitative research
   content analysis 186, 192–4, 195–9
   production analysis 130–4
   reception analysis 222–3, 226–31
quantitative research
   content analysis 186, 192–4
   reception analysis 222–3

race *see* ethnicity
Radio Telefis Éireann (RTÉ) 130, 133–4
Radway, Janice 171, 223
rationality 46
Rayner, P. 92
'reading against the grain' 162